LETTERS FROM A STOIC

Lucius Seneca

COLLINS
CLASSICS

William Collins
An imprint of HarperCollins*Publishers*
1 London Bridge Street
London SE1 9GF

WilliamCollinsBooks.com

HarperCollins*Publishers*
Macken House, 39/40 Mayor Street Upper
Dublin 1, D01 C9W8, Ireland

This William Collins paperback edition published in Great Britain in 2020

4

A catalogue record for this book
is available from the British Library

A ISBN: 978-0-00-842505-0
B ISBN: 978-0-00-842504-3

Classic Literature: Words and Phrases adapted from
Collins English Dictionary

Typesetting in Kalix by Palimpsest Book Production Limited,
Falkirk, Stirlingshire

Printed and Bound in the UK using 100% Renewable Electricity at
CPI Group (UK) Ltd

MIX
Paper | Supporting
responsible forestry
FSC™ C007454

This book is produced from independently certified FSC™ paper
to ensure responsible forest management.

For more information visit: www.harpercollins.co.uk/green

Find out more about HarperCollins and the environment at
www.harpercollins.co.uk/green

History of William Collins

In 1819, millworker William Collins from Glasgow, Scotland, set up a company for printing and publishing pamphlets, sermons, hymn books, and prayer books. That company was Collins and was to mark the birth of HarperCollins Publishers as we know it today. The long tradition of Collins dictionary publishing can be traced back to the first dictionary William co-published in 1825, *Greek and English Lexicon*. Indeed, from 1840 onwards, he began to produce illustrated dictionaries and even obtained a licence to print and publish the Bible.

Soon after, William published the first Collins novel; however, it was the time of the Long Depression, where harvests were poor, prices were high, potato crops had failed, and violence was erupting in Europe. As a result, many factories across the country were forced to close down and William chose to retire in 1846, partly due to the hardships he was facing.

Aged 30, William's son, William II, took over the business. A keen humanitarian with a warm heart and a generous spirit, William II was truly "Victorian" in his outlook. He introduced new, up-to-date steam presses and published affordable editions of Shakespeare's works and *The Pilgrim's Progress*, making them available to the masses for the first time.

A new demand for educational books meant that success came with the publication of travel books, scientific books, encyclopedias, and dictionaries. This demand to be educated led to the later publication of atlases, and Collins also held the monopoly on scripture writing at the time.

In the 1860s Collins began to expand and diversify and the idea of "books for the millions" was developed, although the phrase wasn't coined until 1907. Affordable editions of classical literature were published, and in 1903 Collins introduced 10 titles in their Collins Handy Illustrated Pocket Novels. These proved so popular that a few years later this had increased to an output of 50 volumes, selling nearly half a million in their year of publication. In the same year, The Everyman's Library was also instituted, with the idea of publishing an affordable library of the most important classical works, biographies, religious and philosophical treatments, plays, poems, travel, and adventure. This series eclipsed all competition at the time, and the introduction of paperback books in the 1950s helped to open that market and marked a high point in the industry.

HarperCollins is and has always been a champion of the classics, and the current Collins Classics series follows in this tradition—publishing classical literature that is afford-able and available to all. Beautifully packaged, highly collectible, and intended to be reread and enjoyed at every opportunity.

CONTENTS

LETTERS
FROM A STOIC

THE EPISTLES
OF SENECA

II. ON DISCURSIVENESS IN READING

[1]Judging by what you write me, and by what I hear, I am forming a good opinion regarding your future. You do not run hither and thither and distract yourself by changing your abode; for such restlessness is the sign of a disordered spirit. The primary indication, to my thinking, of a well-ordered mind is a man's ability to remain in one place and linger in his own company. [2]Be careful, however, lest this reading of many authors and books of every sort may tend to make you discursive and unsteady. You must linger among a limited number of master thinkers, and digest their works, if you would derive ideas which shall win firm hold in your mind. Everywhere means nowhere. When a person spends all his time in foreign travel, he ends by having many acquaintances, but no friends. And the same thing must hold true of men who seek intimate acquaintance with no single author, but visit them all in a hasty and hurried manner. [3]Food does no good and is not assimilated into the body if it leaves the stomach as soon as it is eaten; nothing hinders a cure so much as frequent change of medicine; no wound will heal when one salve is tried after another; a plant which is often moved can never grow strong. There is nothing so efficacious that it can be helpful while it

is being shifted about. And in reading of many books is distraction.

Accordingly, since you cannot read all the books which you may possess, it is enough to possess only as many books as you can read. [4]"But," you reply, "I wish to dip first into one book and then into another." I tell you that it is the sign of an overnice appetite to toy with many dishes; for when they are manifold and varied, they cloy but do not nourish. So you should always read standard authors; and when you crave a change, fall back upon those whom you read before. Each day acquire something that will fortify you against poverty, against death, indeed against other misfortunes as well; and after you have run over many thoughts, select one to be thoroughly digested that day. [5]This is my own custom; from the many things which I have read, I claim some one part for myself.

The thought for today is one which I discovered in Epicurus;[a] for I am wont to cross over even into the enemy's camp, – not as a deserter, but as a scout. [6]He says: "Contented poverty is an honourable estate." Indeed, if it be contented, it is not poverty at all. It is not the man who has too little, but the man who craves more, that is poor.

What does it matter how much a man has laid up in his safe, or in his warehouse, how large are his flocks and how fat his dividends, if he covets his neighbour's property, and reckons, not his past gains, but his hopes of gains to come? Do you ask what is the proper limit to wealth? It is, first, to have what is necessary, and, second, to have what is enough. Farewell.

[a] Frag. 475 Usener

III. ON TRUE AND FALSE FRIENDSHIP

[1]You have sent a letter to me through the hand of a "friend" of yours, as you call him. And in your very next sentence you warn me not to discuss with him all the matters that concern you, saying that even you yourself are not accustomed to do this; in other words, you have in the same letter affirmed and denied that he is your friend. [2]Now if you used this word of ours[a] in the popular sense, and called him "friend" in the same way in which we speak of all candidates for election as "honourable gentlemen," and as we greet all men whom we meet casually, if their names slip us for the moment, with the salutation "my dear sir," – so be it. But if you consider any man a friend whom you do not trust as you trust yourself, you are mightily mistaken and you do not sufficiently understand what true friendship means. Indeed, I would have you discuss everything with a friend; but first of all discuss the man himself. When friendship is settled, you must trust; before friendship is formed, you must pass judgment. Those persons indeed put last first and confound their duties, who, violating the rules of

---

[a] i.e., a word which has a special significance to the Stoics; see Ep. xlviii, note.

Theophrastus,[a] judge a man after they have made him their friend, instead of making him their friend after they have judged him. Ponder for a long time whether you shall admit a given person to your friendship; but when you have decided to admit him, welcome him with all your heart and soul. Speak as boldly with him as with yourself. [3]As to yourself, although you should live in such a way that you trust your own self with nothing which you could not entrust even to your enemy, yet, since certain matters occur which convention keeps secret, you should share with a friend at least all your worries and reflections. Regard him as loyal, and you will make him loyal. Some, for example, fearing to be deceived, have taught men to deceive; by their suspicions they have given their friend the right to do wrong. Why need I keep back any words in the presence of my friend? Why should I not regard myself as alone when in his company?

[4]There is a class of men who communicate, to anyone whom they meet, matters which should be revealed to friends alone, and unload upon the chance listener whatever irks them. Others, again, fear to confide in their closest intimates; and if it were possible, they would not trust even themselves, burying their secrets deep in their hearts. But we should do neither. It is equally faulty to trust everyone and to trust no one. Yet the former fault is, I should say, the more ingenuous, the latter the more safe. [5]In like manner you should rebuke these two kinds of men, – both those who always lack repose, and those who are always in repose. For love of bustle is not industry, – it is only the restlessness of a hunted mind. And true repose does not consist in condemning all motion as merely vexation; that kind of repose is slackness and inertia. [6]Therefore, you should note the following saying, taken from my reading in

[a] Frag. 74 Wimmer.

6

Pomponius: "Some men shrink into dark corners, to such a degree that they see darkly by day." No, men should combine these tendencies, and he who reposes should act and he who acts should take repose. Discuss the problem with Nature; she will tell you that she has created both day and night. Farewell.

V. ON THE PHILOSOPHER'S MEAN

[1]I commend you and rejoice in the fact that you are persistent in your studies, and that, putting all else aside, you make it each day your endeavour to become a better man. I do not merely exhort you to keep at it; I actually beg you to do so. I warn you, however, not to act after the fashion of those who desire to be conspicuous rather than to improve, by doing things which will rouse comment as regards your dress or general way of living. [2]Repellent attire, unkempt hair, slovenly beard, open scorn of silver dishes, a couch on the bare earth, and any other perverted forms of self-display, are to be avoided. The mere name of philosophy, however quietly pursued, is an object of sufficient scorn; and what would happen if we should begin to separate ourselves from the customs of our fellow-men? Inwardly, we ought to be different in all respects, but our exterior should conform to society. [3]Do not wear too fine, nor yet too frowzy, a toga. One needs no silver plate, encrusted and embossed in solid gold; but we should not believe the lack of silver and gold to be proof of the simple life. Let us try to maintain a higher standard of life than that of the multitude, but not a contrary standard; otherwise, we shall frighten away and repel the very persons whom we are trying to improve. We also bring it about that

they are unwilling to imitate us in anything, because they are afraid lest they might be compelled to imitate us in everything.

[4]The first thing which philosophy undertakes to give is fellow-feeling with all men; in other words, sympathy and sociability. We part company with our promise if we are unlike other men. We must see to it that the means by which we wish to draw admiration be not absurd and odious. Our motto,[a] as you know, is "Live according to Nature"; but it is quite contrary to nature to torture the body, to hate un-laboured elegance, to be dirty on purpose, to eat food that is not only plain, but disgusting and forbidding. [5]Just as it is a sign of luxury to seek out dainties, so it is madness to avoid that which is customary and can be purchased at no great price. Philosophy calls for plain living, but not for penance; and we may perfectly well be plain and neat at the same time. This is the mean of which I approve; our life should observe a happy medium between the ways of a sage and the ways of the world at large; all men should admire it, but they should understand it also.

[6]"Well then, shall we act like other men? Shall there be no distinction between ourselves and the world?" Yes, a very great one; let men find that we are unlike the common herd, if they look closely. If they visit us at home, they should admire us, rather than our household appointments. He is a great man who uses earthenware dishes as if they were silver; but he is equally great who uses silver as if it were earthen-ware. It is the sign of an unstable mind not to be able to endure riches.

[7]But I wish to share with you today's profit also. I find in the writings of our[b] Hecato that the limiting of desires helps also to cure fears: "Cease to hope," he says, "and you will cease to fear." "But how," you will reply, "can things so

[a] i.e., of the Stoic school.

[b] Frag. 25 Fowler.

different go side by side?" In this way, my dear Lucilius: though they do seem at variance, yet they are really united. Just as the same chain fastens the prisoner and the soldier who guards him, so hope and fear, dissimilar as they are, keep step together; fear follows hope. [8]I am not surprised that they proceed in this way; each alike belongs to a mind that is in suspense, a mind that is fretted by looking forward to the future. But the chief cause of both these ills is that we do not adapt ourselves to the present, but send our thoughts a long way ahead. And so foresight, the noblest blessing of the human race, becomes perverted. [9]Beasts avoid the dangers which they see, and when they have escaped them are free from care; but we men torment ourselves over that which is to come as well as over that which is past. Many of our blessings bring bane to us; for memory recalls the tortures of fear, while foresight anticipates them. The present alone can make no man wretched. Farewell.

VI. ON SHARING KNOWLEDGE

[1]I feel, my dear Lucilius, that I am being not only reformed, but transformed. I do not yet, however, assure myself, or indulge the hope, that there are no elements left in me which need to be changed. Of course there are many that should be made more compact, or made thinner, or be brought into greater prominence. And indeed this very fact is proof that my spirit is altered into something better, – that it can see its own faults, of which it was previously ignorant. In certain cases sick men are congratulated because they themselves have perceived that they are sick.

[2]I therefore wish to impart to you this sudden change in myself; I should then begin to place a surer trust in our friendship, – the true friendship which hope and fear and self-interest cannot sever, the friendship in which and for the sake of which men meet death. [3]I can show you many who have lacked, not a friend, but a friendship; this, however, cannot possibly happen when souls are drawn together by identical inclinations into an alliance of honourable desires. And why can it not happen? Because in such cases men know that they have all things in common, especially their troubles.

You cannot conceive what distinct progress I notice that

each day brings to me. [4]And when you say: "Give me also a share in these gifts which you have found so helpful," I reply that I am anxious to heap all these privileges upon you, and that I am glad to learn in order that I may teach. Nothing will ever please me, no matter how excellent or beneficial, if I must retain the knowledge of it to myself. And if wisdom were given me under the express condition that it must be kept hidden and not uttered, I should refuse it. No good thing is pleasant to possess, without friends to share it.

[5]I shall therefore send to you the actual books; and in order that you may not waste time in searching here and there for profitable topics, I shall mark certain passages, so that you can turn at once to those which I approve and admire. Of course, however, the living voice and the intimacy of a common life will help you more than the written word. You must go to the scene of action, first, because men put more faith in their eyes than in their ears,[a] and second, because the way is long if one follows precepts, but short and helpful, if one follows patterns. [6]Cleanthes could not have been the express image of Zeno, if he had merely heard his lectures; he shared in his life, saw into his hidden purposes, and watched him to see whether he lived according to his own rules. Plato, Aristotle, and the whole throng of sages who were destined to go each his different way, derived more benefit from the character than from the words of Socrates. It was not the class-room of Epicurus, but living together under the same roof, that made great men of Metrodorus, Hermarchus, and Polyaenus. Therefore I summon you, not merely that you may derive benefit, but that you may confer benefit; for we can assist each other greatly.

[7]Meanwhile, I owe you my little daily contribution; you

[a] Cf. Herodotus, i. 8 ὦτα τυγχάνει ἀνθρώποισι ἐόντα ἀπιστότερα ὀφθαλμῶν.

shall be told what pleased me today in the writings of Hecato;[a] it is these words: "What progress, you ask, have I made? I have begun to be a friend to myself." That was indeed a great benefit; such a person can never be alone. You may be sure that such a man is a friend to all mankind. Farewell.

[a] Frag. 26 Fowler.

VII. ON CROWDS

[1]Do you ask me what you should regard as especially to be avoided? I say, crowds; for as yet you cannot trust yourself to them with safety. I shall admit my own weakness, at any rate; for I never bring back home the same character that I took abroad with me. Something of that which I have forced to be calm within me is disturbed; some of the foes that I have routed return again. Just as the sick man, who has been weak for a long time, is in such a condition that he cannot be taken out of the house without suffering a relapse, so we ourselves are affected when our souls are recovering from a lingering disease. [2]To consort with the crowd is harmful; there is no person who does not make some vice attractive to us, or stamp it upon us, or taint us unconsciously therewith. Certainly, the greater the mob with which we mingle, the greater the danger.

But nothing is so damaging to good character as the habit of lounging at the games; for then it is that vice steals subtly upon one through the avenue of pleasure. [3]What do you think I mean? I mean that I come home more greedy, more ambitious, more voluptuous, and even more cruel and inhuman, because I have been among human beings. By chance I attended a mid-day exhibition, expecting some fun, wit, and relaxation, – an exhibition at which men's eyes have respite from the slaughter of their fellow-men. But it was quite the reverse. The previous combats were the essence of compassion; but now all the trifling is put aside and it is pure murder.[a] The men have no defensive armour. They are exposed to blows at all points, and no one ever strikes in vain. [4]Many persons prefer this programme to the usual pairs and to the bouts "by request." Of course they do; there is no helmet or shield to deflect the weapon. What is the need of defensive armour, or of skill? All these mean delaying death. In the morning they throw men to the lions and the bears; at noon, they throw them to the spectators. The spectators demand that the slayer shall face the man who is to slay him in his turn; and they always reserve the latest conqueror for another butchering. The outcome of every fight is death, and the means are fire and sword. This sort of thing goes on while the arena is empty.

[5]You may retort: "But he was a highway robber; he killed a man!" And what of it? Granted that, as a murderer, he deserved this punishment, what crime have you committed, poor fellow, that you should deserve to sit and see this show? In the morning they cried "Kill him! Lash him! Burn him! Why does he meet the sword in so cowardly a way? Why does he strike so feebly? Why doesn't he die game? Whip him to meet his wounds! Let them receive blow for blow, with chests bare and exposed to the stroke!" And when the games stop for the intermission, they announce: "A little throatcutting in the meantime, so that there may still be something going on!"

Come now; do you[b] not understand even this truth, that a bad example reacts on the agent? Thank the immortal gods

---

[a] During the luncheon interval condemned criminals were often driven into the arena and compelled to fight, for the amusement of those spectators who remained throughout the day.

[b] The remark is addressed to the brutalized spectators.

that you are teaching cruelty to a person who cannot learn to be cruel. ⁶The young character, which cannot hold fast to righteousness, must be rescued from the mob; it is too easy to side with the majority. Even Socrates, Cato, and Laelius might have been shaken in their moral strength by a crowd that was unlike them; so true it is that none of us, no matter how much he cultivates his abilities, can withstand the shock of faults that approach, as it were, with so great a retinue. ⁷Much harm is done by a single case of indulgence or greed; the familiar friend, if he be luxurious, weakens and softens us imperceptibly; the neighbour, if he be rich, rouses our covetousness; the companion, if he be slanderous, rubs off some of his rust upon us, even though we be spotless and sincere. What then do you think the effect will be on character, when the world at large assaults it! You must either imitate or loathe the world.

⁸But both courses are to be avoided; you should not copy the bad simply because they are many, nor should you hate the many because they are unlike you. Withdraw into yourself, as far as you can. Associate with those who will make a better man of you. Welcome those whom you yourself can improve. The process is mutual; for men learn while they teach. ⁹There is no reason why pride in advertising your abilities should lure you into publicity, so that you should desire to recite or harangue before the general public. Of course I should be willing for you to do so if you had a stock-in-trade that suited such a mob; as it is, there is not a man of them who can understand you. One or two individuals will perhaps come in your way, but even these will have to be moulded and trained by you so that they will understand you. You may say: "For what purpose did I learn all these things?" But you need not fear that you have wasted your efforts; it was for yourself that you learned them.

¹⁰In order, however, that I may not today have learned exclusively for myself, I shall share with you three excellent

sayings, of the same general purport, which have come to my attention. This letter will give you one of them as payment of my debt; the other two you may accept as a contribution in advance. Democritus[a] says: "One man means as much to me as a multitude, and a multitude only as much as one man." [11]The following also was nobly spoken by someone or other, for it is doubtful who the author was; they asked him what was the object of all this study applied to an art that would reach but very few. He replied: "I am content with few, content with one, content with none at all." The third saying – and a noteworthy one, too – is by Epicurus,[b] written to one of the partners of his studies: "I write this not for the many, but for you; each of us is enough of an audience for the other." [12]Lay these words to heart, Lucilius, that you may scorn the pleasure which comes from the applause of the majority. Many men praise you; but have you any reason for being pleased with yourself, if you are a person whom the many can understand? Your good qualities should face inwards. Farewell.

[a] Frag. 302[a] Diels[2].
[b] Frag. 208 Usener.

IX. ON PHILOSOPHY
AND FRIENDSHIP

[1]You desire to know whether Epicurus[a] is right when, in one of his letters, he rebukes those who hold that the wise man is self-sufficient and for that reason does not stand in need of friendships. This is the objection raised by Epicurus against Stilbo and those who believe[b] that the Supreme Good is a soul which is insensible to feeling.

[2]We are bound to meet with a double meaning if we try to express the Greek term "lack of feeling" summarily, in a single word, rendering it by the Latin word impatientia. For it may be understood in the meaning the opposite to that which we wish it to have. What we mean to express is, a soul which rejects any sensation of evil; but people will interpret the idea as that of a soul which can endure no evil. Consider, therefore, whether it is not better to say "a soul that cannot be harmed," or "a soul entirely beyond the realm of suffering." [3]There is this difference between ourselves and the other school:[c] our ideal wise man feels his troubles, but overcomes them; their wise man does not even feel them.

[a] Frag. 174 Usener.

[b] i.e., the Cynics.

[c] i.e., the Cynics.

But we and they alike hold this idea, – that the wise man is self-sufficient. Nevertheless, he desires friends, neighbours, and associates, no matter how much he is sufficient unto himself. [4]And mark how self-sufficient he is; for on occasion he can be content with a part of himself. If he lose a hand through disease or war, or if some accident puts out one or both of his eyes, he will be satisfied with what is left, taking as much pleasure in his impaired and maimed body as he took when it was sound. But while he does not pine for these parts if they are missing, he prefers not to lose them. [5]In this sense the wise man is self-sufficient, that he can do without friends, not that he desires to do without them. When I say "can," I mean this: he endures the loss of a friend with equanimity.

But he need never lack friends, for it lies in his own control how soon he shall make good a loss. Just as Phidias, if he lose a statue, can straightway carve another, even so our master in the art of making friendships can fill the place of a friend he has lost. [6]If you ask how one can make oneself a friend quickly, I will tell you, provided we are agreed that I may pay my debt[a] at once and square the account, so far as this letter is concerned. Hecato,[b] says: "I can show you a philtre, compounded without drugs, herbs, or any witch's incantation: 'If you would be loved, love.'" Now there is great pleasure, not only in maintaining old and established friendships, but also in beginning and acquiring new ones. [7]There is the same difference between winning a new friend and having already won him, as there is between the farmer who sows and the farmer who reaps. The philosopher Attalus used to say: "It is more pleasant to make than to keep a friend, as it is more pleasant to the artist to paint than to have finished painting." When one is busy and absorbed in

[a] i.e., the *diurna mercedula*; see Ep. vi, [7].
[b] Frag. 27 Fowler.

one's work, the very absorption affords great delight; but when one has withdrawn one's hand from the completed masterpiece, the pleasure is not so keen. Henceforth it is the fruits of his art that he enjoys; it was the art itself that he enjoyed while he was painting. In the case of our children, their young manhood yields the more abundant fruits, but their infancy was sweeter.

[8]Let us now return to the question. The wise man, I say, self-sufficient though he be, nevertheless desires friends if only for the purpose of practising friendship, in order that his noble qualities may not lie dormant. Not, however, for the purpose mentioned by Epicurus[a] in the letter quoted above: "That there may be someone to sit by him when he is ill, to help him when he is in prison or in want;" but that he may have someone by whose sick-bed he himself may sit, someone a prisoner in hostile hands whom he himself may set free. He who regards himself only, and enters upon friendships for this reason, reckons wrongly. The end will be like the beginning: he has made friends with one who might assist him out of bondage; at the first rattle of the chain such a friend will desert him. [9]These are the so-called "fair-weather" friendships; one who is chosen for the sake of utility will be satisfactory only so long as he is useful. Hence prosperous men are blockaded by troops of friends; but those who have failed stand amid vast loneliness their friends fleeing from the very crisis which is to test their worth. Hence, also, we notice those many shameful cases of persons who, through fear, desert or betray. The beginning and the end cannot but harmonize. He who begins to be your friend because it pays will also cease because it pays. A man will be attracted by some reward offered in exchange for his friendship, if he be attracted by aught in friendship other than friendship itself.

[10]For what purpose, then, do I make a man my friend?

[a] Frag. 175 Usener.

In order to have someone for whom I may die, whom I may follow into exile, against whose death I may stake my own life, and pay the pledge, too. The friendship which you portray is a bargain and not a friendship; it regards convenience only, and looks to the results. [11]Beyond question the feeling of a lover has in it something akin to friendship; one might call it friendship run mad. But, though this is true, does anyone love for the sake of gain, or promotion, or renown? Pure[a] love, careless of all other things, kindles the soul with desire for the beautiful object, not without the hope of a return of the affection. What then? Can a cause which is more honourable produce a passion that is base? [12]You may retort: "We are now discussing the question whether friendship is to be cultivated for its own sake." On the contrary, nothing more urgently requires demonstration; for if friendship is to be sought for its own sake, he may seek it who is self-sufficient. "How, then," you ask, "does he seek it?" Precisely as he seeks an object of great beauty, not attracted to it by desire for gain, nor yet frightened by the instability of Fortune. One who seeks friendship for favourable occasions, strips it of all its nobility.

[13]"The wise man is self-sufficient." This phrase, my dear Lucilius, is incorrectly explained by many; for they withdraw the wise man from the world, and force him to dwell within his own skin. But we must mark with care what this sentence signifies and how far it applies; the wise man is sufficient unto himself for a happy existence, but not for mere existence. For he needs many helps towards mere existence; but for a happy existence he needs only a sound and upright soul, one that despises Fortune.

[14]I should like also to state to you one of the distinctions of Chrysippus,[b] who declares that the wise man is in want of

---

[a] "Pure love," i.e., love in its essence, unalloyed with other emotions.

[b] Cf. his Frag. moral. 674 von Arnim.

nothing, and yet needs many things.[a] "On the other hand," he says, "nothing is needed by the fool, for he does not understand how to use anything, but he is in want of everything." The wise man needs hands, eyes, and many things that are necessary for his daily use; but he is in want of nothing. For want implies a necessity, and nothing is necessary to the wise man. [15]Therefore, although he is self-sufficient, yet he has need of friends. He craves as many friends as possible, not, however, that he may live happily; for he will live happily even without friends. The Supreme Good calls for no practical aids from outside; it is developed at home, and arises entirely within itself. If the good seeks any portion of itself from without, it begins to be subject to the play of Fortune.

[16]People may say: "But what sort of existence will the wise man have, if he be left friendless when thrown into prison, or when stranded in some foreign nation, or when delayed on a long voyage, or when out upon a lonely shore?" His life will be like that of Jupiter, who, amid the dissolution of the world, when the gods are confounded together and Nature rests for a space from her work, can retire into himself and give himself over to his own thoughts.[b] In some such way as this the sage will act; he will retreat into himself, and live with himself. [17]As long as he is allowed to order his affairs according to his judgment, he is self-sufficient – and marries a wife; he is self-sufficient – and brings up children; he is self-sufficient – and yet could not live if he had to live without the society of man. Natural promptings, and not his own selfish needs, draw him into Friendships. For just as other

[a] The distinction is based upon the meaning of *egere*, "to be in want of" something indispensible, and *opus esse*, "to have need of" something which one can do without.

[b] This refers to the Stoic conflagration: after certain cycles their world was destroyed by fire. Cf. E. V. Arnold, *Roman Stoicism*, pp. 192 f; cf. also Chrysippus, Frag. phys. 1065 von Arnim.

things have for us an inherent attractiveness, so has friend-ship. As we hate solitude and crave society, as nature draws men to each other, so in this matter also there is an attraction which makes us desirous of friendship. [18]Nevertheless, though the sage may love his friends dearly, often comparing them with himself, and putting them ahead of himself, yet all the good will be limited to his own being, and he will speak the words which were spoken by the very Stilbo whom Epicurus criticizes in his letter. For Stilbo, after his country was captured and his children and his wife lost, as he emerged from the general desolation alone and yet happy, spoke as follows to Demetrius, called Sacker of Cities because of the destruction he brought upon them, in answer to the question whether he had lost anything: "I have all my goods with me!" [19]There is a brave and stout-hearted man for you! The enemy conquered, but Stilbo conquered his conqueror. "I have lost nothing!" Aye, he forced Demetrius to wonder whether he himself had conquered after all. "My goods are all with me!" In other words, he deemed nothing that might be taken from him to be a good.

We marvel at certain animals because they can pass through fire and suffer no bodily harm; but how much more marvellous is a man who has marched forth unhurt and unscathed through fire and sword and devastation! Do you understand now how much easier it is to conquer a whole tribe than to conquer one man? This saying of Stilbo[a] makes common ground with Stoicism; the Stoic also can carry his goods unimpaired through cities that have been burned to ashes; for he is self-sufficient. Such are the bounds which he sets to his own happiness.

[20]But you must not think that our school alone can utter noble words; Epicurus himself, the reviler of Stilbo, spoke

---

[a] *Gnomologici Vaticani* 515[a] Sternberg

similar language;[a] put it down to my credit, though I have already wiped out my debt for the present day.[b] He says: "Whoever does not regard what he has as most ample wealth, is unhappy, though he be master of the whole world." Or, if the following seems to you a more suitable phrase, – for we must try to render the meaning and not the mere words: "A man may rule the world and still be unhappy, if he does not feel that he is supremely happy." [21]In order, however, that you may know that these sentiments are universal,[c] suggested, of course, by Nature, you will find in one of the comic poets this verse;

Unblest is he who thinks himself unblest.[d]

or what does your condition matter, if it is bad in your own eyes? [22]You may say; "What then? If yonder man, rich by base means, and yonder man, lord of many but slave of more, shall call themselves happy, will their own opinion make them happy?" It matters not what one says, but what one feels; also, not how one feels on one particular day, but how one feels at all times. There is no reason, however, why you should fear that this great privilege will fall into unworthy hands; only the wise man is pleased with his own. Folly is ever troubled with weariness of itself. Farewell.

[a] Frag. 474 Usener.

[b] Cf. above § 6.

[c] i.e., not confined to the Stoics, etc.

[d] Author unknown; perhaps, as Buecheler thinks, adapted from the Greek.

XI. ON THE BLUSH OF MODESTY

[1]Your friend and I have had a conversation. He is a man of ability; his very first words showed what spirit and understanding he possesses, and what progress he has already made. He gave me a foretaste, and he will not fail to answer thereto. For he spoke not from forethought, but was suddenly caught off his guard. When he tried to collect himself, he could scarcely banish that hue of modesty, which is a good sign in a young man; the blush that spread over his face seemed so to rise from the depths. And I feel sure that his habit of blushing will stay with him after he has strengthened his character, stripped off all his faults, and become wise. For by no wisdom can natural weaknesses of the body be removed. That which is implanted and inborn can be toned down by training, but not overcome. [2]The steadiest speaker, when before the public, often breaks into a perspiration, as if he had wearied or over-heated himself; some tremble in the knees when they rise to speak; I know of some whose teeth chatter, whose tongues falter, whose lips quiver. Training and experience can never shake off this habit; nature exerts her own power and through such a weakness makes her presence known even to the strongest. [3]I know that the blush, too, is a habit of this sort, spreading suddenly over the faces of the

most dignified men. It is, indeed more prevalent in youth, because of the warmer blood and the sensitive countenance; nevertheless, both seasoned men and aged men are affected by it. Some are most dangerous when they redden, as if they were letting all their sense of shame escape. [4]Sulla, when the blood mantled his cheeks, was in his fiercest mood. Pompey had the most sensitive cast of countenance; he always blushed in the presence of a gathering, and especially at a public assembly. Fabianus also, I remember, reddened when he appeared as a witness before the senate; and his embarrassment became him to a remarkable degree. [5]Such a habit is not due to mental weakness, but to the novelty of a situation; an inexperienced person is not necessarily confused, but is usually affected, because he slips into this habit by natural tendency of the body. Just as certain men are full-blooded, so others are of a quick and mobile blood, that rushes to the face at once.

[6]As I remarked, Wisdom can never remove this habit; for if she could rub out all our faults, she would be mistress of the universe. Whatever is assigned to us by the terms of our birth and the blend in our constitutions, will stick with us, no matter how hard or how long the soul may have tried to master itself. And we cannot forbid these feelings any more than we can summon them. [7]Actors in the theatre, who imitate the emotions, who portray fear and nervousness, who depict sorrow, imitate bashfulness by hanging their heads, lowering their voices, and keeping their eyes fixed and rooted upon the ground. They cannot, however, muster a blush; for the blush cannot be prevented or acquired. Wisdom will not assure us of a remedy, or give us help against it; it comes or goes unbidden, and is a law unto itself.

[8]But my letter calls for its closing sentence. Hear and take to heart this useful and wholesome motto:[a] "Cherish

---

[a] Epicurus. 210 Usener.

some man of high character, and keep him ever before your eyes, living as if he were watching you, and ordering all your actions as if he beheld them." [9]Such, my dear Lucilius, is the counsel of Epicurus;[a] he has quite properly given us a guardian and an attendant. We can get rid of most sins, if we have a witness who stands near us when we are likely to go wrong. The soul should have someone whom it can respect, – one by whose authority it may make even its inner shrine more hallowed.[b] Happy is the man who can make others better, not merely when he is in their company, but even when he is in their thoughts! And happy also is he who can so revere a man as to calm and regulate himself by calling him to mind! One who can so revere another, will soon be himself worthy of reverence. [10]Choose therefore a Cato; or, if Cato seems too severe a model, choose some Laelius, a gentler spirit. Choose a master whose life, conversation, and soul-expressing face have satisfied you; picture him always to yourself as your protector or your pattern. For we must indeed have someone according to whom we may regulate our characters; you can never straighten that which is crooked unless you use a ruler. Farewell.

[a] Frag. 210 Usener.

[b] The figure is taken from the ἄδυτον, the Holy of Holies in a temple. Cf. Vergil, *Aeneid*, vi. 10 *secreta Sibyllas*.

XII. ON OLD AGE

[1]Wherever I turn, I see evidences of my advancing years. I visited lately my country-place, and protested against the money which was spent on the tumble-down building. My bailiff maintained that the flaws were not due to his own carelessness; "he was doing everything possible, but the house was old." And this was the house which grew under my own hands! What has the future in store for me, if stones of my own age are already crumbling? [2]I was angry, and I embraced the first opportunity to vent my spleen in the bailiff's presence. "It is clear," I cried, "that these plane-trees are neglected; they have no leaves. Their branches are so gnarled and shrivelled; the boles are so rough and unkempt! This would not happen, if someone loosened the earth at their feet, and watered them." The bailiff swore by my protecting deity that "he was doing everything possible, and never relaxed his efforts, but those trees were old." Between you and me, I had planted those trees myself, I had seen them in their first leaf. [3]Then I turned to the door and asked: "Who is that brokendown dotard? You have done well to place him at the entrance; for he is outward bound.[a] Where did you get him?

[a] A jesting allusion to the Roman funeral; the corpse's feet pointing towards the door.

What pleasure did it give you to take up for burial some other man's dead?"[a] But the slave said: "Don't you know me, sir? I am Felicio; you used to bring me little images.[b] My father was Philositus the steward, and I am your pet slave." "The man is clean crazy," I remarked. "Has my pet slave become a little boy again? But it is quite possible; his teeth are just dropping out."[c]

[4] I owe it to my country-place that my old age became apparent whithersoever I turned. Let us cherish and love old age; for it is full of pleasure if one knows how to use it. Fruits are most welcome when almost over; youth is most charming at its close; the last drink delights the toper, the glass which souses him and puts the finishing touch on his drunkenness. [5] Each pleasure reserves to the end the greatest delights which it contains. Life is most delightful when it is on the downward slope, but has not yet reached the abrupt decline. And I myself believe that the period which stands, so to speak, on the edge of the roof, possesses pleasures of its own. Or else the very fact of our not wanting pleasures has taken the place of the pleasures themselves. How comforting it is to have tired out one's appetites, and to have done with them! [6] "But," you say, "it is a nuisance to be looking death in the face!" Death, however, should be looked in the face by young and old alike. We are not summoned according to our rating on the censor's list.[d] Moreover, no one is so old that it would be improper for him to hope for another day of existence. And one day, mind you, is a stage on life's journey.

[a] His former owner should have kept him and buried him.

[b] Small figures, generally of terra-cotta, were frequently given to children as presents at the Saturnalia. Cf. Macrobius, i. 11 49 *sigila . . . pro se atque suis piaculum.*

[c] i.e., the old slave resembles a child in that he is losing his teeth (but for the second time).

[d] i.e., *seniores*, as contrasted with *iuniores*.

Our span of life is divided into parts; it consists of large circles enclosing smaller. One circle embraces and bounds the rest; it reaches from birth to the last day of existence. The next circle limits the period of our young manhood. The third confines all of childhood in its circumference. Again, there is, in a class by itself, the year; it contains within itself all the divisions of time by the multiplication of which we get the total of life. The month is bounded by a narrower ring. The smallest circle of all is the day; but even a day has its beginning and its ending, its sunrise and its sunset. [7]Hence Heraclitus, whose obscure style gave him his surname,[a] remarked: "One day is equal to every day." Different persons have interpreted the saying in different ways. Some hold that days are equal in number of hours, and this is true; for if by "day" we mean twenty-four hours' time, all days must be equal, inasmuch as the night acquires what the day loses. But others maintain that one day is equal to all days through resemblance, because the very longest space of time possesses no element which cannot be found in a single day, – namely, light and darkness, – and even to eternity day makes these alternations[b] more numerous, not different when it is shorter and different again when it is longer. [8]Hence, every day ought to be regulated as if it closed the series, as if it rounded out and completed our existence.

Pacuvius, who by long occupancy made Syria his own,[c] used to hold a regular burial sacrifice in his own honour, with wine and the usual funeral feasting, and then would have

---

[a] ὁ σκοτεινός, "the Obscure," Frag. 106 Diels[2].

[b] i.e., of light and darkness.

[c] *Usus* was the mere enjoyment of a piece of property; *dominium* was the exclusive right to its control. Possession for one, or two, years conferred ownership. See Leage, *Roman Private Law*, pp. 133, 152, and 16[4] Although Pacuvius was governor so long that the province seemed to belong to him, yet he knew he might die any day.

himself carried from the dining-room to his chamber, while eunuchs applauded and sang in Greek to a musical accompaniment: "He has lived his life, he has lived his life!" [9]Thus Pacuvius had himself carried out to burial every day. Let us, however, do from a good motive what he used to do from a debased motive; let us go to our sleep with joy and gladness; let us say:

I have lived; the course which Fortune set for me
Is finished.[a]

And if God is pleased to add another day, we should welcome it with glad hearts. That man is happiest, and is secure in his own possession of himself, who can await the morrow without apprehension. When a man has said: "I have lived!", every morning he arises he receives a bonus.

[10]But now I ought to close my letter. "What?" you say; "shall it come to me without any little offering?" "Be not afraid; it brings something, – nay, more than something, a great deal. For what is more noble than the following saying[b] of which I make this letter the bearer: "It is wrong to live under constraint; but no man is constrained to live under constraint." Of course not. On all sides lie many short and simple paths to freedom; and let us thank God that no man can be kept in life. We may spurn the very constraints that hold us. [11]"Epicurus," you reply, "uttered these words; what are you doing with another's property?" Any truth, I maintain, is my own property. And I shall continue to heap quotations from Epicurus upon you, so that all persons who swear by the words of another, and put a value upon the speaker and not upon the thing spoken, may understand that the best ideas are common property. Farewell.

[a] Vergil, *Aeneid*, iv. 653.

[b] Epicurus, Sprüche, 9 Wokte.

XVI. ON PHILOSOPHY, THE GUIDE OF LIFE

[1]It is clear to you, I am sure, Lucilius, that no man can live a happy life, or even a supportable life, without the study of wisdom; you know also that a happy life is reached when our wisdom is brought to completion, but that life is at least endurable even when our wisdom is only begun. This idea, however, clear though it is, must be strengthened and implanted more deeply by daily reflection; it is more important for you to keep the resolutions you have already made than to go on and make noble ones. You must persevere, must develop new strength by continuous study, until that which is only a good inclination becomes a good settled purpose. [2]Hence you no longer need to come to me with much talk and protestations; I know that you have made great progress. I understand the feelings which prompt your words; they are not feigned or specious words. Nevertheless I shall tell you what I think, – that at present I have hopes for you, but not yet perfect trust. And I wish that you would adopt the same attitude towards yourself; there is no reason why you should put confidence in yourself too quickly and readily. Examine yourself; scrutinize and observe yourself in divers ways; but mark, before all else, whether it is in

philosophy or merely in life itself[a] that you have made progress. [3]Philosophy is no trick to catch the public; it is not devised for show. It is a matter, not of words, but of facts. It is not pursued in order that the day may yield some amusement before it is spent, or that our leisure may be relieved of a tedium that irks us. It moulds and constructs the soul; it orders our life, guides our conduct, shows us what we should do and what we should leave undone; it sits at the helm and directs our course as we waver amid uncertainties. Without it, no one can live fearlessly or in peace of mind. Countless things that happen every hour call for advice; and such advice is to be sought in philosophy.

[4]Perhaps someone will say: "How can philosophy help me, if Fate exists? Of what avail is philosophy, if God rules the universe? Of what avail is it, if Chance governs everything? For not only is it impossible to change things that are determined, but it is also impossible to plan beforehand against what is undetermined; either God has forestalled my plans, and decided what I am to do, or else Fortune gives no free play to my plans." [5]Whether the truth, Lucilius, lies in one or in all of these views, we must be philosophers; whether Fate binds us down by an inexorable law, or whether God as arbiter of the universe has arranged everything, or whether Chance drives and tosses human affairs without method, philosophy ought to be our defence. She will encourage us to obey God cheerfully, but Fortune defiantly; she will teach us to follow God and endure Chance. [6]But it is not my purpose now to be led into a discussion as to what is within our own control, – if foreknowledge is supreme, or if a chain of fated events drags us along in its clutches, or if the sudden and the unexpected play the tyrant over us; I return now to my warning and my exhortation, that you should not allow the impulse of your spirit to weaken and grow cold. Hold fast to

[a] i.e., have merely advanced in years.

it and establish it firmly, in order that what is now impulse may become a habit of the mind.

[7]If I know you well, you have already been trying to find out, from the very beginning of my letter, what little contribution it brings to you. Sift the letter, and you will find it. You need not wonder at any genius of mine; for as yet I am lavish only with other men's property. – But why did I say "other men"? Whatever is well said by anyone is mine. This also is a saying of Epicurus:[a] "If you live according to nature, you will never be poor; if you live according to opinion, you will never be rich." [8]Nature's wants are slight; the demands of opinion are boundless. Suppose that the property of many millionaires is heaped up in your possession. Assume that fortune carries you far beyond the limits of a private income, decks you with gold, clothes you in purple, and brings you to such a degree of luxury and wealth that you can bury the earth under your marble floors; that you may not only possess, but tread upon, riches. Add statues, paintings, and whatever any art has devised for the luxury; you will only learn from such things to crave still greater.

[9]Natural desires are limited; but those which spring from false opinion can have no stopping-point. The false has no limits. When you are travelling on a road, there must be an end; but when astray, your wanderings are limitless. Recall your steps, therefore, from idle things, and when you would know whether that which you seek is based upon a natural or upon a misleading desire, consider whether it can stop at any definite point. If you find, after having travelled far, that there is a more distant goal always in view, you may be sure that this condition is contrary to nature. Farewell.

[a] Frag. 201 Usener.

XVIII. ON FESTIVALS
AND FASTING

[1]It is the month of December, and yet the city is at this very moment in a sweat. License is given to the general merry-making. Everything resounds with mighty preparations, – as if the Saturnalia differed at all from the usual business day! So true it is that the difference is nil, that I regard as correct the remark of the man who said: "Once December was a month; now it is a year."[a]

[2]If I had you with me, I should be glad to consult you and find out what you think should be done, – whether we ought to make no change in our daily routine, or whether, in order not to be out of sympathy with the ways of the public, we should dine in gayer fashion and doff the toga.[b] As it is now, we Romans have changed our dress for the sake of pleasure and holiday-making, though in former times that was only customary when the State was disturbed and had fallen on evil days. [3]I am sure that, if I know you aright, playing the part of an umpire you would have wished that we should be neither like the

---

[a] i.e., the whole year is a Saturnalia.

[b] For a dinner dress.

liberty-capped[a] throng in all ways, nor in all ways unlike them; unless, perhaps, this is just the season when we ought to lay down the law to the soul, and bid it be alone in refraining from pleasures just when the whole mob has let itself go in pleasures; for this is the surest proof which a man can get of his own constancy, if he neither seeks the things which are seductive and allure him to luxury, nor is led into them. [4]It shows much more courage to remain dry and sober when the mob is drunk and vomiting; but it shows greater self-control to refuse to withdraw oneself and to do what the crowd does, but in a different way, – thus neither making oneself conspicuous nor becoming one of the crowd. For one may keep holiday without extravagance.

[5]I am so firmly determined, however, to test the constancy of your mind that, drawing from the teachings of great men, I shall give you also a lesson: Set aside a certain number of days, during which you shall be content with the scantiest and cheapest fare, with coarse and rough dress, saying to yourself the while: "Is this the condition that I feared?" [6]It is precisely in times of immunity from care that the soul should toughen itself beforehand for occasions of greater stress, and it is while Fortune is kind that it should fortify itself against her violence. In days of peace the soldier performs manoeuvres, throws up earthworks with no enemy in sight, and wearies himself by gratuitous toil, in order that he may be equal to unavoidable toil. If you would not have a man flinch when the crisis comes, train him before it comes. Such is the course which those men[b] have followed who, in their imitation of poverty, have every month come almost to

---

[a] The *pilleus* was worn by newly freed slaves and by the Roman populace on festal occasions.

[b] The Epicurians. Cf. § 9 and Epicurus, Frag. 15[8] Usener.

want, that they might never recoil from what they had so
often rehearsed.

[7]You need not suppose that I mean meals like Timon's,
or "paupers' huts,"[a] or any other device which luxurious
millionaires use to beguile the tedium of their lives. Let the
pallet be a real one, and the coarse cloak; let the bread be
hard and grimy. Endure all this for three or four days at a
time, sometimes for more, so that it may be a test of yourself
instead of a mere hobby. Then, I assure you, my dear
Lucilius, you will leap for joy when filled with a pennyworth
of food, and you will understand that a man's peace of mind
does not depend upon Fortune; for, even when angry she
grants enough for our needs.

[8]There is no reason, however, why you should think that
you are doing anything great; for you will merely be doing
what many thousands of slaves and many thousands of poor
men are doing every day. But you may credit yourself with
this item, – that you will not be doing it under compulsion,
and that it will be as easy for you to endure it permanently
as to make the experiment from time to time. Let us practise
our strokes on the "dummy";[b] let us become intimate with
poverty, so that Fortune may not catch us off our guard. We
shall be rich with all the more comfort, if we once learn how
far poverty is from being a burden.

[9]Even Epicurus, the teacher of pleasure, used to observe
stated intervals, during which he satisfied his hunger in
niggardly fashion; he wished to see whether he thereby fell
short of full and complete happiness, and, if so, by what
amount he fell short, and whether this amount was worth
purchasing at the price of great effort. At any rate, he makes
such a statement in the well known letter written to Polyaenus

[a] Cf. Ep. c. 6 and Martial, iii. 48.

[b] The post which gladiators used when preparing themselves for combats
in the arena.

in the archonship of Charinus.[a] Indeed, he boasts that he himself lived on less than a penny, but that Metrodorus, whose progress was not yet so great, needed a whole penny. [10]Do you think that there can be fullness on such fare? Yes, and there is pleasure also, – not that shifty and fleeting Pleasure which needs a fillip now and then, but a pleasure that is steadfast and sure. For though water, barley-meal, and crusts of barley-bread, are not a cheerful diet, yet it is the highest kind of Pleasure to be able to derive pleasure from this sort of food, and to have reduced one's needs to that modicum which no unfairness of Fortune can snatch away. [11]Even prison fare is more generous; and those who have been set apart for capital punishment are not so meanly fed by the man who is to execute them. Therefore, what a noble soul must one have, to descend of one's own free will to a diet which even those who have been sentenced to death have not to fear! This is indeed forestalling the spearthrusts of Fortune.

[12]So begin, my dear Lucilius, to follow the custom of these men, and set apart certain days on which you shall withdraw from your business and make yourself at home with the scantiest fare. Establish business relations with poverty.

> Dare, O my friend, to scorn the sight of wealth,
> And mould thyself to kinship with thy God.[b]

[13]For he alone is in kinship with God who has scorned wealth. Of course I do not forbid you to possess it, but I would have you reach the point at which you possess it dauntlessly; this can be accomplished only by persuading yourself that you

[a] Usually identified with Chaerimus, 307–8 B.C. But Wilhelm, *Öster Jahreshefte*, V.136, has shown that there is probably no confusion of names. A Charinus was archon at Athens in 290–89; see Johnson, *Class. Phil.* ix. p. 256.

[b] Vergil, *Aeneid*, viii. 364 f.

can live happily without it as well as with it, and by regarding riches always as likely to elude you.

[14]But now I must begin to fold up my letter. "Settle your debts first," you cry. Here is a draft on Epicurus; he will pay down the sum: "Ungoverned anger begets madness."[a] You cannot help knowing the truth of these words, since you have had not only slaves, but also enemies. [15]But indeed this emotion blazes out against all sorts of persons; it springs from love as much as from hate, and shows itself not less in serious matters than in jest and sport. And it makes no difference how important the provocation may be, but into what kind of soul it penetrates. Similarly with fire; it does not matter how great is the flame, but what it falls upon. For solid timbers have repelled a very great fire; conversely, dry and easily inflammable stuff nourishes the slightest spark into a conflagration. So it is with anger, my dear Lucilius; the outcome of a mighty anger is madness, and hence anger should be avoided, not merely that we may escape excess, but that we may have a healthy mind. Farewell.

[a] Frag. 484 Usener.

XXVII. ON OLD AGE AND DEATH

[1]I was just lately telling you that I was within sight of old age.[a] I am now afraid that I have left old age behind me. For some other word would now apply to my years, or at any rate to my body; since old age means a time of life that is weary rather than crushed. You may rate me in the worn-out class, – of those who are nearing the end.

[2]Nevertheless, I offer thanks to myself, with you as witness; for I feel that age has done no damage to my mind, though I feel its effects on my constitution. Only my vices, and the outward aids to these vices, have reached senility; my mind is strong and rejoices that it has but slight connexion with the body. It has laid aside the greater part of its load. It is alert; it takes issue with me on the subject of old age; it declares that old age is its time of bloom. [3]Let me take it at its word, and let it make the most of the advantages it possesses. The mind bids me do some thinking and consider how much of this peace of spirit and moderation of character I owe to wisdom and how much to my time of life; it bids me distinguish carefully what I cannot do and what I do not

[a] See the twelfth letter. Seneca was by this time at least sixty-five years old, and probably older.

want to do. . . .[a] For why should one complain or regard it as a disadvantage, if powers which ought to come to an end have failed? [4]"But," you say, "it is the greatest possible disadvantage to be worn out and to die off, or rather, if I may speak literally, to melt away! For we are not suddenly smitten and laid low; we are worn away, and every day reduces our powers to a certain extent."

But is there any better end to it all than to glide off to one's proper haven, when nature slips the cable? Not that there is anything painful in a shock and a sudden departure from existence; it is merely because this other way of departure is easy, – a gradual withdrawal. I, at any rate, as if the test were at hand and the day were come which is to pronounce its decision concerning all the years of my life, watch over myself and commune thus with myself: [5]"The showing which we have made up to the present time, in word or deed, counts for nothing. All this is but a trifling and deceitful pledge of our spirit, and is wrapped in much charlatanism. I shall leave it to Death to determine what progress I have made. Therefore with no faint heart I am making ready for the day when, putting aside all stage artifice and actor's rouge, I am to pass judgment upon myself, – whether I am merely declaiming brave sentiments, or whether I really feel them; whether all the bold threats I have uttered against fortune are a pretence and a farce. [6]Put aside the opinion of the world; it is always wavering and always takes both sides. Put aside the studies which you have pursued throughout your life; Death will deliver the final judgment in your case. This is what I mean: your debates and learned talks, your maxims gathered from the teachings of the wise, your cultured conversation, – all these afford no proof of

[a] This passage is hopelessly corrupt. The course of the argument requires something like this: For it is just as much to my advantage not to be able to do what I do not want to do, as it is to be able to do whatever gives me pleasure.

the real strength of your soul. Even the most timid man can deliver a bold speech. What you have done in the past will be manifest only at the time when you draw your last breath. I accept the terms; I do not shrink from the decision." [7]This is what I say to myself, but I would have you think that I have said it to you also. You are younger; but what does that matter? There is no fixed count of our years. You do not know where death awaits you; so be ready for it everywhere.

[8]I was just intending to stop, and my hand was making ready for the closing sentence; but the rites are still to be performed and the travelling money for the letter disbursed. And just assume that I am not telling where I intend to borrow the necessary sum; you know upon whose coffers I depend. Wait for me but a moment, and I will pay you from my own account;[a] meanwhile, Epicurus will oblige me with these words:[b] "Think on death," or rather, if you prefer the phrase, on "migration to heaven." [9]The meaning is clear, – that it is a wonderful thing to learn thoroughly how to die. You may deem it superfluous to learn a text that can be used only once; but that is just the reason why we ought to think on a thing. When we can never prove whether we really know a thing, we must always be learning it. [10]"Think on death." In saying this, he bids us think on freedom. He who has learned to die has unlearned slavery; he is above any external power, or, at any rate, he is beyond it. What terrors have prisons and bonds and bars for him? His way out is clear. There is only one chain which binds us to life, and that is the love of life. The chain may not be cast off, but it may be rubbed away, so that, when necessity shall demand, nothing may retard or hinder us from being ready to do at once that which at some time we are bound to do. Farewell.

[a] i.e., the money will be brought from home, – the saying will be one of Seneca's own.
[b] Epicurus, Frag. 205 Usener.

XXVII. ON THE GOOD WHICH ABIDES

[1]"What," say you, "are you giving me advice? Indeed, have you already advised yourself, already corrected your own faults? Is this the reason why you have leisure to reform other men?" No, I am not so shameless as to undertake to cure my fellow-men when I am ill myself. I am, however, discussing with you troubles which concern us both, and sharing the remedy with you, just as if we were lying ill in the same hospital. Listen to me, therefore, as you would if I were talking to myself. I am admitting you to my inmost thoughts, and am having it out with myself, merely making use of you as my pretext. [2]I keep crying out to myself: "Count your years, and you will be ashamed to desire and pursue the same things you desired in your boyhood days. Of this one thing make sure against your dying day, – let your faults die before you die. Away with those disordered pleasures, which must be dearly paid for; it is not only those which are to come that harm me, but also those which have come and gone. Just as crimes, even if they have not been detected when they were committed, do not allow anxiety to end with them; so with guilty pleasures, regret remains even after the pleasures are over. They are not substantial, they are not trustworthy; even if they do not harm us, they are fleeting. [3]Cast about rather

for some good which will abide. But there can be no such good except as the soul discovers it for itself within itself. Virtue alone affords everlasting and peace-giving joy; even if some obstacle arise, it is but like an intervening cloud, which floats beneath the sun but never prevails against it."

[4]When will it be your lot to attain this joy? Thus far, you have indeed not been sluggish, but you must quicken your pace. Much toil remains; to confront it, you must yourself lavish all your waking hours, and all your efforts, if you wish the result to be accomplished. This matter cannot be delegated to someone else. [5]The other kind of literary activity[a] admits of outside assistance. Within our own time there was a certain rich man named Calvisius Sabinus; he had the bank-account and the brains of a freedman.[b] I never saw a man whose good fortune was a greater offence against propriety. His memory was so faulty that he would sometimes forget the name of Ulysses, or Achilles, or Priam, – names which we know as well as we know those of our own attendants. No major-domo in his dotage, who cannot give men their right names, but is compelled to invent names for them, – no such man, I say, calls off the names[c] of his master's tribesmen so atrociously as Sabinus used to call off the Trojan and Achaean heroes. But none the less did he desire to appear learned. [6]So he devised this short cut to learning: he paid fabulous prices for slaves, – one to know Homer by heart and another to know Hesiod; he also delegated a special slave to each of the nine lyric poets. You need not wonder that he paid high prices for these slaves; if he did not find them ready to hand he had

---

[a] i.e., ordinary studies, or literature, as contrasted with philosophy.

[b] Compare with the following the vulgarities of Trimalchio in the Satire of Petronius, and the bad taste of Nasidienus in Horace (Sat. ii. 8).

[c] At the *salutatio*, or morning call. The position of *nomenclator*, "caller-of-names," was originally devoted more strictly to political purposes. Here it is primarily social.

them made to order. After collecting this retinue, he began to make life miserable for his guests; he would keep these fellows at the foot of his couch, and ask them from time to time for verses which he might repeat, and then frequently break down in the middle of a word. [7]Satellius Quadratus, a feeder, and consequently a fawner, upon addle-pated millionaires, and also (for this quality goes with the other two) a flouter of them, suggested to Sabinus that he should have philologists to gather up the bits.[a] Sabinus remarked that each slave cost him one hundred thousand sesterces; Satellius replied: "You might have bought as many book-cases for a smaller sum." But Sabinus held to the opinion that what any member of his household knew, he himself knew also. [8]This same Satellius began to advise Sabinus to take wrestling lessons, – sickly, pale, and thin as he was, Sabinus answered: "How can I? I can scarcely stay alive now." "Don't say that, I implore you," replied the other, "consider how many perfectly healthy slaves you have!" No man is able to borrow or buy a sound mind; in fact, as it seems to me, even though sound minds were for sale, they would not find buyers. Depraved minds, however, are bought and sold every day.

[9]But let me pay off my debt and say farewell: "Real wealth is poverty adjusted to the law of Nature."[b] Epicurus has this saying in various ways and contexts; but it can never be repeated too often, since it can never be learned too well. For some persons the remedy should be merely prescribed; in the case of others, it should be forced down their throats. Farewell.

---

[a] i.e., all the ideas that dropped out of the head of Sabinus. The slave who picked up the crumbs was called *analecta*.

[b] Epicurus, Frag. 477 Usener.

XXVIII. ON TRAVEL AS A CURE FOR DISCONTENT

[1]Do you suppose that you alone have had this experience? Are you surprised, as if it were a novelty, that after such long travel and so many changes of scene you have not been able to shake off the gloom and heaviness of your mind? You need a change of soul rather than a change of climate.[a] Though you may cross vast spaces of sea, and though, as our Vergil[b] remarks,

> Lands and cities are left astern,

your faults will follow you whithersoever you travel. [2]Socrates made the same remark to one who complained; he said: "Why do you wonder that globe-trotting does not help you, seeing that you always take yourself with you? The reason which set you wandering is ever at your heels." What pleasure is there in seeing new lands? Or in surveying cities and spots of interest? All your bustle is useless. Do you ask why such flight does not help you? It is because

---

[a] Cf. Horace, Ep. i. 11, 27 *caelum non animum mutant qui trans mare currunt.*

[b] *Aeneid*, iii. 72, vi. 78 f.

you flee along with yourself. You must lay aside the burdens of the mind; until you do this, no place will satisfy you. [3]Reflect that your present behaviour is like that of the prophetess whom Vergil describes: she is excited and goaded into fury, and contains within herself much inspiration that is not her own:

> The priestess raves, if haply she may shake
> The great god from her heart.

You wander hither and yon, to rid yourself of the burden that rests upon you, though it becomes more troublesome by reason of your very restlessness, just as in a ship the cargo when stationary makes no trouble, but when it shifts to this side or that, it causes the vessel to heel more quickly in the direction where it has settled. Anything you do tells against you, and you hurt yourself by your very unrest; for you are shaking up a sick man.

[4]That trouble once removed, all change of scene will become pleasant; though you may be driven to the uttermost ends of the earth, in whatever corner of a savage land you may find yourself, that place, however forbidding, will be to you a hospitable abode. The person you are matters more than the place to which you go; for that reason we should not make the mind a bondsman to any one place. Live in this belief: "I am not born for any one corner of the universe; this whole world is my country." [5]If you saw this fact clearly, you would not be surprised at getting no benefit from the fresh scenes to which you roam each time through weariness of the old scenes. For the first would have pleased you in each case, had you believed it wholly yours.[a] As it is, however, you are not journeying; you are drifting and being driven, only exchanging one place for another, although that which you

---

[a] i.e., had you been able to say *patria mea totus mundus est.*

seek, – to live well, – is found everywhere.[a] [6]Can there be any spot so full of confusion as the Forum? Yet you can live quietly even there, if necessary. Of course, if one were allowed to make one's own arrangements, I should flee far from the very sight and neighbourhood of the Forum. For just as pestilential places assail even the strongest constitution, so there are some places which are also unwholesome for a healthy mind which is not yet quite sound, though recovering from its ailment. [7]I disagree with those who strike out into the midst of the billows and, welcoming a stormy existence, wrestle daily in hardihood of soul with life's problems. The wise man will endure all that, but will not choose it; he will prefer to be at peace rather than at war. It helps little to have cast out your own faults if you must quarrel with those of others. [8]Says one: "There were thirty tyrants surrounding Socrates, and yet they could not break his spirit"; but what does it matter how many masters a man has? "Slavery" has no plural; and he who has scorned it is free, – no matter amid how large a mob of over-lords he stands.

[9]It is time to stop, but not before I have paid duty. "The knowledge of sin is the beginning of salvation." This saying of Epicurus[b] seems to me to be a noble one. For he who does not know that he has sinned does not desire correction; you must discover yourself in the wrong before you can reform yourself. [10]Some boast of their faults. Do you think that the man has any thought of mending his ways who counts over his vices as if they were virtues? Therefore, as far as possible, prove yourself guilty, hunt up charges against yourself; play the part, first of accuser, then of judge, last of intercessor. At times be harsh with yourself.[c] Farewell.

[a] Cf. Horace, Ep. i. 11, 28 – *navibus atque Quadrigis petimus bene vivere; quod petis, hic est.*

[b] Frag. 522 Usener.

[c] i.e., refuse your own intercession.

XXXIII. ON THE FUTILITY OF LEARNING MAXIMS

[1]You wish me to close these letters also, as I closed my former letters, with certain utterances taken from the chiefs of our school. But they did not interest themselves in choice extracts; the whole texture of their work is full of strength. There is unevenness, you know, when some objects rise conspicuous above others. A single tree is not remarkable if the whole forest rises to the same height. [2]Poetry is crammed with utterances of this sort, and so is history. For this reason I would not have you think that these utterances belong to Epicurus. they are common property and are emphatically our own.[a] They are, however, more noteworthy in Epicurus, because they appear at infrequent intervals and when you do not expect them, and because it is surprising that brave words should be spoken at any time by a man who made a practice of being effeminate. For that is what most persons maintain. In my own opinion, however, Epicurus is really a brave man, even though he did wear long sleeves.[b] Fortitude,

[a] Stoic as well as Epicurean.

[b] Contrasted with *alte cinctos*. The sleeveless and "girt-up" tunic is the sign of energy; cf. Horace, *Sat*. i. [5] 5, and Suetonius, *Caligula*, 52: the effeminate Caligula would "appear in public with a long-sleeved tunic and bracelets."

energy, and readiness for battle are to be found among the Persians,[a] just as much as among men who have girded themselves up high.

[3]Therefore, you need not call upon me for extracts and quotations; such thoughts as one may extract here and there in the works of other philosophers run through the whole body of our writings. Hence we have no "show-window goods," nor do we deceive the purchaser in such a way that, if he enters our shop, he will find nothing except that which is displayed in the window. We allow the purchasers themselves to get their samples from anywhere they please. [4]Suppose we should desire to sort out each separate motto from the general stock; to whom shall we credit them? To Zeno, Cleanthes, Chrysippus, Panaetius, or Posidonius? We Stoics are not subjects of a despot: each of us lays claim to his own freedom. With them,[b] on the other hand, whatever Hermarchus says or Metrodorus, is ascribed to one source.

In that brotherhood, everything that any man utters is spoken under the leadership and commanding authority[c] of one alone. We cannot, I maintain, no matter how we try, pick out anything from so great a multitude of things equally good.

Only the poor man counts his flock.[d]

Wherever you direct your gaze, you will meet with something that might stand out from the rest, if the context in which you read it were not equally notable.

[5]For this reason, give over hoping that you can skim, by

[a] Who wore sleeves.

[b] i.e., the Epicureans.

[c] For the phrase *ductu et auspiciis* see Plautus, *Amph.* i. [1] 41 *ut gesserit rem publicam ductu imperio auspicio suo*; and Horace, *Od.* i. [7] 27 *Teucro duce et auspice Teucro*. The original significance of the phrase refers to the right of the commander-in-chief to take the auspices.

[d] Ovid, *Metamorphosis*, xiii. 824.

means of epitomes, the wisdom of distinguished men. Look into their wisdom as a whole; study it as a whole. They are working out a plan and weaving together, line upon line, a masterpiece, from which nothing can be taken away without injury to the whole. Examine the separate parts, if you like, provided you examine them as parts of the man himself. She is not a beautiful woman whose ankle or arm is praised, but she whose general appearance makes you forget to admire her single attributes.

[6]If you insist, however, I shall not be niggardly with you, but lavish; for there is a huge multitude of these passages; they are scattered about in profusion, – they do not need to be gathered together, but merely to be picked up. They do not drip forth occasionally; they flow continuously. They are unbroken and are closely connected. Doubtless they would be of much benefit to those who are still novices and worshipping outside the shrine; for single maxims sink in more easily when they are marked off and bounded like a line of verse. [7]That is why we give to children a proverb, or that which the Greeks call Chria,[a] to be learned by heart; that sort of thing can be comprehended by the young mind, which cannot as yet hold more. For a man, however, whose progress is definite, to chase after choice extracts and to prop his weakness by the best known and the briefest sayings and to depend upon his memory, is disgraceful; it is time for him to lean on himself. He should make such maxims and not memorize them. For it is disgraceful even for an old man, or one who has sighted old age, to have a note-book knowledge. "This is what Zeno said." But what have you yourself said? "This is the opinion of Cleanthes." But what is your own opinion? How long shall you march under another man's orders? Take command, and utter some word which posterity will remember. Put forth

[a] Either "maxims" or "outlines," "themes." For a discussion of them see Quintilian, *Inst. Orat.* i. [9] 3 ff.

something from your own stock. [8]For this reason I hold that there is nothing of eminence in all such men as these, who never create anything themselves, but always lurk in the shadow of others, playing the rôle of interpreters, never daring to put once into practice what they have been so long in learning. They have exercised their memories on other men's material. But it is one thing to remember, another to know. Remembering is merely safeguarding something entrusted to the memory; knowing, however, means making everything your own; it means not depending upon the copy and not all the time glancing back at the master. [9]"Thus said Zeno, thus said Cleanthes, indeed!" Let there be a difference between yourself and your book! How long shall you be a learner? From now on be a teacher as well! "But why," one asks,[a] "should I have to continue hearing lectures on what I can read?" "The living voice," one replies, "is a great help." Perhaps, but not the voice which merely makes itself the mouthpiece of another's words, and only performs the duty of a reporter.

[10]Consider this fact also. Those who have never attained their mental independence begin, in the first place, by following the leader in cases where everyone has deserted the leader; then, in the second place, they follow him in matters where the truth is still being investigated. However, the truth will never be discovered if we rest contented with discoveries already made. Besides, he who follows another not only discovers nothing but is not even investigating. [11]What then? Shall I not follow in the footsteps of my predecessors? I shall indeed use the old road, but if I find one that makes a shorter cut and is smoother to travel, I shall open the new road. Men who have made these discoveries before us are not our masters,

---

[a] The objector is the assumed auditor. The answer to the objection gives the usual view as to the power of the living voice; to this Seneca assents, provided that the voice has a message of its own.

but our guides. Truth lies open for all; it has not yet been monopolized. And there is plenty of it left even for posterity to discover. Farewell.

XL. ON THE PROPER STYLE FOR A PHILOSOPHER'S DISCOURSE

[1]I thank you for writing to me so often; for you are revealing your real self to me in the only way you can. I never receive a letter from you without being in your company forthwith. If the pictures of our absent friends are pleasing to us, though they only refresh the memory and lighten our longing by a solace that is unreal and unsubstantial, how much more pleasant is a letter, which brings us real traces, real evidences, of an absent friend! For that which is sweetest when we meet face to face is afforded by the impress of a friend's hand upon his letter, – recognition.

[2]You write me that you heard a lecture by the philosopher Serapio,[a] when he landed at your present place of residence. "He is wont," you say, "to wrench up his words with a mighty rush, and he does not let them flow forth one by one, but makes them crowd and dash upon each other.[b] For the words come in such quantity that a single voice is inadequate to utter them." I do not approve of this in a

---

[a] This person cannot be identified.

[b] The explanation of Professor Summers seems sound, that the metaphor is taken from a mountain-torrent. Compare the description of Cratinus' style in Aristophanes, *Ach.* 526, or that of Pindar in Horace, *Od.* iv. [2]5 ff.

philosopher; his speech, like his life, should be composed; and nothing that rushes headlong and is hurried is well ordered. That is why, in Homer, the rapid style, which sweeps down without a break like a snow-squall, is assigned to the younger speaker; from the old man eloquence flows gently, sweeter than honey.[a]

[3]Therefore, mark my words; that forceful manner of speech, rapid and copious, is more suited to a mountebank than to a man who is discussing and teaching an important and serious subject. But I object just as strongly that he should drip out his words as that he should go at top speed; he should neither keep the ear on the stretch, nor deafen it. For that poverty-stricken and thin-spun style also makes the audience less attentive because they are weary of its stammering slowness; nevertheless, the word which has been long awaited sinks in more easily than the word which flits past us on the wing. Finally, people speak of "handing down" precepts to their pupils; but one is not "handing down" that which eludes the grasp. [4]Besides, speech that deals with the truth should be unadorned and plain. This popular style has nothing to do with the truth; its aim is to impress the common herd, to ravish heedless ears by its speed; it does not offer itself for discussion, but snatches itself away from discussion. But how can that speech govern others which cannot itself be governed? May I not also remark that all speech which is employed for the purpose of healing our minds, ought to sink into us? Remedies do not avail unless they remain in the system.

[5]Besides, this sort of speech contains a great deal of sheer emptiness; it has more sound than power. My terrors should be quieted, my irritations soothed, my illusions shaken off, my indulgences checked, my greed rebuked. And which of these cures can be brought about in a hurry? What physician

---

[a] *Iliad*, iii. 222 (Odysseus), and i. 249 (Nestor).

can heal his patient on a flying visit? May I add that such a jargon of confused and ill-chosen words cannot afford pleasure, either? [6]No; but just as you are well satisfied, in the majority of cases, to have seen through tricks which you did not think could possibly be done,[a] so in the case of these word-gymnasts to have heard them once is amply sufficient. For what can a man desire to learn or to imitate in them? What is he to think of their souls, when their speech is sent into the charge in utter disorder, and cannot be kept in hand? [7]Just as, when you run down hill, you cannot stop at the point where you had decided to stop, but your steps are carried along by the momentum of your body and are borne beyond the place where you wished to halt; so this speed of speech has no control over itself, nor is it seemly for philosophy; since philosophy should carefully place her words, not fling them out, and should proceed step by step.

[8]"What then?" you say; "should not philosophy sometimes take a loftier tone?" Of course she should; but dignity of character should be preserved, and this is stripped away by such violent and excessive force. Let philosophy possess great forces, but kept well under control; let her stream flow unceasingly, but never become a torrent. And I should hardly allow even to an orator a rapidity of speech like this, which cannot be called back, which goes lawlessly ahead; for how could it be followed by jurors, who are often inexperienced and untrained? Even when the orator is carried away by his desire to show off his powers, or by uncontrollable emotion, even then he should not quicken his pace and heap up words to an extent greater than the ear can endure.

---

[a] Seneca's phrase, *quae fieri posse non crederes*, has been interpreted as a definition of αράδοξα. It is more probable, however, that he is comparing with the juggler's tricks the verbal performances of certain lecturers, whose jargon one marvels at but does not care to hear again.

[9]You will be acting rightly, therefore, if you do not regard those men who seek how much they may say, rather than how they shall say it, and if for yourself you choose, provided a choice must be made, to speak as Publius Vinicius the stammerer does. When Asellius was asked how Vinicius spoke, he replied: "Gradually"! (It was a remark of Geminus Varius, by the way: "I don't see how you can call that man 'eloquent'; why, he can't get out three words together.") Why, then, should you not choose to speak as Vinicius does? [10]Though of course some wag may cross your path, like the person who said, when Vinicius was dragging out his words one by one, as if he were dictating and not speaking. "Say, haven't you anything to say?" And yet that were the better choice, for the rapidity of Quintus Haterius, the most famous orator of his age, is, in my opinion, to be avoided by a man of sense. Haterius never hesitated, never paused; he made only one start, and only one stop.

[11]However, I suppose that certain styles of speech are more or less suitable to nations also; in a Greek you can put up with the unrestrained style, but we Romans, even when writing, have become accustomed to separate our words.[a] And our compatriot Cicero, with whom Roman oratory sprang into prominence, was also a slow pacer.[b] The Roman language is more inclined to take stock of itself, to weigh, and to offer something worth weighing. [12]Fabianius, a man noteworthy because of his life, his knowledge, and, less important than either of these, his eloquence also, used to discuss a subject with dispatch rather than with haste; hence you might call it ease rather than speed. I approve this quality in the wise man; but I do not demand it; only let his speech proceed unhampered,

[a] The Greek texts were still written without separation of the words, in contrast with the Roman.

[b] *Gradarius* may be contrasted with *tolutarius*, "trotter." The word might also mean one who walks with dignified step, as in a religious procession.

though I prefer that it should be deliberately uttered rather than spouted.

[13]However, I have this further reason for frightening you away from the latter malady, namely, that you could only be successful in practising this style by losing your sense of modesty; you would have to rub all shame from your countenance,[a] and refuse to hear yourself speak. For that heedless flow will carry with it many expressions which you would wish to criticize.

[14]And, I repeat, you could not attain it and at the same time preserve your sense of shame. Moreover, you would need to practise every day, and transfer your attention from subject matter to words. But words, even if they came to you readily and flowed without any exertion on your part, yet would have to be kept under control. For just as a less ostentatious gait becomes a philosopher, so does a restrained style of speech, far removed from boldness. Therefore, the ultimate kernel of my remarks is this: I bid you be slow of speech. Farewell

[a] Cf. Martial, xi. 2[7] 7 *aut cum perfricuit frontem posuitque pudorem.* After a violent rubbing, the face would not show blushes.

XLI. ON THE GOD WITHIN US

[1]You are doing an excellent thing, one which will be wholesome for you, if, as you write me, you are persisting in your effort to attain sound understanding; it is foolish to pray for this when you can acquire it from yourself. We do not need to uplift our hands towards heaven, or to beg the keeper of a temple to let us approach his idol's ear, as if in this way our prayers were more likely to be heard. God is near you, he is with you, he is within you. [2]This is what I mean, Lucilius: a holy spirit indwells within us, one who marks our good and bad deeds, and is our guardian. As we treat this spirit, so are we treated by it. Indeed, no man can be good without the help of God. Can one rise superior to fortune unless God helps him to rise? He it is that gives noble and upright counsel. In each good man

A god doth dwell, but what god know we not.[a]

[a] Vergil, Aeneid, viii. 352, *Hoc nemus, hunc, inquit, frondoso vertice collem, Quis deus incertum est, habitat deus,* and cf. Quintillian, i. 1⁰ 88, where he is speaking of Ennius, whom "*sicut sacros vetustate lucos adoremus, in quibus grandia et antiqua robora iam non tantum habent speciem quantem religionem.*"

[3]If ever you have come upon a grove that is full of ancient trees which have grown to an unusual height, shutting out a view of the sky by a veil of pleached and intertwining branches, then the loftiness of the forest, the seclusion of the spot, and your marvel at the thick unbroken shade in the midst of the open spaces, will prove to you the presence of deity. Or if a cave, made by the deep crumbling of the rocks, holds up a mountain on its arch, a place not built with hands but hollowed out into such spaciousness by natural causes, your soul will be deeply moved by a certain intimation of the existence of God. We worship the sources of mighty rivers; we erect altars at places where great streams burst suddenly from hidden sources; we adore springs of hot water as divine, and consecrate certain pools because of their dark waters or their immeasurable depth. [4]If you see a man who is unterrified in the midst of dangers, untouched by desires, happy in adversity, peaceful amid the storm, who looks down upon men from a higher plane, and views the gods on a footing of equality, will not a feeling of reverence for him steal over you, will you not say: "This quality is too great and too lofty to be regarded as resembling this petty body in which it dwells? A divine power has descended upon that man." [5]When a soul rises superior to other souls, when it is under control, when it passes through every experience as if it were of small account, when it smiles at our fears and at our prayers, it is stirred by a force from heaven. A thing like this cannot stand upright unless it be propped by the divine. Therefore, a greater part of it abides in that place from whence it came down to earth. Just as the rays of the sun do indeed touch the earth, but still abide at the source from which they are sent; even so the great and hallowed soul, which has come down in order that we may have a nearer knowledge of divinity, does indeed associate with us, but still cleaves to its origin; on that source it depends, thither it turns its gaze and strives to go, and

it concerns itself with our doings only as a being superior to ourselves.

[6]What, then, is such a soul? One which is resplendent with no external good, but only with its own. For what is more foolish than to praise in a man the qualities which come from without? And what is more insane than to marvel at characteristics which may at the next instant be passed on to someone else? A golden bit does not make a better horse. The lion with gilded mane, in process of being trained and forced by weariness to endure the decoration, is sent into the arena in quite a different way from the wild lion whose spirit is unbroken; the latter, indeed, bold in his attack, as nature wished him to be, impressive because of his wild appearance, – and it is his glory that none can look upon him without fear, – is favoured[a] in preference to the other lion, that languid and gilded brute.

[7]No man ought to glory except in that which is his own. We praise a vine if it makes the shoots teem with increase, if by its weight it bends to the ground the very poles which hold its fruit; would any man prefer to this vine one from which golden grapes and golden leaves hang down? In a vine the virtue peculiarly its own is fertility; in man also we should praise that which is his own. Suppose that he has a retinue of comely slaves and a beautiful house, that his farm is large and large his income; none of these things is in the man himself; they are all on the outside. [8]Praise the quality in him which cannot be given or snatched away, that which is the peculiar property of the man. Do you ask what this is? It is soul, and reason brought to perfection in the soul. For man is a reasoning animal. Therefore, man's highest good is attained, if he has fulfilled the good for which nature designed him at birth. [9]And what is it which this reason demands

---

[a] The spectators of the fight, which is to take place between the two lions, applaud the wild lion and bet on him.

of him? The easiest thing in the world, – to live in accordance with his own nature. But this is turned into a hard task by the general madness of mankind; we push one another into vice. And how can a man be recalled to salvation, when he has none to restrain him, and all mankind to urge him on? Farewell.

XLVII. ON MASTER AND SLAVE

[1]I am glad to learn, through those who come from you, that you live on friendly terms with your slaves. This befits a sensible and well-educated man like yourself. "They are slaves," people declare.[a] Nay, rather they are men. "Slaves!" No, comrades. "Slaves!" No, they are unpretentious friends. "Slaves!" No, they are our fellow-slaves, if one reflects that Fortune has equal rights over slaves and free men alike.

[2]That is why I smile at those who think it degrading for a man to dine with his slave. But why should they think it degrading? It is only because purse-proud etiquette surrounds a householder at his dinner with a mob of standing slaves. The master eats more than he can hold, and with monstrous greed loads his belly until it is stretched and at length ceases to do the work of a belly; so that he is at greater pains to discharge all the food than he was to stuff it down. [3]All this time the poor slaves may not move their lips, even to speak. The slightest murmur

---

[a] Much of the following is quoted by Macrobius, *Sat.* i. 1[1] 7 ff., in the passage beginning *vis tu cogitare eos, quos ios tuum vocas, isdem seminibus ortos eodem frui caelo*, etc.

is repressed by the rod; even a chance sound, – a cough, a sneeze, or a hiccup, – is visited with the lash. There is a grievous penalty for the slightest breach of silence. All night long they must stand about, hungry and dumb.

[4]The result of it all is that these slaves, who may not talk in their master's presence, talk about their master. But the slaves of former days, who were permitted to converse not only in their master's presence, but actually with him, whose mouths were not stitched up tight, were ready to bare their necks for their master, to bring upon their own heads any danger that threatened him; they spoke at the feast, but kept silence during torture. [5]Finally, the saying, in allusion to this same high-handed treatment, becomes current: "As many enemies as you have slaves." They are not enemies when we acquire them; we make them enemies.

I shall pass over other cruel and inhuman conduct towards them; for we maltreat them, not as if they were men, but as if they were beasts of burden. When we recline at a banquet, one slave mops up the disgorged food, another crouches beneath the table and gathers up the left-overs of the tipsy guests. [6]Another carves the priceless game birds; with unerring strokes and skilled hand he cuts choice morsels along the breast or the rump. Hapless fellow, to live only for the purpose of cutting fat capons correctly – unless, indeed, the other man is still more unhappy than he, who teaches this art for pleasure's sake, rather than he who learns it because he must. [7]Another, who serves the wine, must dress like a woman and wrestle with his advancing years; he cannot get away from his boyhood; he is dragged back to it; and though he has already acquired a soldier's figure, he is kept beardless by having his hair smoothed away or plucked out by the roots, and he must remain awake throughout the night, dividing his time between his master's drunkenness and his lust; in the chamber he must be a man, at the feast a boy.[a] [8]Another, whose duty it is to put a valuation on the guests, must stick to his task, poor fellow, and watch to see whose flattery and whose immodesty, whether of appetite or of language, is to get them an invitation for tomorrow. Think also of the poor purveyors of food, who note their masters' tastes with delicate skill, who know what special flavours will sharpen their appetite, what will please their eyes, what new combinations will rouse their cloyed stomachs, what food will excite their loathing through sheer satiety, and what will stir them to hunger on that particular day. With slaves like these the master cannot bear to dine; he would think it beneath his dignity to associate with his slave at the same table! Heaven forfend!

But how many masters is he creating in these very men! [9]I have seen standing in the line, before the door of Callistus, the former master,[b] of Callistus; I have seen the master himself shut out while others were welcomed, – the master who once fastened the "For Sale" ticket on Callistus and put him in the market along with the good-for-nothing slaves. But he has been paid off by that slave who was shuffled into the first lot of those on whom the crier practises his lungs; the slave, too, in his turn has cut his name from the list and in his turn has adjudged him unfit to enter his house. The master sold Callistus, but how much has Callistus made his master pay for!

[10]Kindly remember that he whom you call your slave sprang from the same stock, is smiled upon by the same skies,

[a] *Glabri, delicati*, or *exoleti* were favourite slaves, kept artifically youthful by Romans of the more dissolute class. Cf. Catullus, lxi. 142, and Seneca, *De Brevitate Vitae*, 1^2 5 (a passage closely resembling the description given above by Seneca), where the master prides himself upon the elegant appearance and graceful gestures of these favourites.

[b] The master of Callistus, before he became the favourite of Caligula, is unknown.

and on equal terms with yourself breathes, lives, and dies. It is just as possible for you to see in him a free-born man as for him to see in you a slave. As a result of the massacres in Marius's[a] day, many a man of distinguished birth, who was taking the first steps toward senatorial rank by service in the army, was humbled by fortune, one becoming a shepherd, another a caretaker of a country cottage. Despise, then, if you dare, those to whose estate you may at any time descend, even when you are despising them.

[11]I do not wish to involve myself in too large a question, and to discuss the treatment of slaves, towards whom we Romans are excessively haughty, cruel, and insulting. But this is the kernel of my advice: Treat your inferiors as you would be treated by your betters. And as often as you reflect how much power you have over a slave, remember that your master has just as much power over you. [12]"But I have no master," you say. You are still young; perhaps you will have one. Do you not know at what age Hecuba entered captivity, or Croesus, or the mother of Darius, or Plato, or Diogenes?[b]

[13]Associate with your slave on kindly, even on affable, terms; let him talk with you, plan with you, live with you. I know that at this point all the exquisites will cry out against me in a body; they will say: "There is nothing more debasing,

[a] There is some doubt whether we should not read Variana, as Lipsius suggests. This method of qualifying for senator suits the Empire better than the Republic. Variana would refer to the defeat of Varus in Germany, A.D. 9.

[b] Plato was about forty years old when he visited Sicily, whence he was afterwards deported by Dionysius the Elder. He was sold into slavery at Aegina and ransomed by a man from Cyrene. Diogenes, while travelling from Athens to Aegina, is said to have been captured by pirates and sold in Crete, where he was purchased by a certain Corinthian and given his freedom.

more disgraceful, than this." But these are the very persons whom I sometimes surprise kissing the hands of other men's slaves. [14]Do you not see even this, how our ancestors removed from masters everything invidious, and from slaves everything insulting? They called the master "father of the household," and the slaves "members of the household," a custom which still holds in the mime. They established a holiday on which masters and slaves should eat together, – not as the only day for this custom, but as obligatory on that day in any case. They allowed the slaves to attain honours in the household and to pronounce judgment;[a] they held that a household was a miniature commonwealth.

[15]"Do you mean to say," comes the retort, "that I must seat all my slaves at my own table?" No, not any more than that you should invite all free men to it. You are mistaken if you think that I would bar from my table certain slaves whose duties are more humble, as, for example, yonder muleteer or yonder herdsman; I propose to value them according to their character, and not according to their duties. Each man acquires his character for himself, but accident assigns his duties. Invite some to your table because they deserve the honor, and others that they may come to deserve it. For if there is any slavish quality in them as the result of their low associations, it will be shaken off by intercourse with men of gentler breeding. [16]You need not, my dear Lucilius, hunt for friends only in the forum or in the Senate-house; if you are careful and attentive, you will find them at home also. Good material often stands idle for want of an artist; make the experiment, and you will find it so. As he is a fool who, when purchasing a horse, does not consider the animal's points, but merely his saddle and bridle; so he is doubly a fool who values a man from his clothes or from his rank, which indeed is only a robe that clothes us.

[a] i.e., as the praetor himself was normally accustomed to do.

[17]"He is a slave." His soul, however, may be that of a freeman. "He is a slave." But shall that stand in his way? Show me a man who is not a slave; one is a slave to lust, another to greed, another to ambition, and all men are slaves to fear. I will name you an ex-consul who is slave to an old hag, a millionaire who is slave to a serving-maid; I will show you youths of the noblest birth in serfdom to pantomime players! No servitude is more disgraceful than that which is self-imposed.

You should therefore not be deterred by these finicky persons from showing yourself to your slaves as an affable person and not proudly superior to them; they ought to respect you rather than fear you. [18]Some may maintain that I am now offering the liberty-cap to slaves in general and toppling down lords from their high estate, because I bid slaves respect their masters instead of fearing them. They say: "This is what he plainly means: slaves are to pay respect as if they were clients or early-morning callers!" Anyone who holds this opinion forgets that what is enough for a god cannot be too little for a master. Respect means love, and love and fear cannot be mingled. [19]So I hold that you are entirely right in not wishing to be feared by your slaves, and in lashing them merely with the tongue; only dumb animals need the thong.

That which annoys us does not necessarily injure us; but we are driven into wild rage by our luxurious lives, so that whatever does not answer our whims arouses our anger. [20]We don the temper of kings. For they, too, forgetful alike of their own strength and of other men's weakness, grow white-hot with rage, as if they had received an injury, when they are entirely protected from danger of such injury by their exalted station. They are not unaware that this is true, but by finding fault they seize upon opportunities to do harm; they insist that they have received injuries, in order that they may inflict them.

[21]I do not wish to delay you longer; for you need no exhortation. This, among other things, is a mark of good character: it forms its own judgments and abides by them; but badness is fickle and frequently changing, not for the better, but for something different. Farewell.

XLVIII. ON QUIBBLING AS UNWORTHY OF THE PHILOSOPHER

[1]In answer to the letter which you wrote me while travelling, – a letter as long as the journey itself, – I shall reply later. I ought to go into retirement, and consider what sort of advice I should give you. For you yourself, who consult me, also reflected for a long time whether to do so; how much more, then, should I myself reflect, since more deliberation is necessary in settling than in propounding a problem! And this is particularly true when one thing is advantageous to you and another to me. Am I speaking again in the guise of an Epicurean?[a] [2]But the fact is, the same thing is advantageous to me which is advantageous to you; for I am not your friend unless whatever is at issue concerning you is my concern also. Friendship produces between us a partnership in all our interests. There is no such thing as good or bad fortune for

[a] The Epicureans, who reduced all goods to "utilities," could not regard a friend's advantage as identical to one's own advantage. And yet they laid great stress upon friendship as one of the chief sources of pleasure. For an attempt to reconcile these two positions see Cicero, *De Finibus*, i. 65 ff. Seneca has inadvertantly used a phrase that implies a difference between a friend's interest and one's own. This leads him to reassert the Stoic view of friendship, which adopted as its motto κοινὰ τὰ τῶν φίλων.

the individual; we live in common. And no one can live happily who has regard to himself alone and transforms everything into a question of his own utility; you must live for your neighbour, if you would live for yourself. ³This fellowship, maintained with scrupulous care, which makes us mingle as men with our fellow-men and holds that the human race have certain rights in common, is also of great help in cherishing the more intimate fellowship which is based on friendship, concerning which I began to speak above. For he that has much in common with a fellow-man will have all things in common with a friend.

⁴And on this point, my excellent Lucilius, I should like to have those subtle dialecticians of yours advise me how I ought to help a friend, or how a fellow man, rather than tell me in how many ways the word "friend" is used, and how many meanings the word "man" possesses. Lo, Wisdom and Folly are taking opposite sides. Which shall I join? Which party would you have me follow? On that side, "man" is the equivalent of "friend"; on the other side, "friend" is not the equivalent of "man." The one wants a friend for his own advantage; the other wants to make himself an advantage to his friend.ᵃ What you have to offer me is nothing but distortion of words and splitting of syllables. ⁵It is clear that unless I can devise some very tricky premises and by false deductions tack on to them a fallacy which springs from the truth, I shall not be able to distinguish between what is desirable and what is to be avoided! I am ashamed! Old men as we are, dealing with a problem so serious, we make play of it!

ᵃ The sides are given in the reverse order in the two clauses: to the Stoic the terms "friend" and "man" are co-extensive; he is the friend of everybody, and his motive in friendship is to be of service; the Epicurean, however, narrows the definition of "friend" and regards him merely as an instrument to his own happiness.

⁶"'Mouse' is a syllable.ᵃ Now a mouse eats its cheese; therefore, a syllable eats cheese." Suppose now that I cannot solve this problem; see what peril hangs over my head as a result of such ignorance! What a scrape I shall be in! Without doubt I must beware, or some day I shall be catching syllables in a mousetrap, or, if I grow careless, a book may devour my cheese! Unless, perhaps, the following syllogism is shrewder still: "'Mouse' is a syllable. Now a syllable does not eat cheese. Therefore a mouse does not eat cheese." ⁷What childish nonsense! Do we knit our brows over this sort of problem? Do we let our beards grow long for this reason? Is this the matter which we teach with sour and pale faces?

Would you really know what philosophy offers to humanity? Philosophy offers counsel. Death calls away one man, and poverty chafes another; a third is worried either by his neighbour's wealth or by his own. So-and-so is afraid of bad luck; another desires to get away from his own good fortune. Some are ill-treated by men, others by the gods. ⁸Why, then, do you frame for me such games as these? It is no occasion for jest; you are retained as counsel for unhappy mankind. You have promised to help those in peril by sea, those in captivity, the sick and the needy, and those whose heads are under the poised axe. Whither are you straying? What are you doing?

This friend, in whose company you are jesting, is in fear. Help him, and take the noose from about his neck. Men are stretching out imploring hands to you on all sides; lives ruined and in danger of ruin are begging for some assistance; men's hopes, men's resources, depend upon you. They ask that you deliver them from all their restlessness, that you reveal to them, scattered and wandering as they are, the

---

ᵃ In this paragraph Seneca exposes the folly of trying to prove a truth by means of logical tricks, and offers a caricature of those which were current among the philosophers whom he derides.

clear light of truth. [9]Tell them what nature has made necessary, and what superfluous; tell them how simple are the laws that she has laid down, how pleasant and unimpeded life is for those who follow these laws, but how bitter and perplexed it is for those who have put their trust in opinion rather than in nature.

I should deem your games of logic to be of some avail in relieving men's burdens, if you could first show me what part of these burdens they will relieve. What among these games of yours banishes lust? Or controls it? Would that I could say that they were merely of no profit! They are positively harmful. I can make it perfectly clear to you whenever you wish, that a noble spirit when involved in such subtleties is impaired and weakened. [10]I am ashamed to say what weapons they supply to men who are destined to go to war with fortune, and how poorly they equip them! Is this the path to the greatest good? Is philosophy to proceed by such claptrap[a] and by quibbles which would be a disgrace and a reproach even for expounders[b] of the law? For what else is it that you men are doing, when you deliberately ensnare the person to whom you are putting questions, than making it appear that the man has lost his case on a technical error?[c]

---

[a] Literally, "or if or if not," words constantly employed by the logicians in legal instruments. For the latter cf. Cicero, *Pro Caecina*, 23 [65] *tum illud, quod dicitur, "sive nive" irrident, tum aucupia verborum et litterarum tendiculas in invidiam vocant.*

[b] Literally, "to those who sit studying the praetor's edicts." The *album* is the bulletin-board, on which the edicts of the praetor were posted, giving the formulae and stipulations for legal processes of various kinds.

[c] In certain actions the praetor appointed a judge and established a formula, indicating the plaintiff's claim and the judge's duty. If the statement was false, or the claim excessive, the plaintiff lost his case; under certain conditions (see last sentence of Seneca § 11) the defendant could claim annulment of the formula and have the case tried again. Such cases were not lost on

But just as the judge can reinstate those who have lost a suit in this way, so philosophy has reinstated these victims of quibbling to their former condition. [11]Why do you men abandon your mighty promises, and, after having assured me in high-sounding language that you will permit the glitter of gold to dazzle my eyesight no more than the gleam of the sword, and that I shall, with mighty steadfastness, spurn both that which all men crave and that which all men fear, why do you descend to the ABC's of scholastic pedants? What is your answer?

Is this the path to heaven?[a]

For that is exactly what philosophy promises to me, that I shall be made equal to God. For this I have been summoned, for this purpose have I come. Philosophy, keep your promise!

[12]Therefore, my dear Lucilius, withdraw yourself as far as possible from these exceptions and objections of so-called philosophers. Frankness, and simplicity beseem true goodness. Even if there were many years left to you, you would have had to spend them frugally in order to have enough for the necessary things; but as it is, when your time is so scant, what madness it is to learn superfluous things! Farewell.

---

their merits, and for that reason the lawyer who purposely took such an advantage was doing a contemptible thing.

[a] Vergil, *Aeneid*, ix. 641.

LIII. ON THE FAULTS OF THE SPIRIT

[1]You can persuade me into almost anything now, for I was recently persuaded to travel by water. We cast off when the sea was lazily smooth; the sky, to be sure, was heavy with nasty clouds, such as usually break into rain or squalls. Still, I thought that the few miles between Puteoli and your dear Parthenope[a] might be run off in quick time, despite the uncertain and lowering sky. So, in order to get away more quickly, I made straight out to sea for Nesis,[b] with the purpose of cutting across all the inlets. [2]But when we were so far out that it made little difference to me whether I returned or kept on, the calm weather, which had enticed me, came to naught. The storm had not yet begun, but the ground-swell was on, and the waves kept steadily coming faster. I began to ask the

[a] The poetical name for Naples; perhaps it was once a town near by which gave a sort of romantic second title to the larger city. Professor Summers thinks that this poetical name, together with *tua*, indicates a reference to a passage from the verse of Lucilius. Perhaps, however, *tua* means nothing more than "the place which you love so well," being in the neighbourhood of Pompeii, the birthplace of Lucilius.

[b] An islet near the mouth of the bay wherein Baiae was situated. Puteoli was on the opposite side of the bay from Baiae.

pilot to put me ashore somewhere; he replied that the coast was rough and a bad place to land, and that in a storm he feared a lee shore more than anything else. [3]But I was suffering too grievously to think of the danger, since a sluggish seasickness which brought no relief was racking me, the sort that upsets the liver without clearing it. Therefore I laid down the law to my pilot, forcing him to make for the shore, willy-nilly. When we drew near, I did not wait for things to be done in accordance with Vergil's orders, until

Prow faced seawards[a]

or

Anchor plunged from bow;[b]

I remembered my profession[c] as a veteran devotee of cold water, and, clad as I was in my cloak, let myself down into the sea, just as a cold-water bather should. [4]What do you think my feelings were, scrambling over the rocks, searching out the path, or making one for myself? I understood that sailors have good reason to fear the land. It is hard to believe what I endured when I could not endure myself; you may be sure that the reason why Ulysses was shipwrecked on every possible occasion was not so much because the sea-god was angry with him from his birth; he was simply subject to seasickness. And in the future I also, if I must go anywhere by sea, shall only reach my destination in the twentieth year.[d]

[5]When I finally calmed my stomach (for you know that

---

[a] *Aeneid*, vi. [3] This was the usual method of mooring a ship in ancient times.

[b] *Aeneid*, iii. 277.

[c] Compare Ep. lxxxiii. 5.

[d] Ulysses took ten years on his journey, because of sea-sickness; Seneca will need twice as many.

one does not escape seasickness by escaping from the sea) and refreshed my body with a rubdown, I began to reflect how completely we forget or ignore our failings, even those that affect the body, which are continually reminding us of their existence, – not to mention those which are more serious in proportion as they are more hidden. 6A slight ague deceives us; but when it has increased and a genuine fever has begun to burn, it forces even a hardy man, who can endure much suffering, to admit that he is ill. There is pain in the foot, and a tingling sensation in the joints; but we still hide the complaint and announce that we have sprained a joint, or else are tired from over-exercise. Then the ailment, uncertain at first, must be given a name; and when it begins to swell the ankles also, and has made both our feet "right" feet,[a] we are bound to confess that we have the gout. 7The opposite holds true of diseases of the soul; the worse one is, the less one perceives it. You need not be surprised, my beloved Lucilius. For he whose sleep is light pursues visions during slumber, and sometimes, though asleep, is conscious that he is asleep; but sound slumber annihilates our very dreams and sinks the spirit down so deep that it has no perception of self. 8Why will no man confess his faults? Because he is still in their grasp; only he who is awake can recount his dream, and similarly a confession of sin is a proof of sound mind.

Let us, therefore, rouse ourselves, that we may be able to correct our mistakes. Philosophy, however, is the only power that can stir us, the only power that can shake off our deep slumber. Devote yourself wholly to philosophy. You are worthy of her; she is worthy of you; greet one another with a loving embrace. Say farewell to all other interests with courage and frankness. Do not study philosophy merely during your spare time.[b]

[a] That is, they are so swollen that left and right look alike.

[b] Literally "on sufferance," whenever other matters permit. Cf. Pliny, *Ep.* vii.

[9]If you were ill, you would stop caring for your personal concerns, and forget your business duties; you would not think highly enough of any client to take active charge of his case during a slight abatement of your sufferings. You would try your hardest to be rid of the illness as soon as possible. What, then? Shall you not do the same thing now? Throw aside all hindrances and give up your time to getting a sound mind; for no man can attain it if he is engrossed in other matters. Philosophy wields her own authority; she appoints her own time and does not allow it to be appointed for her. She is not a thing to be followed at odd times, but a subject for daily practice; she is mistress, and she commands our attendance. [10]Alexander, when a certain state promised him a part of its territory and half its entire property, replied: "I invaded Asia with the intention, not of accepting what you might give, but of allowing you to keep what I might leave." Philosophy likewise keeps saying to all occupations: "I do not intend to accept the time which you have left over, but I shall allow you to keep what I myself shall leave."

[11]Turn to her, therefore, with all your soul, sit at her feet, cherish her; a great distance will then begin to separate you from other men. You will be far ahead of all mortals, and even the gods will not be far ahead of you. Do you ask what will be the difference between yourself and the gods? They will live longer. But, by my faith, it is the sign of a great artist to have confined a full likeness to the limits of a miniature. The wise man's life spreads out to him over as large a surface as does all eternity to a god. There is one point in which the sage has an advantage over the god; for a god is freed from terrors by the bounty of nature, the wise man by his own bounty. [12]What a wonderful privilege, to have the weaknesses of a man and the serenity of a god! The power of philosophy to blunt the blows of chance is beyond belief. No missile can

---

[30] *precario studeo*, – "subject to interruption from others."

settle in her body; she is well-protected and impenetrable. She spoils the force of some missiles and wards them off with the loose folds of her gown, as if they had no power to harm; others she dashes aside, and hurls them back with such force that they recoil upon the sender. Farewell.

LV. ON VATIA'S VILLA

[1]I have just returned from a ride in my litter; and I am as weary as if I had walked the distance, instead of being seated. Even to be carried for any length of time is hard work, perhaps all the more so because it is an unnatural exercise; for Nature gave us legs with which to do our own walking, and eyes with which to do our own seeing. Our luxuries have condemned us to weakness; we have ceased to be able to do that which we have long declined to do. [2]Nevertheless, I found it necessary to give my body a shaking up, in order that the bile which had gathered in my throat, if that was my trouble, might be shaken out, or, if the very breath within me had become, for some reason, too thick, that the jolting, which I have felt was a good thing for me, might make it thinner. So I insisted on being carried longer than usual, along an attractive beach, which bends between Cumae and Servilius Vatia's country-house,[a] shut in by the sea on one side and the lake on the

[a] Cumae was on the coast about six miles north of Cape Misenum. Lake Acheron (see § 6) was a salt-water pool between those two points, separated from the sea by a sandbar; it lay near Lake Avernus and probably derived its name from that fact. The Vatia mentioned here is unknown; he must not be confused with Isauricus.

other, just like a narrow path. It was packed firm under foot, because of a recent storm; since, as you know, the waves, when they beat upon the beach hard and fast, level it out; but a continuous period of fair weather loosens it, when the sand, which is kept firm by the water, loses its moisture.

[3]As my habit is, I began to look about for something there that might be of service to me, when my eyes fell upon the villa which had once belonged to Vatia. So this was the place where that famous praetorian millionaire passed his old age! He was famed for nothing else than his life of leisure, and he was regarded as lucky only for that reason. For whenever men were ruined by their friendship with Asinius Gallus[a] whenever others were ruined by their hatred of Sejanus, and later[b] by their intimacy with him, – for it was no more dangerous to have offended him than to have loved him, – people used to cry out: "O Vatia, you alone know how to live!" [4]But what he knew was how to hide, not how to live; and it makes a great deal of difference whether your life be one of leisure or one of idleness. So I never drove past his country-place during Vatia's lifetime without saying to myself: "Here lies Vatia!"

But, my dear Lucilius, philosophy is a thing of holiness, something to be worshipped, so much so that the very counterfeit pleases. For the mass of mankind consider that a person is at leisure who has withdrawn from society, is free from care, self-sufficient, and lives for himself; but these privileges can be the reward only of the wise man. Does he who is a victim of anxiety know how to live for himself? What? Does he even know (and that is of first importance) how to live at

[a] Son of Asinius Pollio; his frankness got him into trouble and he died of starvation in a dungeon in A.D. 3[3] Tacitus, *Ann.* i. 3[2] 2, quotes Augustus, discussing his own successor, as saying of Gallus *avidus et minor*. Sejanus was overthrown and executed in A.D. 31.

[b] i.e., after his fall.

all? [5]For the man who has fled from affairs and from men, who has been banished to seclusion by the unhappiness which his own desires have brought upon him, who cannot see his neighbour more happy than himself, who through fear has taken to concealment, like a frightened and sluggish animal. – this person is not living for himself he is living for his belly, his sleep, and his lust, – and that is the most shameful thing in the world. He who lives for no one does not necessarily live for himself. Nevertheless, there is so much in steadfastness and adherence to one's purpose that even sluggishness, if stubbornly maintained, assumes an air of authority[a] with us.

[6]I could not describe the villa accurately; for I am familiar only with the front of the house, and with the parts which are in public view and can be seen by the mere passer-by. There are two grottoes, which cost a great deal of labour, as big as the most spacious hall, made by hand. One of these does not admit the rays of the sun, while the other keeps them until the sun sets. There is also a stream running through a grove of plane-trees, which draws for its supply both on the sea and on Lake Acheron; it intersects the grove just like a race-way[b] and is large enough to support fish, although its waters are continually being drawn off. When the sea is calm, however, they do not use the stream, only touching the well-stocked waters when the storms give the fishermen a forced holiday. [7]But the most convenient thing about the villa is the fact that Baiae is next door, it is free from all the inconveniences of that resort, and yet enjoys its pleasures. I myself understand these attractions, and I believe that it is a villa suited to every season of the year. It fronts the west wind, which it intercepts in such a way that Baiae is denied it.

[a] i.e., imposes on us.

[b] Literally, "like a Euripus," referring to the narrow strait which divides Euboea from Boeotia at Chalcis. Its current is swift.

So it seems that Vatia was no fool when he selected this place as the best in which to spend his leisure when it was already unfruitful and decrepit.

[8]The place where one lives, however, can contribute little towards tranquillity; it is the mind which must make everything agreeable to itself. I have seen men despondent in a gay and lovely villa, and I have seen them to all appearance full of business in the midst of a solitude. For this reason you should not refuse to believe that your life is well-placed merely because you are not now in Campania. But why are you not there? Just let your thoughts travel, even to this place. [9]You may hold converse with your friends when they are absent, and indeed as often as you wish and for as long as you wish. For we enjoy this, the greatest of pleasures, all the more when we are absent from one another. For the presence of friends makes us fastidious; and because we can at any time talk or sit together, when once we have parted we give not a thought to those whom we have just beheld. [10]And we ought to bear the absence of friends cheerfully, just because everyone is bound to be often absent from his friends even when they are present. Include among such cases, in the first place, the nights spent apart, then the different engagements which each of two friends has, then the private studies of each and their excursions into the country, and you will see that foreign travel does not rob us of much. [11]A friend should be retained in the spirit; such a friend can never be absent. He can see every day whomsoever he desires to see.

I would therefore have you share your studies with me, your meals, and your walks. We should be living within too narrow limits if anything were barred to our thoughts. I see you, my dear Lucilius, and at this very moment I hear you; I am with you to such an extent that I hesitate whether I should not begin to write you notes instead of letters. Farewell.

LVI. ON QUIET AND STUDY

[1]Beshrew me[a] if I think anything more requisite than silence for a man who secludes himself in order to study! Imagine what a variety of noises reverberates about my ears! I have lodgings right over a bathing establishment. So picture to yourself the assortment of sounds, which are strong enough to make me hate my very powers of hearing! When your strenuous gentleman, for example, is exercising himself by flourishing leaden weights; when he is working hard, or else pretends to be working hard, I can hear him grunt; and whenever he releases his imprisoned breath, I can hear him panting in wheezy and high-pitched tones. Or perhaps I notice some lazy fellow, content with a cheap rubdown, and hear the crack of the pummelling hand on his shoulder, varying in sound according as the hand is laid on flat or hollow. Then, perhaps, a professional[b] comes along, shouting out the score; that is the finishing touch. [2]Add to this the arresting of an occasional roisterer or pickpocket, the racket of the man who

---

[a] That is 'Curse me' or 'Damn me.'

[b] *Pilicrepus* probably means "ball-counter," – one who keeps a record of the strokes. Compare our "billiard-marker."

always likes to hear his own voice in the bathroom,[a] or the enthusiast who plunges into the swimming-tank with unconscionable noise and splashing. Besides all those whose voices, if nothing else, are good, imagine the hair-plucker with his penetrating, shrill voice, – for purposes of advertisement, – continually giving it vent and never holding his tongue except when he is plucking the armpits and making his victim yell instead. Then the cakeseller with his varied cries, the sausageman, the confectioner, and all the vendors of food hawking their wares, each with his own distinctive intonation.

[3]So you say: "What iron nerves or deadened ears, you must have, if your mind can hold out amid so many noises, so various and so discordant, when our friend Chrysippus[b] is brought to his death by the continual good-morrows that greet him!" But I assure you that this racket means no more to me than the sound of waves or falling water; although you will remind me that a certain tribe once moved their city merely because they could not endure the din of a Nile cataract.[c] [4]Words seem to distract me more than noises; for words demand attention, but noises merely fill the ears and beat upon them. Among the sounds that din round me without distracting, I include passing carriages, a machinist in the same block, a saw-sharpener near by, or some fellow who is demonstrating with little pipes and flutes at the Trickling Fountain,[d] shouting rather than singing.

---

[a] This was especially true of poets, cf. Horace, *Sat.* i. [4] [76] *suave locus voci resonat conclusus*, and Martial, iii. 44.

[b] It is nowhere else related of the famous Stoic philosopher Chrysippus that he objected to the salutations of his friends; and, besides, the morning salutation was a Roman, not a Greek, custom. Lipsius, therefore, was probably right when he proposed to read here, for Chrysippus, Crispus, one of Seneca's friends; cf. *Epigr.* 6.

[c] The same story is told in *Naturalis Quaestiones*, iv. [2] 5

[d] A cone-shaped fountain, resembling a turning-post (*meta*) in the circus,

⁵Furthermore, an intermittent noise upsets me more than a steady one. But by this time I have toughened my nerves against all that sort of thing, so that I can endure even a boatswain marking the time in high-pitched tones for his crew. For I force my mind to concentrate, and keep it from straying to things outside itself; all outdoors may be bedlam, provided that there is no disturbance within, provided that fear is not wrangling with desire in my breast, provided that meanness and lavishness are not at odds, one harassing the other. For of what benefit is a quiet neighbourhood, if our emotions are in an uproar?

⁶'Twas night, and all the world was lulled to rest.[a]

This is not true; for no real rest can be found when reason has not done the lulling. Night brings our troubles to the light, rather than banishes them; it merely changes the form of our worries. For even when we seek slumber, our sleepless moments are as harassing as the daytime. Real tranquillity is the state reached by an unperverted mind when it is relaxed. ⁷Think of the unfortunate man who courts sleep by surrendering his spacious mansion to silence, who, that his ear may be disturbed by no sound, bids the whole retinue of his slaves be quiet and that whoever approaches him shall walk on tiptoe; he tosses from this side to that and seeks a fitful slumber amid his frettings! ⁸He complains that he has heard sounds, when he has not heard them at all. The reason, you ask? His soul's in an uproar; it must be soothed, and its rebellious murmuring checked. You need not suppose that the soul is at peace when the body is still. Sometimes quiet means disquiet.

We must therefore rouse ourselves to action and busy

---

from which the water spouted through many jets; hence the "sweating" (*sudans*). Its remains may still be seen now not far from the Colosseum on the Velia.

[a] A fragment from the Argonautica of Varro Atacinus.

ourselves with interests that are good, as often as we are in the grasp of an uncontrollable sluggishness. [9]Great generals, when they see that their men are mutinous, check them by some sort of labour or keep them busy with small forays. The much occupied man has no time for wantonness, and it is an obvious commonplace that the evils of leisure can be shaken off by hard work. Although people may often have thought that I sought seclusion because I was disgusted with politics and regretted my hapless and thankless position,[a] yet, in the retreat to which apprehension and weariness have driven me, my ambition sometimes develops afresh. For it is not because my ambition was rooted out that it has abated, but because it was wearied or perhaps even put out of temper by the failure of its plans. [10]And so with luxury, also, which sometimes seems to have departed, and then when we have made a profession of frugality, begins to fret us and, amid our economies, seeks the pleasures which we have merely left but not condemned. Indeed, the more stealthily it comes, the greater is its force. For all unconcealed vices are less serious; a disease also is farther on the road to being cured when it breaks forth from concealment and manifests its power. So with greed, ambition, and the other evils of the mind, – you may be sure that they do most harm when they are hidden behind a pretence of soundness.

[11]Men think that we are in retirement, and yet we are not. For if we have sincerely retired, and have sounded the signal for retreat, and have scorned outward attractions, then, as I remarked above,[b] no outward thing will distract us; no music of men or of birds[c] can interrupt good thoughts, when they have once become steadfast and sure. [12]The mind which starts at words or at chance sounds is unstable and has not

---

[a] See Introduction, page viii.

[b] § 4 of this letter.

[c] An allusion to the Sirens and Ulysses, cf. § 15 below.

yet withdrawn into itself; it contains within itself an element of anxiety and rooted fear, and this makes one a prey to care, as our Vergil says:

> I, whom of yore no dart could cause to flee,
> Nor Greeks, with crowded lines of infantry.
> Now shake at every sound, and fear the air,
> Both for my child and for the load I bear.[a]

[13]This man in his first state is wise; he blenches neither at the brandished spear, nor at the clashing armour of the serried foe, nor at the din of the stricken city. This man in his second state lacks knowledge fearing for his own concerns, he pales at every sound; any cry is taken for the battle-shout and overthrows him; the slightest disturbance renders him breathless with fear. It is the load that makes him afraid.[b] [14]Select anyone you please from among your favourites of Fortune, trailing their many responsibilities, carrying their many burdens, and you will behold a picture of Vergil's hero, "fearing both for his child and for the load he bears."

You may therefore be sure that you are at peace with yourself, when no noise readies you, when no word shakes you out of yourself, whether it be of flattery or of threat, or merely an empty sound buzzing about you with unmeaning din. [15]"What then?" you say, "is it not sometimes a simpler matter just to avoid the uproar?" I admit this. Accordingly, I shall change from my present quarters. I merely wished to test myself and to give myself practice. Why need I be tormented any longer, when Ulysses found so simple a cure for his comrades[c] even against the songs of the Sirens? Farewell.

---

[a] Aeneas is escaping from Troy, *Aeneid*, ii. 726 ff.

[b] Aeneas carries Anchises; the rich man carries his burden of wealth.

[c] Not merely by stopping their ears with wax, but also by bidding them row past the Sirens as quickly as possible. *Odyssey*, xii. 182.

LVII. ON THE TRIALS OF TRAVEL

[1]When it was time for me to return to Naples from Baiae, I easily persuaded myself that a storm was raging, that I might avoid another trip by sea; and yet the road was so deep in mud, all the way, that I may be thought none the less to have made a voyage. On that day I had to endure the full fate of an athlete; the anointing[a] with which we began was followed by the sand-sprinkle in the Naples tunnel.[b] [2] No place could be longer than that prison; nothing could be dimmer than those torches, which enabled us, not to see amid the darkness, but to see the darkness. But, even supposing that there was light in the place, the dust, which is an oppressive and disagreeable thing even in the open air, would destroy the light; how much worse the dust is there, where it rolls back upon itself, and, being shut in without ventilation, blows back in the faces of those who set it going! So we endured two

[a] i.e., an "anointing" with mud.

[b] A characteristic figure. After anointing, the wrestler was sprinkled with sand, so that the opponent's hand might not slip. The Naples tunnel furnished a shortcut to those who, like Seneca in this letter, did not wish to take the time to travel by the shore route along the promontory of Pausilipum.

inconveniences at the same time, and they were diametrically different: we struggled both with mud and with dust on the same road and on the same day.

[3]The gloom, however, furnished me with some food for thought; I felt a certain mental thrill, and a transformation unaccompanied by fear, due to the novelty and the unpleasantness of an unusual occurrence. Of course I am not speaking to you of myself at this point, because I am far from being a perfect person, or even a man of middling qualities; I refer to one over whom fortune has lost her control. Even such a man's mind will be smitten with a thrill and he will change colour. [4]For there are certain emotions, my dear Lucilius, which no courage can avoid; nature reminds courage how perishable a thing it is. And so he will contract his brow when the prospect is forbidding, will shudder at sudden apparitions, and will become dizzy when he stands at the edge of a high precipice and looks down. This is not fear; it is a natural feeling which reason cannot rout. [5]That is why certain brave men, most willing to shed their own blood, cannot bear to see the blood of others. Some persons collapse and faint at the sight of a freshly inflicted wound; others are affected similarly on handling or viewing an old wound which is festering. And others meet the sword-stroke more readily than they see it dealt.

[6]Accordingly, as I said, I experienced a certain transformation, though it could not be called confusion. Then at the first glimpse of restored daylight my good spirits returned without forethought or command. And I began to muse and think how foolish we are to fear certain objects to a greater or less degree, since all of them end in the same way. For what difference does it make whether a watchtower or a mountain crashes down upon us? No difference at all, you will find. Nevertheless, there will be some men who fear the latter mishap to a greater degree, though both accidents are equally deadly; so true it is that fear looks not to the effect,

but to the cause of the effect. [7]Do you suppose that I am now referring to the Stoics,[a] who hold that the soul of a man crushed by a great weight cannot abide, and is scattered forthwith, because it has not had a free opportunity to depart? That is not what I am doing; those who think thus are, in my opinion, wrong. [8]Just as fire cannot be crushed out, since it will escape round the edges of the body which overwhelms it; just as the air cannot be damaged by lashes and blows, or even cut into, but flows back about the object to which it gives place; similarly the soul, which consists of the subtlest particles, cannot be arrested or destroyed inside the body, but, by virtue of its delicate substance, it will rather escape through the very object by which it is being crushed. Just as lightning, no matter how widely it strikes and flashes, makes its return through a narrow opening,[b] so the soul, which is still subtler than fire, has a way of escape through any part of the body. [9]We therefore come to this question, – whether the soul can be immortal. But be sure of this: if the soul survives the body after the body is crushed, the soul can in no wise be crushed out, precisely because it does not perish; for the rule of immortality never admits of exceptions, and nothing can harm that which is everlasting. Farewell.

[a] Cf. Hicks, *Stoic and Epicurean*, p. 61, on the doctrine of interpenetration, explaining the diffusion of the soul throughout the body; and Rohde, *Psyche*, ii. 319, on the popular superstition that one who dies in a whirlwind has his soul snatched away by the wind-spirits. The doctrine referred to by Seneca is not, however, a purely Stoic doctrine.

[b] For this belief compare Xenophon, *Mem.* iv. 3 14, "No one sees the bolt either on its way down or on its way back." Seneca himself was much interested in lightning cf. *N. Q.* ii. 4[0] 2.

LVIII. ON BEING

[1]How scant of words our language is, nay, how poverty-stricken, I have not fully understood until today. We happened to be speaking of Plato, and a thousand subjects came up for discussion, which needed names and yet possessed none; and there were certain others which once possessed, but have since lost, their words because we were too nice about their use. But who can endure to be nice in the midst of poverty?[a] [2]There is an insect, called by the Greeks oestrus,[b] which drives cattle wild and scatters them all over their pasturing grounds; it used to be called asilus in our language, as you may believe on the authority of Vergil:-

Near Silarus groves, and eke Alburnus' shades
Of green-clad oak-trees flits an insect, named
Asilus by the Romans; in the Greek
The word is rendered oestrus. With a rough

[a] This theme was emphasized by Lucretius, i. 136 and 832, and iii. 26⁰ Munro thinks, however, that "Lucretius had too much instead of too little technical language for a poet." Seneca knew Lucretius; cf. Epp. lviii. 12, xc. 11, etc.

[b] The gad-fly.

And strident sound it buzzes and drives wild
The terror-stricken herds throughout the woods.[a]

[3]By which I infer that the word has gone out of use. And, not to keep you waiting too long, there were certain uncompounded words current, like cernere ferro inter se, as will be proved again by Vergil:-

Great heroes, born in various lands, had come
To settle matters mutually with the sword.[b]

This "settling matters" we now express by decernere. The plain word has become obsolete. [4]The ancients used to say iusso, instead of iussero, in conditional clauses. You need not take my word, but you may turn again to Vergil:-

The other soldiers shall conduct the fight
With me, where I shall bid.[c]

[5]It is not in my purpose to show, by this array of examples, how much time I have wasted on the study of language; I merely wish you to understand how many words, that were current in the works of Ennius and Accius, have become mouldy with age; while even in the case of Vergil, whose works are explored daily, some of his words have been filched away from us.

[6]You will say, I suppose: "What is the purpose and meaning of this preamble?" I shall not keep you in the dark; I desire, if possible, to say the word essentia to you and obtain a favourable hearing. If I cannot do this, I shall risk it even

[a] *Georgics*, iii. 146 ff.
[b] *Aeneid*, xii. 708 f.
[c] *Aeneid*, xi. 467.

though it put you out of humour. I have Cicero,[a] as authority
for the use of this word, and I regard him as a powerful
authority. If you desire testimony of a later date, I shall cite
Fabianus,[b] careful of speech, cultivated, and so polished in
style that he will suit even our nice tastes. For what can we
do, my dear Lucilius? How otherwise can we find a word for
that which the Greeks call οὐσία, something that is indispensable, something that is the natural substratum of everything?
I beg you accordingly to allow me to use this word essentia. I
shall nevertheless take pains to exercise the privilege, which
you have granted me, with as sparing a hand as possible;
perhaps I shall be content with the mere right. [7]Yet what good
will your indulgence do me, if, lo and behold, I can in no
wise express in Latin[c] the meaning of the word which gave
me the opportunity to rail at the poverty of our language?
And you will condemn our narrow Roman limits even more,
when you find out that there is a word of one syllable which
I cannot translate. "What is this?" you ask. It is the word ὄν.
You think me lacking in facility; you believe that the word is
ready to hand, that it might be translated by quod est. I notice,
however, a great difference; you are forcing me to render a
noun by a verb. [8]But if I must do so, I shall render it by quod
est. There are six ways[d] in which Plato expresses this idea,
according to a friend of ours, a man of great learning, who

[a] Cicero usually says *natura*. The word, according to Quintilian, was first
used by a certain Sergius Flavus. It is also found in Apulcius, Macrobius,
and Sidonius.

[b] See Ep. c. Papirius Fabianus, who lived in the times of Tiberius and
Caligula, was a pupil of the Sextius of Ep. lix., and was (Pliny, *N. H.* xxxvi.
1[5] 24) *naturae rerum peritissimus*. He is praised by the elder Seneca (*Cont.*
[2] *Praef.*) who, however, says of him *deerat robur – splendor aderat*.

[c] i.e., I must not use other imported words to explain *essentia*, which is not
a native Latin word, but invented as a literal translation of οὐσία.

[d] Cf. § 16.

mentioned the fact today. And I shall explain all of them to you, if I may first point out that there is something called genus and something called species.

For the present, however, we are seeking the primary idea of genus, on which the others, the different species, depend, which is the source of all classification, the term under which universal ideas are embraced. And the idea of genus will be reached if we begin to reckon back from particulars; for in this way we shall be conducted back to the primary notion. [9]Now "man" is a species, as Aristotle[a] says; so is "horse," or "dog." We must therefore discover some common bond for all these terms, one which embraces them and holds them subordinate to itself. And what is this? It is "animal." And so there begins to be a genus "animal," including all these terms, "man," "horse," and "dog." [10]But there are certain things which have life (anima) and yet are not "animals." For it is agreed that plants and trees possess life, and that is why we speak of them as living and dying. Therefore the term "living things" will occupy a still higher place, because both animals and plants are included in this category. Certain objects, however, lack life, – such as rocks. There will therefore be another term to take precedence over "living things," and that is "substance." I shall classify "substance" by saying that all substances are either animate or inanimate. [11]But there is still something superior to "substance"; for we speak of certain things as possessing substance, and certain things as lacking substance. What, then, will be the term from which these things are derived? It is that to which we lately gave an inappropriate name, "that which exists." For by using this term they will be divided into species, so that we can say: that which exists either possesses, or lacks, substance.

[12]This, therefore, is what genus is, – the primary, original, and (to play upon the word) "general." Of course there are

---

[a] *Categories* 2 b 11 and often.

the other genera: but they are "special" genera: "man" being, for example, a genus. For "man" comprises species: by nations, – Greek, Roman, Parthian; by colours, – white, black, yellow. The term comprises individuals also: Cato, Cicero, Lucretius. So "man" falls into the category genus, in so far as it includes many kinds; but in so far as it is subordinate to another term, it falls into the category species. But the genus "that which exists" is general, and has no term superior to it. It is the first term in the classification of things, and all things are included under it.

[13]The Stoics would set ahead of this still another genus, even more primary; concerning which I shall immediately speak, after proving that the genus which has been discussed above, has rightly been placed first, being, as it is, capable of including everything. [14]I therefore distribute "that which exists" into these two species, – things with, and things without, substance. There is no third class. And how do I distribute "substance"? By saying that it is either animate or inanimate. And how do I distribute the "animate"? By saying: "Certain things have mind, while others have only life." Or the idea may be expressed as follows: "Certain things have the power of movement, of progress, of change of position, while others are rooted in the ground; they are fed and they grow only through their roots." Again, into what species do I divide "animals"? They are either perishable or imperishable. [15]Certain of the Stoics regard the primary genus[a] as the "something." I shall add the reasons they give for their belief; they say: "in the order of nature some things exist, and other things do not exist. And even the things that do not exist are really part of the order of nature. What these are will readily occur to the mind, for example centaurs, giants, and all other figments of unsound reasoning, which have begun to have a definite shape, although they have no bodily consistency."

[a] i.e., the *genus* beyond "that which exists."

[16]But I now return to the subject which I promised to discuss for you, namely, how it is that Plato[a] divides all existing things in six different ways. The first class of "that which exists" cannot be grasped by the sight or by the touch, or by any of the senses; but it can be grasped by the thought. Any generic conception, such as the generic idea "man," does not come within the range of the eyes; but "man" in particular does; as, for example, Cicero, Cato. The term "animal" is not seen; it is grasped by thought alone. A particular animal, however, is seen, for example, a horse, a dog.

[17]The second class of "things which exist," according to Plato, is that which is prominent and stands out above everything else; this, he says, exists in a pre-eminent degree.[b] The word "poet" is used indiscriminately, for this term is applied to all writers of verse; but among the Greeks it has come to be the distinguishing mark of a single individual. You know that Homer is meant when you hear men say "the poet." What, then, is this pre-eminent Being? God, surely, one who is greater and more powerful than anyone else.

[18]The third class is made up of those things which exist in the proper sense of the term;[c] they are countless in number, but are situated beyond our sight. "What are these?" you ask. They are Plato's own furniture, so to speak; he calls them "ideas," and from them all visible things are created, and according to their pattern all things are fashioned. They are

---

[a] Cf. § [8] Plato's usual division was threefold, – αἰσθητά, μαθηματικά, εἴδη (*sensibilia, mathematica, ideae*), – a division which is often quoted by Aristotle.

[b] Εἶναι κατ᾽ ἐξοχήν. After illustrating the poet κατ᾽ ἐξοχήν, Homer, he passes to τὸ ὂν κατ᾽ ἐξοχήν, God.

[c] Ὄντως τὰ ὄντα. "Each idea is a single, independent, separate, self-existing, perfect, and eternal essence"; Adam, *The Republic of Plato*, ii. 16[9] See Zeller's *Plato* (p. 237) for a list of Greek words used by Plato to indicate the reality of these ideas.

immortal, unchangeable, inviolable. [19]And this "idea," or rather, Plato's conception of it,[a] is as follows: "The 'idea' is the everlasting pattern of those things which are created by nature." I shall explain this definition, in order to set the subject before you in a clearer light: Suppose that I wish to make a likeness of you; I possess in your own person the pattern of this picture, wherefrom my mind receives a certain outline, which it is to embody in its own handiwork. That outward appearance, then, which gives me instruction and guidance, this pattern for me to imitate, is the "idea." Such patterns, therefore, nature possesses in infinite number, – of men, fish, trees, according to whose model everything that nature has to create is worked out.

[20]In the fourth place we shall put "form."[b] And if you would know what "form" means, you must pay close attention, calling Plato, and not me, to account for the difficulty of the subject. However, we cannot make fine distinctions without encountering difficulties. A moment ago I made use of the artist as an illustration. When the artist desired to reproduce Vergil in colours he would gaze upon Vergil himself. The "idea" was Vergil's outward appearance, and this was the pattern of the intended work. That which the artist draws from this "idea" and has embodied in his own work, is the "form." [21]Do you ask me where the difference lies? The former is the pattern; while the latter is the shape taken from the pattern and embodied in the work. Our artist follows the one, but the other he creates. A statue has a certain external appearance; this external appearance of the statue is the "form." And the pattern[c] itself has a certain external appearance, by gazing upon which the sculptor has fashioned his statue; this

[a] Cf., for example, *Parmenides* 132 D. What follows is not a direct quotation, and the same thought is found elsewhere.

[b] Εἶδος.

[c] i.e., the "original."

is the "idea." If you desire a further distinction, I will say that the "form" is in the artist's work, the "idea" outside his work, and not only outside it, but prior to it.

²²The fifth class is made up of the things which exist in the usual sense of the term. These things are the first that have to do with us; here we have all such things as men, cattle, and things. In the sixth class goes all that which has a fictitious existence, like void, or time.

Whatever is concrete to the sight or touch, Plato does not include among the things which he believes to be existent in the strict sense of the term.ᵃ These things are the first that have to do with us: here we have all such things as men, cattle, and things. For they are in a state of flux, constantly diminishing or increasing. None of us is the same man in old age that he was in youth; nor the same on the morrow as on the day preceding. Our bodies are burned along like flowing waters; every visible object accompanies time in its flight; of the things which we see, nothing is fixed. Even I myself as I comment on this change, am changed myself. ²³This is just what Heraclitusᵇ says: "We go down twice into the same river, and yet into a different river." For the stream still keeps the same name, but the water has already flowed past. Of course this is much more evident in rivers than in human beings. Still, we mortals are also carried past in no less speedy a course; and this prompts me to marvel at our madness in cleaving with great affection to such a fleeting thing as the body, and in fearing lest some day we may die, when every instant means the death of our previous condition.ᶜ Will you not stop fearing lest that may happen once which really happens every day? ²⁴So much for man, – a substance that

---

ᵃ i.e., κυρίως ὄντα. See above, § 16f

ᵇ Frag. 49ᵃ Diels² ποταμοῖς τοῖς αὐτοῖς ἐμβαίνομέν τε καὶ οὐκ ἐμβαίνομεν, εἰμέν τε καὶ οὐκ εἰμεν.

ᶜ This idea Seneca has already developed in Ep. xxiv. 20.

flows away and falls, exposed to every influence; but the universe, too, immortal and enduring as it is, changes and never remains the same. For though it has within itself all that it has had, it has it in a different way from that in which it has had it; it keeps changing its arrangement.

[25]"Very well," say you, "what good shall I get from all this fine reasoning?" None, if you wish me to answer your question. Nevertheless, just as an engraver rests his eyes when they have long been under a strain and are weary, and calls them from their work, and "feasts" them, as the saying is; so we at times should slacken our minds and refresh them with some sort of entertainment. But let even your entertainment be work; and even from these various forms of entertainment you will select, if you have been watchful, something that may prove wholesome. [26]That is my habit, Lucilius: I try to extract and render useful some element from every field of thought, no matter how far removed it may be from philosophy. Now what could be less likely to reform character than the subjects which we have been discussing? And how can I be made a better man by the "ideas" of Plato? What can I draw from them that will put a check on my appetites? Perhaps the very thought, that all these things which minister to our senses, which arouse and excite us, are by Plato denied a place among the things that really exist. [27]Such things are therefore imaginary, and though they for the moment present a certain external appearance, yet they are in no case permanent or substantial; none the less, we crave them as if they were always to exist, or as if we were always to possess them.

We are weak, watery beings standing in the midst of unrealities; therefore let us turn our minds to the things that are everlasting. Let us look up to the ideal outlines of all things, that flit about on high, and to the God who moves among them and plans how he may defend from death that which he could not make imperishable because its substance forbade, and so by reason may overcome the defects of the body. [28]For all things abide, not because they are everlasting, but because they are protected by the care of him who governs all things; but that which was imperishable would need no guardian. The Master Builder keeps them safe, overcoming the weakness of their fabric by his own power. Let us despise everything that is so little an object of value that it makes us doubt whether it exists at all. [29]Let us at the same time reflect, seeing that Providence rescues from its perils the world itself, which is no less mortal than we ourselves, that to some extent our petty bodies can be made to tarry longer upon earth by our own providence, if only we acquire the ability to control and check those pleasures whereby the greater portion of mankind perishes. [30]Plato himself, by taking pains, advanced to old age. To be sure, he was the fortunate possessor of a strong and sound body (his very name was given him because of his broad chest);[a] but his strength was much impaired by sea voyages and desperate adventures. Nevertheless, by frugal living, by setting a limit upon all that rouses the appetites, and by painstaking attention to himself, he reached that advanced age in spite of many hindrances. [31]You know, I am sure, that Plato had the good fortune, thanks to his careful living, to die on his birthday, after exactly completing his eighty-first year. For this reason wise men of the East, who happened to be in Athens at that time, sacrificed to him after his death, believing that his length of days was too full for a mortal man, since he had rounded out the perfect number of nine times nine. I do not doubt that he would have been quite willing to forgo a few days from this total, as well as the sacrifice.

[32]Frugal living can bring one to old age; and to my mind old age is not to be refused any more than is to be craved. There is a pleasure in being in one's own company as long as

---

[a] Diogenes Laertius, iii. 1, who records also other explanations of the name Plato, which replaced the given name Aristocles.

possible, when a man has made himself worth enjoying. The question, therefore, on which we have to record our judgment is, whether one should shrink from extreme old age and should hasten the end artificially, instead of waiting for it to come. A man who sluggishly awaits his fate is almost a coward, just as he is immoderately given to wine who drains the jar dry and sucks up even the dregs. [33]But we shall ask this question also: "Is the extremity of life the dregs, or is it the clearest and purest part of all, provided only that the mind is unimpaired, and the senses, still sound, give their support to the spirit, and the body is not worn out and dead before its time?" For it makes a great deal of difference whether a man is lengthening his life or his death. [34]But if the body is useless for service, why should one not free the struggling soul? Perhaps one ought to do this a little before the debt is due, lest, when it falls due, he may be unable to perform the act. And since the danger of living in wretchedness is greater than the danger of dying soon, he is a fool who refuses to stake a little time and win a hazard of great gain.[a]

Few have lasted through extreme old age to death without impairment, and many have lain inert, making no use of themselves. How much more cruel, then, do you suppose it really is to have lost a portion of your life, than to have lost your right to end that life? [35]Do not hear me with reluctance, as if my statement applied directly to you, but weigh what I have to say. It is this, that I shall not abandon old age, if old age preserves me intact for myself, and intact as regards the better part of myself; but if old age begins to shatter my mind, and to pull its various faculties to pieces, if it leaves me, not life, but only the breath of life, I shall rush out of a house that is crumbling and tottering. [36]I shall not avoid illness by seeking death, as long as the

[a] Cf. Plato, *Phaedo*, 114 D καὶ ἄξιον κινδυνεῦσαι, οἰομένῳ οὕτως ἔχειν· καλὸς γὰρ ὁ κίνδυνος, the "chance" being immortality.

illness is curable and does not impede my soul. I shall not lay violent hands upon myself just because I am in pain; for death under such circumstances is defeat. But if I find out that the pain must always be endured, I shall depart, not because of the pain but because it will be a hindrance to me as regards all my reasons for living. He who dies just because he is in pain is a weakling, a coward; but he who lives merely to brave out this pain, is a fool.

[37]But I am running on too long; and, besides, there is matter here to fill a day. And how can a man end his life, if he cannot end a letter? So farewell. This last word[a] you will read with greater pleasure than all my deadly talk about death. Farewell.

---

[a] Since *vale* means "keep well" no less than "good bye."

LXV. ON THE FIRST CAUSE

[1]I shared my time yesterday with ill health;[a] it claimed for itself all the period before noon; in the afternoon, however, it yielded to me. And so I first tested my spirit by reading; then, when reading was found to be possible, I dared to make more demands upon the spirit, or perhaps I should say, to make more concessions to it. I wrote a little, and indeed with more concentration than usual, for I am struggling with a difficult subject and do not wish to be downed. In the midst of this, some friends visited me, with the purpose of employing force and of restraining me, as if I were a sick man indulging in some excess. [2]So conversation was substituted for writing; and from this conversation I shall communicate to you the topic which is still the subject of debate; for we have appointed you referee.[b] You have more of a task on your hands than you suppose, for the argument is threefold.

Our Stoic philosophers, as you know, declare that there are two things in the universe which are the source of every-

---

[a] For Seneca's troubles in this regard see also Epp. liv. and civ.

[b] The *arbiter* was a judge appointed to try a case according to *bona fides* (equity), as contrasted with the *iudex* proper, whose duty was defined by the magistrate.

thing, – namely, cause and matter.[a] Matter lies sluggish, a substance ready for any use, but sure to remain unemployed if no one sets it in motion. Cause, however, by which we mean reason, moulds matter and turns it in whatever direction it will, producing thereby various concrete results. Accordingly, there must be, in the case of each thing, that from which it is made, and, next, an agent by which it is made. The former is its material, the latter its cause.

[3]All art is but imitation of nature; therefore, let me apply these statements of general principles to the things which have to be made by man. A statue, for example, has afforded matter which was to undergo treatment at the hands of the artist, and has had an artist who was to give form to the matter. Hence, in the case of the statue, the material was bronze, the cause was the workman. And so it goes with all things, – they consist of that which is made and of the maker. [4]The Stoics believe in one cause only – the maker; but Aristotle thinks that the word "cause" can be used in three ways: "The first cause," he says, "is the actual matter, without which nothing can be created. The second is the workman. The third is the form, which is impressed upon every work, – a statue, for example." This last is what Aristotle calls the idols.[b] "There is, too," says he, "a fourth, – the purpose of the work as a whole." [5]Now I shall show you what this last means. Bronze is the "first cause" of the statue, for it could never

---

[a] See Zeller's *Stoics* (translated by Reichel), pp. 139 ff.

[b] The statue figure is a frequent one in philosophy; cf. Ep. ix. [5] The "form" of Aristotle goes back to the "idea" of Plato. These four causes are the causes of Aristotle, matter (ὕλη), form (εἶδος), force (τὸ κινοῦν), and the end (τὸ τέλος); when they all concur, we pass from possibility to fact. Aristotle gives eight categories in *Phys.* 225 b 5; and ten in *Categ.* 1 b 25, – substance, quantity, quality, relation, place, time, situation, possession, action, passion. For a definition of εἶδος see Aristotle, *Phys* 190 b 20 γίγνεται πᾶν ἔκ τε τοῦ ὑποκειμένου καὶ τῆς μορφῆς (i.e. τοῦ εἴδους).

have been made unless there had been something from which it could be cast and moulded. The "second cause" is the artist; for without the skilled hands of a workman that bronze could not have been shaped to the outlines of the statue. The "third cause" is the form, inasmuch as our statue could never be called The Lance-Bearer or The Boy Binding his Hair[a] had not this special shape been stamped upon it. The "fourth cause" is the purpose of the work. For if this purpose had not existed, the statue would not have been made. [6]Now what is this purpose? It is that which attracted the artist which he followed when he made the statue. It may have been money, if he has made it for sale; or renown, if he has worked for reputation; or religion, if he has wrought it as a gift for a temple. Therefore this also is a cause contributing towards the making of the statue; or do you think that we should avoid including, among the causes of a thing which has been made, that element without which the thing in question would not have been made?

[7]To these four Plato adds a fifth cause, – the pattern which he himself calls the "idea"; for it is this that the artist gazed upon[b] when he created the work which he had decided to carry out. Now it makes no difference whether he has this pattern outside himself, that he may direct his glance to it, or within himself, conceived and placed there by himself. God has within himself these patterns of all things, and his mind comprehends the harmonies and the measures of the whole totality of things which are to be carried out; he is filled with

[a] Well-known works of Polyclitus, fifth century B.C.

[b] Explaining the derivation of the Greek word, – ἰδεῖν, "to behold." For a discussion of Plato's "ideas," those "independent, separate, self-existing, perfect, and eternal essences" (*Republic* vi. and vii.) see Adam, *The Republic of Plato*, ii. 168-17[9] According to Adam, Plato owes his theory of ideas to Socrates, the Eleatics, and the study of geometry; but his debt is not so great as his discovery.

these shapes which Plato calls the "ideas," – imperishable, unchangeable, not subject to decay. And therefore, though men die, humanity itself, or the idea of man, according to which man is moulded, lasts on, and though men toil and perish, it suffers no change. [8]Accordingly, there are five causes, as Plato says:[a] the material, the agent, the make-up, the model, and the end in view. Last comes the result of all these. Just as in the case of the statue, – to go back to the figure with which we began, – the material is the bronze, the agent is the artist, the make-up is the form which is adapted to the material, the model is the pattern imitated by the agent, the end in view is the purpose in the maker's mind, and, finally, the result of all these is the statue itself. [9]The universe also, in Plato's opinion, possesses all these elements. The agent is God; the source, matter; the form, the shape and the arrangement of the visible world. The pattern is doubtless the model according to which God has made this great and most beautiful creation. [10]The purpose is his object in so doing. Do you ask what God's purpose is? It is goodness. Plato, at any rate, says: "What was God's reason for creating the world? God is good, and no good person is grudging of anything that is good. Therefore, God made it the best world possible." Hand down your opinion, then, O judge; state who seems to you to say what is truest, and not who says what is absolutely true. For to do that is as far beyond our ken as truth itself.

[11]This throng of causes, defined by Aristotle and by Plato, embraces either too much or too little.[b] For if they regard as

[a] i.e., the four categories as established by Aristotle, plus the "idea" of Plato.
[b] The Stoic view (see § 2 of this letter), besides making the four categories of "substance," "form," "variety," and "variety of relation," regarded material things as the only things which possessed being. The Stoics thus differ from Aristotle and Plato in holding that nothing is real except matter; besides, they relate everything to one ultimate cause, the acting force or efficient cause.

"causes" of an object that is to be made everything without which the object cannot be made, they have named too few. Time must be included among the causes; for nothing can be made without time. They must also include place; for if there be no place where a thing can be made, it will not be made. And motion too; nothing is either made or destroyed without motion. There is no art without motion, no change of any kind. [12]Now, however, I am searching for the first, the general cause; this must be simple, inasmuch as matter, too, is simple. Do we ask what cause is? It is surely Creative Reason,[a] – in other words, God. For those elements to which you referred are not a great series of independent causes; they all hinge on one alone, and that will be the creative cause. [13]Do you maintain that form is a cause? This is only what the artist stamps upon his work; it is part of a cause, but not the cause. Neither is the pattern a cause, but an indispensable tool of the cause. His pattern is as indispensable to the artist as the chisel or the file; without these, art can make no progress. But for all that, these things are neither parts of the art, nor causes of it. [14]"Then," perhaps you will say, "the purpose of the artist, that which leads him to undertake to create something, is the cause." It may be a cause; it is not, however, the efficient cause, but only an accessory cause. But there are countless accessory causes; what we are discussing is the general cause. Now the statement of Plato and Aristotle is not in accord with their usual penetration, when they maintain that the whole universe, the perfectly wrought work, is a cause. For there is a great difference between a work and the cause of a work.

[15]Either give your opinion, or, as is easier in cases of this kind, declare that the matter is not clear and call for another

---

[a] i.e., the λόγος σπερματικός, the creative force in nature, that is, Providence, or the will of Zeus.

hearing.[a] But you will reply: "What pleasure do you get from wasting your time on these problems, which relieve you of none of your emotions, rout none of your desires?" So far as I am concerned, I treat and discuss them as matters which contribute greatly toward calming the spirit, and I search myself first, and then the world about me. [16]And not even now am I, as you think, wasting my time. For all these questions, provided that they be not chopped up and torn apart into such unprofitable refinements, elevate and lighten the soul, which is weighted down by a heavy burden and desires to be freed and to return to the elements of which it was once a part. For this body of ours is a weight upon the soul and its penance; as the load presses down the soul is crushed and is in bondage, unless philosophy has come to its assistance and has bid it take fresh courage by contemplating the universe, and has turned it from things earthly to things divine. There it has its liberty, there it can roam abroad;[b] meantime it escapes the custody in which it is bound, and renews its life in heaven. [17]Just as skilled workmen, who have been engaged upon some delicate piece of work which wearies their eyes with straining, if the light which they have is niggardly or uncertain, go forth into the open air and in some park devoted to the people's recreation delight their eyes in the generous light of day; so the soul, imprisoned as it has been in this gloomy and darkened house, seeks the open sky whenever it can, and in the contemplation of the universe finds rest.

[a] i.e., restate the question and hear the evidence again.

[b] According to the Stoics the soul, which consisted of fire or breath and was a part of the divine essence, rose at death into the ether and became one with the stars. Seneca elsewhere (*Consolatio ad Marciam*) states that the soul went through a sort of purifying process, – a view which may have had some influence on Christian thought. The souls of the good, the Stoics maintained, were destined to last until the end of the world, the souls of the bad to be extinguished before that time.

[18]The wise man, the seeker after wisdom, is bound closely, indeed, to his body, but he is an absentee so far as his better self is concerned, and he concentrates his thoughts upon lofty things. Bound, so to speak, to his oath of allegiance, he regards the period of life as his term of service. He is so trained that he neither loves nor hates life; he endures a mortal lot, although he knows that an ampler lot is in store for him. [19]Do you forbid me to contemplate the universe? Do you compel me to withdraw from the whole and restrict me to a part? May I not ask what are the beginnings of all things, who moulded the universe, who took the confused and conglomerate mass of sluggish matter, and separated it into its parts? May I not inquire who is the Master-Builder of this universe, how the mighty bulk was brought under the control of law and order, who gathered together the scattered atoms, who separated the disordered elements and assigned an outward form to elements that lay in one vast shapelessness? Or whence came all the expanse of light? And whether is it fire, or even brighter than fire?[a] [20]Am I not to ask these questions? Must I be ignorant of the heights whence I have descended? Whether I am to see this world but once, or to be born many times? What is my destination afterwards? What abode awaits my soul on its release from the laws of slavery among men? Do you forbid me to have a share in heaven? In other words, do you bid me live with my head bowed down? [21]No, I am above such an existence; I was born to a greater destiny than to be a mere chattel of my body, and I regard this body as nothing but a chain[b] which manacles my freedom. Therefore,

[a] The sequence of elements from the earth outwards and upwards was earth, water, air, and fire. The upper fire was ether. Zeno (quoted by Cicero, *Acad.* i. 1[1] 39) refused to acknowledge a fifth essence: *statuebat enim ignem esse ipsam naturam, quae quaeque gigneret, et mentem et sensus.*

[b] The "prison of the body" is a frequent figure in Stoic as in all philosophy. See, for example, § 16 of this letter, "the soul in bondage."

I offer it as a sort of buffer to fortune, and shall allow no wound to penetrate through to my soul. For my body is the only part of me which can suffer injury. In this dwelling, which is exposed to peril, my soul lives free. [22]Never shall this flesh drive me to feel fear or to assume any pretence that is unworthy of a good man. Never shall I lie in order to honour this petty body. When it seems proper, I shall sever my connexion with it. And at present, while we are bound together, our alliance shall nevertheless not be one of equality; the soul shall bring all quarrels before its own tribunal. To despise our bodies is sure freedom.

[23]To return to our subject; this freedom will be greatly helped by the contemplation of which we were just speaking. All things are made up of matter and of God;[a] God controls matter, which encompasses him and follows him as its guide and leader. And that which creates, in other words, God, is more powerful and precious than matter, which is acted upon by God. [24]God's place in the universe corresponds to the soul's relation to man. World-matter corresponds to our mortal body; therefore let the lower serve the higher. Let us be brave in the face of hazards. Let us not fear wrongs, or wounds, or bonds, or poverty. And what is death? It is either the end, or a process of change. I have no fear of ceasing to exist; it is the same as not having begun. Nor do I shrink from changing into another state, because I shall, under no conditions, be as cramped as I am now. Farewell.

[a] A restatement of the previous remark made in this letter; see note on § 11.

LXXVII. ON TAKING ONE'S OWN LIFE

[1]Suddenly there came into our view today the "Alexandrian" ships, – I mean those which are usually sent ahead to announce the coming of the fleet; they are called "mail-boats." The Campanians are glad to see them; all the rabble of Puteoli[a] stand on the docks, and can recognize the "Alexandrian" boats, no matter how great the crowd of vessels, by the very trim of their sails. For they alone may keep spread their topsails, which all ships use when out at sea, [2]because nothing sends a ship along so well as its upper canvas; that is where most of the speed is obtained. So when the breeze has stiffened and becomes stronger than is comfortable, they set their yards lower; for the wind has less force near the surface of the water. Accordingly, when they have made Capreae and the headland whence

Tall Pallas watches on the stormy peak,[b]

[a] Puteoli, in the bay of Naples, was the head-quarters in Italy of the important grain-trade with Egypt, on which the Roman magistrates relied to feed the populace.

[b] Author unknown.

all other vessels are bidden to be content with the mainsail, and the topsail stands out conspicuously on the "Alexandrian" mail-boats.

[3]While everybody was bustling about and hurrying to the water-front, I felt great pleasure in my laziness, because, although I was soon to receive letters from my friends, I was in no hurry to know how my affairs were progressing abroad, or what news the letters were bringing; for some time now I have had no losses, nor gains either. Even if I were not an old man, I could not have helped feeling pleasure at this; but as it is, my pleasure was far greater. For, however small my possessions might be, I should still have left over more travelling-money than journey to travel, especially since this journey upon which we have set out is one which need not be followed to the end. [4]An expedition will be incomplete if one stops half-way, or anywhere on this side of one's destination; but life is not incomplete if it is honourable. At whatever point you leave off living, provided you leave off nobly, your life is a whole.[a] Often, however, one must leave off bravely, and our reasons therefore need not be momentous; for neither are the reasons momentous which hold us here.

[5]Tullius Marcellinus,[b] a man whom you knew very well, who in youth was a quiet soul and became old prematurely, fell ill of a disease which was by no means hopeless; but it was protracted and troublesome, and it demanded much attention; hence he began to think about dying. He called many of his friends together. Each one of them gave Marcellinus advice, – the timid friend urging him to do what he had made up his mind to do; the flattering and wheedling

[a] This thought, found in Ep. xii. 6 and often elsewhere, is a favourite with Seneca.

[b] It is not likely that this Marcellinus is the same person as the Marcellinus Ep. xxix., because of their different views on philosophy (Summers). But there is no definite evidence for or against.

friend giving counsel which he supposed would be more pleasing to Marcellinus when he came to think the matter over; [6]but our Stoic friend, a rare man, and, to praise him in language which he deserves, a man of courage and vigour[a] admonished him best of all, as it seems to me. For he began as follows: "Do not torment yourself, my dear Marcellinus, as if the question which you are weighing were a matter of importance. It is not an important matter to live; all your slaves live, and so do all animals; but it is important to die honourably, sensibly, bravely. Reflect how long you have been doing the same thing: food, sleep, lust, – this is one's daily round. The desire to die may be felt, not only by the sensible man or the brave or unhappy man, but even by the man who is merely surfeited."

[7]Marcellinus did not need someone to urge him, but rather someone to help him; his slaves refused to do his bidding. The Stoic therefore removed their fears, showing them that there was no risk involved for the household except when it was uncertain whether the master's death was self-sought or not; besides, it was as bad a practice to kill one's master as it was to prevent him forcibly from killing himself. [8]Then he suggested to Marcellinus himself that it would be a kindly act to distribute gifts to those who had attended him throughout his whole life, when that life was finished, just as, when a banquet is finished,[b] the remaining portion is divided among the attendants who stand about the table. Marcellinus was of a compliant and generous disposition, even when it was a question of his own property; so he distributed

---

[a] A Roman compliment; the Greeks would have used καλὸς κἀγαθός; cf. Horace, *Ep.* i. [7]46

> *Strenuus et fortis causisque Philippus agendis*
> Clarus.

[b] For this frequent "banquet of life" simile see Ep. xcviii. [15]*ipse vitae plenus est*, etc.

little sums among his sorrowing slaves, and comforted them besides. [9]No need had he of sword or of bloodshed; for three days he fasted and had a tent put up in his very bedroom.[a] Then a tub was brought in; he lay in it for a long time, and, as the hot water was continually poured over him, he gradually passed away, not without a feeling of pleasure, as he himself remarked, – such a feeling as a slow dissolution is wont to give. Those of us who have ever fainted know from experience what this feeling is.

[10]This little anecdote into which I have digressed will not be displeasing to you. For you will see that your friend departed neither with difficulty nor with suffering. Though he committed suicide, yet he withdrew most gently, gliding out of life. The anecdote may also be of some use; for often a crisis demands just such examples. There are times when we ought to die and are unwilling; sometimes we die and are unwilling. [11]No one is so ignorant as not to know that we must at some time die; nevertheless, when one draws near death, one turns to flight, trembles, and laments. Would you not think him an utter fool who wept because he was not alive a thousand years ago? And is he not just as much of a fool who weeps because he will not be alive a thousand years from now? It is all the same; you will not be, and you were not. Neither of these periods of time belongs to you. [12]You have been cast upon this point of time;[b] if you would make it longer, how much longer shall you make it? Why weep? Why pray? You are taking pains to no purpose.

[a] So that the steam might not escape. One thinks of Seneca's last hours: Tac. *Ann.* xv. [64]*stagnum calidae aquae introiit . . . exin balneo inlatus et vapore eius exanimatus.*

[b] For the same thought cf. Ep. xlix. [3]*punctum est quod vivimus et adhuc puncto minus.*

> Give over thinking that your prayers can bend
> Divine decrees from their predestined end.[a]

These decrees are unalterable and fixed; they are governed by a mighty and everlasting compulsion. Your goal will be the goal of all things. What is there strange in this to you? You were born to be subject to this law; this fate befell your father, your mother, your ancestors, all who came before you; and it will befall all who shall come after you. A sequence which cannot be broken or altered by any power binds all things together and draws all things in its course. [13]Think of the multitudes of men doomed to death who will come after you, of the multitudes who will go with you! You would die more bravely, I suppose, in the company of many thousands; and yet there are many thousands, both of men and of animals, who at this very moment, while you are irresolute about death, are breathing their last, in their several ways. But you, – did you believe that you would not some day reach the goal towards which you have always been travelling? No journey but has its end.

[14]You think, I suppose, that it is now in order for me to cite some examples of great men. No, I shall cite rather the case of a boy. The story of the Spartan lad has been preserved: taken captive while still a stripling, he kept crying in his Doric dialect, "I will not be a slave!" and he made good his word; for the very first time he was ordered to perform a menial and degrading service, – and the command was to fetch a chamber-pot, – he dashed out his brains against the wall.[b] [15]So near at hand is freedom, and is anyone still a slave? Would you not

---

[a] Vergil, *Aeneid*, vi. 376.

[b] See Plutarch, *Mor.* 234 b, for a similar act of the Spartan boy captured by King Antigonus. Hense (*Rhein. Mus.* xlvii. pp. 220 f.) thinks that this story may be taken from Bion, the third-century satirist and moral philosopher.

rather have your own son die thus than reach old age by weakly yielding? Why therefore are you distressed, when even a boy can die so bravely? Suppose that you refuse to follow him; you will be led. Take into your own control that which is now under the control of another. Will you not borrow that boy's courage, and say: "I am no slave!"? Unhappy fellow, you are a slave to men, you are a slave to your business, you are a slave to life. For life, if courage to die be lacking, is slavery.

[16]Have you anything worth waiting for? Your very pleasures, which cause you to tarry and hold you back, have already been exhausted by you. None of them is a novelty to you, and there is none that has not already become hateful because you are cloyed with it. You know the taste of wine and cordials. It makes no difference whether a hundred or a thousand measures[a] pass through your bladder; you are nothing but a wine-strainer.[b] You are a connoisseur in the flavour of the oyster and of the mullet;[c] your luxury has not left you anything untasted for the years that are to come; and yet these are the things from which you are torn away unwillingly. [17]What else is there which you would regret to have taken from you? Friends? But who can be a friend to you? Country? What? Do you think enough of your country to be late to dinner? The light of the sun? You would extinguish it, if you could; for what have you ever done that was fit to be seen in the light? Confess the truth; it is not because you long for the senate chamber or the forum, or even for the world of nature, that you would fain put off dying; it is because you are loth to leave the fish-market, though you have exhausted its stores.[d]

---

[a] About 5¾ gallons.

[b] Cf. Pliny, xiv. [22]*quin immo ut plus capiamus, sacco frangimus vires.* Strained wine could be drunk in greater quantities without intoxication.

[c] Cf. Dio Cassius, xl. 54, for the exiled Milo's enjoyment of the mullets of Marseilles.

[d] Probably the strong tone of disapproval used in this paragraph is directed

[18]You are afraid of death; but how can you scorn it in the midst of a mushroom supper?[a] You wish to live; well, do you know how lo live? You are afraid to die. But come now: is this life of yours anything but death? Gaius Caesar was passing along the Via Latina, when a man stepped out from the ranks of the prisoners, his grey beard hanging down even to his breast, and begged to be put to death. "What!" said Caesar, "are you alive now?" That is the answer which should be given to men to whom death would come as a relief. "You are afraid to die; what! are you alive now?" [19]"But," says one, "I wish to live, for I am engaged in many honourable pursuits. I am loth to leave life's duties, which I am fulfilling with loyalty and zeal." Surely you are aware that dying is also one of life's duties? You are deserting no duty; for there is no definite number established which you are bound to complete. [20]There is no life that is not short. Compared with the world of nature, even Nestor's life was a short one, or Sattia's,[b] the woman who bade carve on her tombstone that she had lived ninety and nine years. Some persons, you see, boast of their long lives; but who could have endured the old lady if she had had the luck to complete her hundredth year? It is with life as it is with a play, – it matters not how long the action is spun out, but how good the acting is. It makes no difference at what point you stop. Stop whenever you choose; only see to it that the closing period is well turned.[c] Farewell.

---

against the Roman in general rather than against the industrious Lucilius. It is characteristic of the diatribe.

[a] Seneca may be recalling the death of the Emperor Claudius.

[b] A traditional example of old age, mentioned by Martial and the elder Pliny.

[c] Compare the last words of the Emperor Augustus: *amicos percontatus ecquid iis videretur mimum vitae commode transegisse* (Suet. *Aug.* 99).

LXXVIII. ON THE HEALING POWER OF THE MIND

[1]That you are frequently troubled by the snuffling of catarrh and by short attacks of fever which follow after long and chronic catarrhal seizures, I am sorry to hear; particularly because I have experienced this sort of illness myself, and scorned it in its early stages. For when I was still young, I could put up with hardships and show a bold front to illness. But I finally succumbed, and arrived at such a state that I could do nothing but snuffle, reduced as I was to the extremity of thinness.[a] [2]I often entertained the impulse of ending my life then and there; but the thought of my kind old father kept me back. For I reflected, not how bravely I had the power to die, but how little power he had to bear bravely the loss of me. And so I commanded myself to live. For sometimes it is an act of bravery even to live.

[3]Now I shall tell you what consoled me during those days, stating at the outset that these very aids to my peace of mind were as efficacious as medicine. Honourable consolation results in a cure; and whatever has uplifted the soul helps the body also. My studies were my salvation. I place

[a] To such a degree that Seneca's enemy Caligula refrained from executing him, on the ground that he would soon die.

119

it to the credit of philosophy that I recovered and regained my strength. I owe my life to philosophy, and that is the least of my obligations! [4]My friends, too, helped me greatly toward good health; I used to be comforted by their cheering words, by the hours they spent at my bedside, and by their conversation. Nothing, my excellent Lucilius, refreshes and aids a sick man so much as the affection of his friends; nothing so steals away the expectation and the fear of death. In fact, I could not believe that, if they survived me, I should be dying at all. Yes, I repeat, it seemed to me that I should continue to live, not with them, but through them. I imagined myself not to be yielding up my soul, but to be making it over to them.

All these things gave me the inclination to succour myself and to endure any torture; besides, it is a most miserable state to have lost one's zest for dying, and to have no zest in living. [5]These, then, are the remedies to which you should have recourse. The physician will prescribe your walks and your exercise; he will warn you not to become addicted to idleness, as is the tendency of the inactive invalid; he will order you to read in a louder voice and to exercise your lungs[a] the passages and cavity of which are affected; or to sail and shake up your bowels by a little mild motion; he will recommend the proper food, and the suitable time for aiding your strength with wine or refraining from it in order to keep your cough from being irritated and hacking. But as for me, my counsel to you is this, – and it is a cure, not merely of this disease of yours, but of your whole life, – "Despise death." There is no sorrow in the world, when we have escaped from the fear of death. [6]There are these three serious elements in every disease: fear of death, bodily pain, and interruption of pleasures. Concerning death enough has been said, and I shall add only a word: this fear

[a] Cf. Ep. xv. 7 f.

is not a fear of disease, but a fear of nature. Disease has often postponed death, and a vision of dying has been many a man's salvation.[a] You will die, not because you are ill, but because you are alive; even when you have been cured, the same end awaits you; when you have recovered, it will be not death, but ill-health, that you have escaped.

[7]Let us now return to the consideration of the characteristic disadvantage of disease: it is accompanied by great suffering. The suffering, however, is rendered endurable by interruptions; for the strain of extreme pain must come to an end.[b] No man can suffer both severely and for a long time; Nature, who loves us most tenderly, has so constituted us as to make pain either endurable or short.[c] [8]The severest pains have their seat in the most slender parts of our body; nerves, joints, and any other of the narrow passages, hurt most cruelly when they have developed trouble within their contracted spaces. But these parts soon become numb, and by reason of the pain itself lose the sensation of pain, whether because the life-force, when checked in its natural course and changed for the worse, loses the peculiar power through which it thrives and through which it warns us, or because the diseased humours of the body, when they cease to have a place into which they may flow, are thrown back upon themselves, and deprive of sensation the parts where they have caused congestion. [9]So gout, both in the feet and in the hands, and all pain in the vertebrae and in the nerves, have their intervals of rest at the times when they have dulled the parts which they before had tortured; the first twinges,[d] in all such cases, are what cause the distress, and

[a] i.e., men have become healthier after passing through serious illness.

[b] Cf. Epicurus, Frag. 446 Usener.

[c] Compare, from among many parallels, Ep. xxiv. [14](dolor) levis es, si ferre possum, brevis es, si ferre non possum.

[d] See also Ep. xcv. 1[7] The word literally means "maggots," "bots," in horses

121

their onset is checked by lapse of time, so that there is an end of pain when numbness has set in. Pain in the teeth, eyes, and ears is most acute for the very reason that it begins among the narrow spaces of the body, – no less acute, indeed, than in the head itself. But if it is more violent than usual, it turns to delirium and stupor. [10]This is, accordingly, a consolation for excessive pain, – that you cannot help ceasing to feel it if you feel it to excess. The reason, however, why the inexperienced are impatient when their bodies suffer is, that they have not accustomed themselves to be contented in spirit. They have been closely associated with the body. Therefore a high-minded and sensible man divorces soul from body, and dwells much with the better or divine part, and only as far as he must with this complaining and frail portion.

[11]"But it is a hardship," men say, "to do without our customary pleasures, – to fast, to feel thirst and hunger." These are indeed serious when one first abstains from them. Later the desire dies down, because the appetites themselves which lead to desire are wearied and forsake us; then the stomach becomes petulant, then the food which we craved before becomes hateful. Our very wants die away. But there is no bitterness in doing without that which you have ceased to desire. [12]Moreover, every pain sometimes stops, or at any rate slackens; moreover, one may take precautions against its return, and, when it threatens, may check it by means of remedies. Every variety of pain has its premonitory symptoms; this is true, at any rate, of pain that is habitual and recurrent. One can endure the suffering which disease entails, if one has come to regard its results with scorn. [13]But do not of your own accord make your troubles heavier to bear and burden yourself with complaining. Pain is slight if opinion has added nothing to it; but if, on the other hand, you begin to encourage

———

or cattle.

yourself and say, "It is nothing, – a trifling matter at most; keep a stout heart and it will soon cease"; then in thinking it slight, you will make it slight. Everything depends on opinion; ambition, luxury, greed, hark back to opinion. It is according to opinion that we suffer. [14]A man is as wretched as he has convinced himself that he is. I hold that we should do away with complaint about past sufferings and with all language like this: "None has ever been worse off than I. What sufferings, what evils have I endured! No one has thought that I shall recover. How often have my family bewailed me, and the physicians given me over! Men who are placed on the rack are not torn asunder with such agony!" However, even if all this is true, it is over and gone. What benefit is there in reviewing past sufferings, and in being unhappy, just because once you were unhappy? Besides, every one adds much to his own ills, and tells lies to himself. And that which was bitter to bear is pleasant to have borne; it is natural to rejoice at the ending of one's ills.

Two elements must therefore be rooted out once for all, – the fear of future suffering, and the recollection of past suffering; since the latter no longer concerns me, and the former concerns me not yet. [15]But when set in the very midst of troubles one should say:

Perchance some day the memory of this sorrow
Will even bring delight.[a]

Let such a man fight against them with all his might: if he once gives way, he will be vanquished; but if he strives against his sufferings, he will conquer. As it is, however, what most men do is to drag down upon their own heads a falling ruin which they ought to try to support. If you begin to withdraw your support from that which thrusts toward

[a] Vergil, *Aeneid*, i. 203.

you and totters and is ready to plunge, it will follow you and lean more heavily upon you; but if you hold your ground and make up your mind to push against it, it will be forced back. [16]What blows do athletes receive on their faces and all over their bodies! Nevertheless, through their desire for fame they endure every torture, and they undergo these things not only because they are fighting but in order to be able to fight. Their very training means torture. So let us also win the way to victory in all our struggles, – for the reward is not a garland or a palm or a trumpeter who calls for silence at the proclamation of our names, but rather virtue, steadfastness of soul, and a peace that is won for all time, if fortune has once been utterly vanquished in any combat. You say, "I feel severe pain." [17]What then; are you relieved from feeling it, if you endure it like a woman? Just as an enemy is more dangerous to a retreating army, so every trouble that fortune brings attacks us all the harder if we yield and turn our backs. "But the trouble is serious." What? Is it for this purpose that we are strong, – that we may have light burdens to bear? Would you have your illness longdrawn-out, or would you have it quick and short? If it is long, it means a respite, allows you a period for resting yourself, bestows upon you the boon of time in plenty; as it arises, so it must also subside. A short and rapid illness will do one of two things: it will quench or be quenched. And what difference does it make whether it is not or I am not? In either case there is an end of pain.

[18]This, too, will help – to turn the mind aside to thoughts of other things and thus to depart from pain. Call to mind what honourable or brave deeds you have done; consider the good side of your own life.[a] Run over in your memory those

---

[a] Literally, perhaps, "the noble rôles which you have played." Summers compares Ep. xiv. [13]*ultimas partes Catonis* – "the closing scenes of Cato's life."

things which you have particularly admired. Then think of all the brave men who have conquered pain: of him who continued to read his book as he allowed the cutting out of varicose veins; of him who did not cease to smile, though that very smile so enraged his torturers that they tried upon him every instrument of their cruelty. If pain can be conquered by a smile, will it not be conquered by reason? [19]You may tell me now of whatever you like – of colds, bad coughing-spells that bring up parts of our entrails, fever that parches our very vitals, thirst, limbs so twisted that the joints protrude in different directions; yet worse than these are the stake, the rack, the red-hot plates, the instrument that reopens wounds while the wounds themselves are still swollen and that drives their imprint still deeper.[a] Nevertheless there have been men who have not uttered a moan amid these tortures. "More yet!" says the torturer; but the victim has not begged for release. "More yet!" he says again; but no answer has come. "More yet!" the victim has smiled, and heartily, too. Can you not bring yourself, after an example like this, to make a mock at pain?

[20]"But," you object, "my illness does not allow me to be doing anything; it has withdrawn me from all my duties." It is your body that is hampered by ill-health, and not your soul as well. It is for this reason that it clogs the feet of the runner and will hinder the handiwork of the cobbler or the artisan; but if your soul be habitually in practice, you will plead and teach, listen and learn, investigate and meditate. What more is necessary? Do you think that you are doing nothing if you possess self-control in your illness? You will be showing that a disease can be overcome, or at any rate endured. [21]There is, I assure you, a place for virtue even upon a bed of sickness. It is not only the sword and the

[a] Cf. Ep. xiv. 4 f. and the *crucibus adfixi, flamma usti*, etc., of Tac. *Ann.* xv. 44.

battle-line that prove the soul alert and unconquered by fear; a man can display bravery even when wrapped in his bed-clothes. You have something to do: wrestle bravely with disease. If it shall compel you to nothing, beguile you to nothing, it is a notable example that you display. O what ample matter were there for renown, if we could have spectators of our sickness! Be your own spectator; seek your own applause.

[22]Again, there are two kinds of pleasures. Disease checks the pleasures of the body, but does not do away with them. Nay, if the truth is to be considered, it serves to excite them; for the thirstier a man is, the more he enjoys a drink; the hungrier he is, the more pleasure he takes in food. Whatever falls to one's lot after a period of abstinence is welcomed with greater zest. The other kind, however, the pleasures of the mind, which are higher and less uncertain, no physician can refuse to the sick man. Whoever seeks these and knows well what they are, scorns all the blandishments of the senses. [23]Men say, "Poor sick fellow!" But why? Is it because he does not mix snow with his wine, or because he does not revive the chill of his drink – mixed as it is in a good-sized bowl – by chipping ice into it? Or because he does not have Lucrine[a] oysters opened fresh at his table? Or because there is no din of cooks about his dining-hall, as they bring in their very cooking apparatus along with their viands? For luxury has already devised this fashion – of having the kitchen accompany the dinner, so that the food may not grow luke-warm, or fail to be hot enough for a palate which has already become hardened. [24]"Poor sick fellow!" – he will eat as much as he can digest. There will be no boar lying before his eyes,[b] banished from the table as if it were a common meat; and on his sideboard there

---

[a] The *lacus Lucrinus* was a salt-water lagoon, near Baiae in Campania.

[b] i.e., to be looked at; there are better dainties on the table.

will be heaped together no breastmeat of birds, because it sickens him to see birds served whole. But what evil has been done to you? You will dine like a sick man, nay, sometimes like a sound man.[a]

[25]All these things, however, can be easily endured – gruel, warm water, and anything else that seems insupportable to a fastidious man, to one who is wallowing in luxury, sick in soul rather than in body – if only we cease to shudder at death. And we shall cease, if once we have gained a knowledge of the limits of good and evil; then, and then only, life will not weary us, neither will death make us afraid. [26]For surfeit of self can never seize upon a life that surveys all the things which are manifold, great, divine; only idle leisure is wont to make men hate their lives. To one who roams[b] through the universe, the truth can never pall; it will be the untruths that will cloy. [27]And, on the other hand, if death comes near with its summons, even though it be untimely in its arrival, though it cut one off in one's prime, a man has had a taste of all that the longest life can give. Such a man has in great measure come to understand the universe. He knows that honourable things do not depend on time for their growth; but any life must seem short to those who measure its length by pleasures which are empty and for that reason unbounded.

[28]Refresh yourself with such thoughts as these, and meanwhile reserve some hours for our letters. There will come a time when we shall be united again and brought together; however short this time may be, we shall make it long by knowing how to employ it. For, as Posidonius says:[c]

[a] *Sanus* is used (1) as signifying "sound in body" and (2) as the opposite of *insanus.*

[b] The Perhaps a reminiscence of Lucretius i. [74] *omne immensum peragravit mente animoque..*

[c] Seneca often quotes Posidonius, as does Cicero also. These words may

"A single day among the learned lasts longer than the longest life of the ignorant." [29]Meanwhile, hold fast to this thought, and grip it close: yield not to adversity; trust not to prosperity; keep before your eyes the full scope of Fortune's power, as if she would surely do whatever is in her power to do. That which has been long expected comes more gently. Farewell.

---

have been taken from his Προτρεπτικά (or Λόγοι προτρεπτικοί), *Exhortations*, a work in which he maintained that men should make a close study of philosophy, in spite of the varying opinions of its expositors.

LXXXIII. ON DRUNKENNESS

[1]You bid me give you an account of each separate day, and of the whole day too; so you must have a good opinion of me if you think that in these days of mine there is nothing to hide. At any rate, it is thus that we should live, – as if we lived in plain sight of all men; and it is thus that we should think, – as if there were someone who could look into our inmost souls; and there is one who can so look. For what avails it that something is hidden from man? Nothing is shut off from the sight of God. He is witness of our souls,[a] and he comes into the very midst of our thoughts – comes into them, I say, as one who may at any time depart. [2]I shall therefore do as you bid, and shall gladly inform you by letter what I am doing, and in what sequence. I shall keep watching myself continually, and – a most useful habit – shall review each day.[b] For this is what makes us wicked: that no one of us looks back over his own life. Our thoughts are devoted only to what we are about to do. And yet our plans for the future always depend on the past.

[a] Cf. Ep. xli. [2]*sacer intra nos spiritus, . . . malorum bonorumque nostrorum observator et custos.*

[b] Cf. Ep. i. [4]*ratio constat inpensae* (referring to his attempt to employ his time profitably).

³Today has been unbroken; no one has filched the slightest part of it from me. The whole time has been divided between rest and reading. A brief space has been given over to bodily exercise, and on this ground I can thank old age – my exercise costs very little effort; as soon as I stir, I am tired. And weariness is the aim and end of exercise, no matter how strong one is. ⁴Do you ask who are my pacemakers? One is enough for me, – the slave Pharius, a pleasant fellow, as you know; but I shall exchange him for another. At my time of life I need one who is of still more tender years. Pharius, at any rate, says that he and I are at the same period of life; for we are both losing our teeth.ª Yet even now I can scarcely follow his pace as he runs, and within a very short time I shall not be able to follow him at all; so you see what profit we get from daily exercise. Very soon does a wide interval open between two persons who travel different ways. My slave is climbing up at the very moment when I am coming down, and you surely know how much quicker the latter is. Nay, I was wrong; for now my life is not coming down; it is falling outright. ⁵Do you ask, for all that, how our race resulted today? We raced to a tie,ᵇ – something which rarely happens in a running contest. After tiring myself out in this way (for I cannot call it exercise), I took a cold bath; this, at my house, means just short of hot. I, the former cold-water enthusiast, who used to celebrate the new year by taking a plunge into the canal, who, just as naturally as I would set out to do some reading or writing, or to compose a speech, used to inaugurate the first of the year with a plunge into the Virgo aqueduct,ᶜ have changed my allegiance, first to the Tiber,

ª See Ep. xii. 3 for a similar witticism.

ᵇ *Hieran* (*coronam*), as Lipsius thinks, when the result was doubtful, the garland was offered to the gods. From the Greek ἱερός, sacred.

ᶜ Constructed by Marcus Agrippa; now the fountain of Trevi.

and then to my favourite tank, which is warmed only by the sun, at times when I am most robust and when there is not a flaw in my bodily processes. I have very little energy left for bathing. [6]After the bath, some stale bread and breakfast without a table; no need to wash the hands after such a meal. Then comes a very short nap. You know my habit; I avail myself of a scanty bit of sleep, – unharnessing, as it were.[a] For I am satisfied if I can just stop staying awake. Sometimes I know that I have slept; at other times, I have a mere suspicion.

[7]Lo, now the din of the Races sounds about me! My ears are smitten with sudden and general cheering. But this does not upset my thoughts or even break their continuity. I can endure an uproar with complete resignation. The medley of voices blended in one note sounds to me like the dashing of waves,[b] or like the wind that lashes the tree-tops, or like any other sound which conveys no meaning.

[8]What is it, then, you ask, to which I have been giving my attention? I will tell you, a thought sticks in my mind, left over from yesterday, – namely, what men of the greatest sagacity have meant when they have offered the most trifling and intricate proofs for problems of the greatest importance, – proofs which may be true, but none the less resemble fallacies. [9]Zeno, that greatest of men, the revered founder of our brave and holy school of philosophy, wishes to discourage us from drunkenness. Listen, then, to his arguments proving that the good man will not get drunk: "No one entrusts a secret to a drunken man; but one will entrust a secret to a

---

[a] The same word is used by Seneca in *De Tranq. An.* xvii. [7]*quidam medio die interiunxerunt et in postmeridianas horas aliquid levioris operae distulerunt.*

[b] Cf. Ep. lvi. [3]*istum fremitum non magis curo quam fluctum aut deiectum aquae.*

good man; therefore, the good man will not get drunk."[a] Mark how ridiculous Zeno is made when we set up a similar syllogism in contrast with his. There are many, but one will be enough: "No one entrusts a secret to a man when he is asleep; but one entrusts a secret to a good man; therefore, the good man does not go to sleep."[b] [10]Posidonius pleads the cause of our master Zeno in the only possible way; but it cannot, I hold, be pleaded even in this way. For Posidonius maintains that the word "drunken" is used in two ways, – in the one case of a man who is loaded with wine and has no control over himself; in the other, of a man who is accustomed to get drunk, and is a slave to the habit. Zeno, he says, meant the latter, – the man who is accustomed to get drunk, not the man who is drunk; and no one would entrust to this person any secret, for it might be blabbed out when the man was in his cups. [11]This is a fallacy. For the first syllogism refers to him who is actually drunk and not to him who is about to get drunk. You will surely admit that there is a great difference between a man who is drunk and a drunkard. He who is actually drunk may be in this state for the first time and may not have the habit, while the drunkard is often free from drunkenness. I therefore interpret the word in its usual meaning, especially since the syllogism is set up by a man who makes a business of the careful use of words, and who weighs his language. Moreover, if this is what Zeno meant, and what he wished it to mean to us, he was trying to avail himself of an equivocal word in order to work in a fallacy; and no man ought to do this when truth is the object of inquiry.

[a] Zeno, Frag. 229 von Arnim, – quoting also Philo's εἰ τῷ μεθύοντι οὐκ ἄν τις εὐλόγως λόγον ἀπόρρητον παρακατάθοιτο . . . οὐκ ἄρα μεθύει ὁ ἀστεῖος.

[b] Cf. Ep. xlix. [8]*quod non perdidisti, habes; cornua autem non perdidisti; cornua ergo habes*, – and the syllogisms given in Ep. xlviii.

[12]But let us admit, indeed, that he meant what Posidonius says; even so, the conclusion is false, that secrets are not entrusted to an habitual drunkard. Think how many soldiers who are not always sober have been entrusted by a general or a captain or a centurion with messages which might not be divulged! With regard to the notorious plot to murder Gaius Caesar, – I mean the Caesar who conquered Pompey and got control of the state, – Tillius Cimber was trusted with it no less than Gaius Cassius. Now Cassius throughout his life drank water; while Tillius Cimber was a sot as well as a brawler. Cimber himself alluded to this fact, saying: "I carry a master? I cannot carry my liquor!" [13]So let each one call to mind those who, to his knowledge, can be ill trusted with wine, but well trusted with the spoken word; and yet one case occurs to my mind, which I shall relate, lest it fall into oblivion. For life should be provided with conspicuous illustrations. Let us not always be harking back to the dim past.

[14]Lucius Piso, the director of Public Safety at Rome, was drunk from the very time of his appointment. He used to spend the greater part of the night at banquets, and would sleep until noon. That was the way he spent his morning hours. Nevertheless, he applied himself most diligently to his official duties, which included the guardianship of the city. Even the sainted Augustus trusted him with secret orders when he placed him in command of Thrace.[a] Piso conquered that country. Tiberius, too, trusted him when he took his holiday in Campania, leaving behind him in the city many a critical matter that aroused both suspicion and hatred. [15]I fancy that it was because Piso's drunkenness turned out well for the Emperor that he appointed to the office of city prefect Cossus, a man of authority and balance,

[a] In 11 B.C., when the Thracians were attacking Macedonia. The campaign lasted for three years, and Piso was rewarded with a triumph at its close.

but so soaked and steeped in drink that once, at a meeting of the Senate, whither he had come after banqueting, he was overcome by a slumber from which he could not be roused, and had to be carried home. It was to this man that Tiberius sent many orders, written in his own hand, – orders which he believed he ought not to trust even to the officials of his household. Cossus never let a single secret slip out, whether personal or public.

[16]So let us abolish all such harangues as this: "No man in the bonds of drunkenness has power over his soul. As the very vats are burst by new wine, and as the dregs at the bottom are raised to the surface by the strength of the fermentation; so, when the wine effervesces, whatever lies hidden below is brought up and made visible. As a man overcome by liquor cannot keep down his food when he has over-indulged in wine, so he cannot keep back a secret either. He pours forth impartially both his own secrets and those of other persons." [17]This, of course, is what commonly happens, but so does this, – that we take counsel on serious subjects with those whom we know to be in the habit of drinking freely. Therefore this proposition, which is laid down in the guise of a defence of Zeno's syllogism, is false, – that secrets are not entrusted to the habitual drunkard.

How much better it is to arraign drunkenness frankly and to expose its vices! For even the middling good man avoids them, not to mention the perfect sage, who is satisfied with slaking his thirst; the sage, even if now and then he is led on by good cheer which, for a friend's sake, is carried somewhat too far, yet always stops short of drunkenness. [18]We shall investigate later the question whether the mind of the sage is upset by too much wine and commits follies like those of the toper; but meanwhile, if you wish to prove that a good man ought not to get drunk, why work it out by logic? Show how base it is to pour down more liquor than one can carry, and not to know the capacity of one's own stomach; show how often the drunkard does things which make him blush when he is sober; state that drunkenness[a] is nothing but a condition of insanity purposely assumed. Prolong the drunkard's condition to several days; will you have any doubt about his madness? Even as it is, the madness is no less; it merely lasts a shorter time. [19]Think of Alexander of Macedon,[b] who stabbed Clitus, his dearest and most loyal friend, at a banquet; after Alexander understood what he had done, he wished to die, and assuredly he ought to have died.

Drunkenness kindles and discloses every kind of vice, and removes the sense of shame that veils our evil undertakings.[c] For more men abstain from, forbidden actions because they are ashamed of sinning than because their inclinations are good. [20]When the strength of wine has become too great and has gained control over the mind, every lurking evil comes forth from its hiding-place. Drunkenness does not create vice, it merely brings it into view; at such times the lustful man does not wait even for the privacy of a bedroom, but without postponement gives free play to the demands of his passions; at such times the unchaste man proclaims and publishes his malady; at such times your cross-grained fellow does not restrain his tongue or his hand. The haughty man increases his arrogance, the ruthless man his cruelty, the slanderer his spitefulness. Every vice is given free play and comes to the front. [21]Besides, we forget who we are, we utter words that are halting and poorly enunciated, the glance is unsteady, the step falters, the head

---

[a] Like anger, which was interpreted by the ancients as "short-lived madness."

[b] For a dramatic account of the murder see Plutarch's *Alexander*, ch. 51.

[c] This is the firm conviction of Seneca, himself a most temperate man. §§ 14 and 15 admit that natural genius may triumph over drunkenness; § 17 may allow (with Chrysippus) a certain amount of hilarity; but the general conclusion is obvious.

is dizzy, the very ceiling moves about as if a cyclone were whirling the whole house, and the stomach suffers torture when the wine generates gas and causes our very bowels to swell. However, at the time, these troubles can be endured, so long as the man retains his natural strength; but what can he do when sleep impairs his powers, and when that which was drunkenness becomes indigestion?

[22]Think of the calamities caused by drunkenness in a nation! This evil has betrayed to their enemies the most spirited and warlike races; this evil has made breaches in walls defended by the stubborn warfare of many years; this evil has forced under alien sway peoples who were utterly unyielding and defiant of the yoke; this evil has conquered by the wine-cup those who in the field were invincible. [23]Alexander, whom I have just mentioned, passed through his many marches, his many battles, his many winter campaigns (through which he worked his way by overcoming disadvantages of time or place), the many rivers which flowed from unknown sources, and the many seas, all in safety; it was intemperance in drinking that laid him low, and the famous death-dealing bowl of Hercules.[a]

[24]What glory is there in carrying much liquor? When you have won the prize, and the other banqueters, sprawling asleep or vomiting, have declined your challenge to still other toasts; when you are the last survivor of the revels; when you have vanquished every one by your magnificent show of prowess and there is no man who has proved himself of so great capacity as you, you are vanquished by the cask. [25]Mark Antony was a great man, a man of distinguished

[a] Lipsius quotes Athenaeus as saying that Boeotian silver cups of large size were so called because the Boeotian Hercules drank from them; Servius, however, on Verg.*Aen.* viii. 278, declared that the name was derived from the large wooden bowl brought by Hercules to Italy and used for sacrificial purposes.

ability; but what ruined him and drove him into foreign habits and un-Roman vices, if it was not drunkenness and – no less potent than wine – love of Cleopatra? This it was that made him an enemy of the state; this it was that rendered him no match for his enemies; this it was that made him cruel, when as he sat at table the heads of the leaders of the state were brought in; when amid the most elaborate feasts and royal luxury he would identify the faces and hands of men whom he had proscribed;[a] when, though heavy with wine, he yet thirsted for blood. It was intolerable that he was getting drunk while he did such things; how much more intolerable that he did these things while actually drunk! [26]Cruelty usually follows wine-bibbing; for a man's soundness of mind is corrupted and made savage. Just as a lingering illness makes men querulous and irritable and drives them wild at the least crossing of their desires, so continued bouts of drunkenness bestialize the soul. For when people are often beside themselves, the habit of madness lasts on, and the vices which liquor generated retain their power even when the liquor is gone.

[27]Therefore you should state why the wise man ought not to get drunk. Explain by facts, and not by mere words, the hideousness of the thing, and its haunting evils. Do that which is easiest of all – namely, demonstrate that what men call pleasures are punishments as soon as they have exceeded due bounds. For if you try to prove that the wise man can souse himself with much wine and yet keep his course straight, even though he be in his cups, you may go on to infer by syllogisms that he will not die if he swallows poison, that he

---

[a] "Antony gave orders to those that were to kill Cicero, to cut off his head and right hand . . .; and, when they were brought before him, he regarded them joyfully, actually bursting out more than once into laughter, and when he had satiated himself with the sight of them, ordered them to be hung up . . . in the forum" (Clough's translation of Plutarch's *Antony*, p. 172).

will not sleep if he takes a sleeping-potion, that he will not vomit and reject the matter which clogs his stomach when you give him hellebore.[a] But, when a man's feet totter and his tongue is unsteady, what reason have you for believing that he is half sober and half drunk? Farewell.

[a] A plant which possessed cathartic properties and was widely used by the ancients. It was also applied in cases of mental derangement. The native Latin term is *veratrum*.

LXXXVIII. ON LIBERAL AND VOCATIONAL STUDIES

[1]You have been wishing to know my views with regard to liberal studies.[a] My answer is this: I respect no study, and deem no study good, which results in money-making. Such studies are profit-bringing occupations, useful only in so far as they give the mind a preparation and do not engage it permanently. One should linger upon them only so long as the mind can occupy itself with nothing greater; they are our apprenticeship, not our real work. [2]Hence you see why "liberal studies" are so called; it is because they are studies worthy of a free-born gentleman. But there is only one really liberal study, – that which gives a man his liberty. It is the study of wisdom, and that is lofty, brave, and great-souled. All other studies are puny and puerile. You surely do not believe that there is good in any of the subjects whose teachers are, as

---

[a] The regular round of education, ἐγκύκλιος παιδεία, including grammar, music, geometry, arithmetic, astrology, and certain phases of rhetoric and dialectic, are in this letter contrasted with liberal studies – those which have for their object the pursuit of virtue. Seneca is thus interpreting *studia liberalia* in a higher sense than his contemporaries would expect. Compare J. R. Lowell's definition of a university, "a place where nothing useful is taught."

you see, men of the most ignoble and base stamp? We ought not to be learning such things; we should have done with learning them.

Certain persons have made up their minds that the point at issue with regard to the liberal studies is whether they make men good; but they do not even profess or aim at a knowledge of this particular subject. [3]The scholar[a] busies himself with investigations into language, and if it be his desire to go farther afield, he works on history, or, if he would extend his range to the farthest limits, on poetry. But which of these paves the way to virtue? Pronouncing syllables, investigating words, memorizing plays, or making rules for the scansion of poetry, what is there in all this that rids one of fear, roots out desire, or bridles the passions? [4]The question is: do such men teach virtue, or not? If they do not teach it, then neither do they transmit it. If they do teach it, they are philosophers. Would you like to know how it happens that they have not taken the chair for the purpose of teaching virtue? See how unlike their subjects are; and yet their subjects would resemble each other if they taught the same thing.[b]

[5]It may be, perhaps, that they make you believe that Homer was a philosopher,[c] although they disprove this by the very arguments through which they seek to prove it. For sometimes they make of him a Stoic, who approves nothing but virtue, avoids pleasures, and refuses to relinquish honour even at the price of immortality; sometimes they make him

[a] *Grammaticus* in classical Greek means "one who is familiar with the alphabet"; in the Alexandrain age a "student of literature"; in the Roman age the equivalent of *litteratus*. Seneca means here a "specialist in linguistic science."

[b] i.e., philosophy (virtue).

[c] This theory was approved by Democritus, Hippias of Elis, and the allegorical interpreters; Xenophanes, Heraclitus, and Plato himself condemned Homer for his supposed unphilosophic fabrications.

an Epicurean, praising the condition of a state in repose, which passes its days in feasting and song; sometimes a Peripatetic, classifying goodness in three ways;[a] sometimes an Academic, holding that all things are uncertain. It is clear, however, that no one of these doctrines is to be fathered upon Homer, just because they are all there; for they are irreconcilable with one another. We may admit to these men, indeed, that Homer was a philosopher; yet surely he became a wise man before he had any knowledge of poetry. So let us learn the particular things that made Homer wise.

[6]It is no more to the point, of course, for me to investigate whether Homer or Hesiod was the older poet, than to know why Hecuba, although younger than Helen,[b] showed her years so lamentably. What, in your opinion, I say, would be the point in trying to determine the respective ages of Achilles and Patroclus? [7]Do you raise the question, "Through what regions did Ulysses stray?" instead of trying to prevent ourselves from going astray at all times? We have no leisure to hear lectures on the question whether he was sea-tost between Italy and Sicily, or outside our known world (indeed, so long a wandering could not possibly have taken place within its narrow bounds); we ourselves encounter storms of the spirit, which toss us daily, and our depravity drives us into all the ills which troubled Ulysses. For us there is never lacking the beauty to tempt our eyes, or the enemy to assail us; on this side are savage monsters that delight in human blood, on that side the treacherous allurements of the ear, and yonder

[a] he *tria genera bonorum* of Cicero's *De Fin* v. 8[4] Cf. *ib*. 18, where the three proper objects of man's search are given as the desire for pleasure, the avoidance of pain, and the attainment of such natural goods as health, strength, and soundness of mind. The Stoics held that the good was absolute.

[b] Summers compares Lucian, *Gall.* 1[7] Seneca, however, does not take such gossip seriously.

is shipwreck and all the varied category of misfortunes.[a] Show me rather, by the example of Ulysses, how I am to love my country, my wife, my father, and how, even after suffering shipwreck, I am to sail toward these ends, honourable as they are. [8]Why try to discover whether Penelope was a pattern of purity,[b] or whether she had the laugh on her contemporaries? Or whether she suspected that the man in her presence was Ulysses, before she knew it was he? Teach me rather what purity is, and how great a good we have in it, and whether it is situated in the body or in the soul.

[9]Now I will transfer my attention to the musician. You, sir, are teaching me how the treble and the bass[c] are in accord with one another, and how, though the strings produce different notes, the result is a harmony; rather bring my soul into harmony with itself, and let not my purposes be out of tune. You are showing me what the doleful keys[d] are; show me rather how, in the midst of adversity, I may keep from uttering a doleful note. [10]The mathematician teaches me how to lay out the dimensions of my estates; but I should rather be taught how to lay out what is enough for a man to own. He teaches me to count, and adapts my fingers to avarice; but I should prefer him to teach me that there is no point in such calculations, and that one is none the happier for tiring out the book-keepers with his possessions – or rather, how useless property is to any man who would find it the greatest misfortune if he should be required to reckon out, by his own wits, the amount of his holdings. [11]What good is there for me in knowing how to parcel out a piece of land, if I know not how to share it with my brother? What good is there in working

[a] This sentence alludes to Calypso, Circe, the Cyclops, and the Sirens.

[b] Unfavourable comment by Lycophron, and by Cicero, *De Nat. Deor.* iii. [22](*Mercurius*) *ex quo et Penelopa Pana natum ferunt.*

[c] With *acutae* and *graves* supply *voces.*

[d] Perhaps the equivalent of a "minor."

out to a nicety the dimensions of an acre, and in detecting the error if a piece has so much as escaped my measuring-rod, if I am embittered when an ill-tempered neighbour merely scrapes off a bit of my land? The mathematician teaches me how I may lose none of my boundaries; I, however, seek to learn how to lose them all with a light heart. [12]"But," comes the reply, "I am being driven from the farm which my father and grandfather owned!" Well? Who owned the land before your grandfather? Can you explain what people (I will not say what person) held it originally? You did not enter upon it as a master, but merely as a tenant. And whose tenant are you? If your claim is successful, you are tenant of the heir. The lawyers say that public property cannot be acquired privately by possession;[a] what you hold and call your own is public property – indeed, it belongs to mankind at large. [13]O what marvellous skill! You know how to measure the circle; you find the square of any shape which is set before you; you compute the distances between the stars; there is nothing which does not come within the scope of your calculations. But if you are a real master of your profession, measure me the mind of man! Tell me how great it is, or how puny! You know what a straight line is; but how does it benefit you if you do not know what is straight in this life of ours?

[14]I come next to the person who boasts his knowledge of the heavenly bodies, who knows

> Whither the chilling star of Saturn hides,
> And through what orbit Mercury doth stray.[b]

Of what benefit will it be to know this? That I shall be disturbed because Saturn and Mars are in opposition, or when

[a] i.e., for a certain term of years; see R. W. Leage, *Roman Private Law*, pp. 133 ff. Compare also Lucretius iii. 971, and Horace, *Ep.* ii. [2]159.

[b] Vergil, *Georg.* i. 336 f.

Mercury sets at eventide in plain view of Saturn, rather than learn that those stars, wherever they are, are propitious,[a] and that they are not subject to change? [15]They are driven along by an unending round of destiny, on a course from which they cannot swerve. They return at stated seasons; they either set in motion, or mark the intervals of the whole world's work. But if they are responsible for whatever happens, how will it help you to know the secrets of the immutable? Or if they merely give indications, what good is there in foreseeing what you cannot escape? Whether you know these things or not, they will take place.

> [16]Behold the fleeting sun,
> The stars that follow in his train, and thou
> Shalt never find the morrow play thee false,
> Or be misled by nights without a cloud.[b]

It has, however, been sufficiently and fully ordained that I shall be safe from anything that may mislead me. [17]"What," you say, "does the 'morrow never play me false'? Whatever happens without my knowledge plays me false." I, for my part, do not know what is to be, but I do know what may come to be. I shall have no misgivings in this matter; I await the future in its entirety; and if there is any abatement in its severity, I make the most of it. If the morrow treats me kindly, it is a sort of deception; but it does not deceive me even at that. For just as I know that all things can happen, so I know,

[a] Saturn and Mars were regarded as unlucky stars. Astrology, which dates back beyond 3000 B.C. in Babylonia, was developed by the Greeks of the Alexandrian age and got a foothold in Rome by the second century B.C., flourished greatly under Tiberius. Cf. Horace, *Od.* i. 1[1] 1 f.; Juv. iii. 42 f., and F. Cumont, *Astrology and Religion among the Greeks and Romans* (trans.), esp. pp. 68 ff. and 84 ff.

[b] Vergil, *Georg.* i. 424 ff.

too, that they will not happen in every case. I am ready for favourable events in every case, but I am prepared for evil.

[18]In this discussion you must bear with me if I do not follow the regular course. For I do not consent to admit painting into the list of liberal arts, any more than sculpture, marble-working, and other helps toward luxury. I also debar from the liberal studies wrestling and all knowledge that is compounded of oil and mud;[a] otherwise, I should be compelled to admit perfumers also, and cooks, and all others who lend their wits to the service of our pleasures. [19]For what "liberal" element is there in these ravenous takers of emetics, whose bodies are fed to fatness while their minds are thin and dull?[b] Or do we really believe that the training which they give is "liberal" for the young men of Rome, who used to be taught by our ancestors to stand straight and hurl a spear, to wield a pike, to guide a horse, and to handle weapons? Our ancestors used to teach their children nothing that could be learned while lying down. But neither the new system nor the old teaches or nourishes virtue. For what good does it do us to guide a horse and control his speed with the curb, and then find that our own passions, utterly uncurbed, bolt with us? Or to beat many opponents in wrestling or boxing, and then to find that we ourselves are beaten by anger?

[20]"What then," you say, "do the liberal studies contribute nothing to our welfare?" Very much in other respects, but nothing at all as regards virtue. For even these arts of which I have spoken, though admittedly of a low grade – depending as they do upon handiwork – contribute greatly toward the equipment of life, but nevertheless have nothing to do with virtue. And if you inquire, "Why, then, do we educate our

---

[a] An allusion to the sand and oil of the wrestling-ring.

[b] Cf. Ep. xv. [3]*copia ciborum subtilitas inpeditur.*

children in the liberal studies?"[a] it is not because they can
bestow virtue, but because they prepare the soul for the recep-
tion of virtue. Just as that "primary course,"[b] as the ancients
called it, in grammar, which gave boys their elementary
training, does not teach them the liberal arts, but prepares
the ground for their early acquisition of these arts, so the
liberal arts do not conduct the soul all the way to virtue, but
merely set it going in that direction.

[21]Posidonius[c] divides the arts into four classes: first we
have those which are common and low, then those which
serve for amusement, then those which refer to the education
of boys, and, finally, the liberal arts. The common sort belong
to workmen and are mere hand-work; they are concerned
with equipping life; there is in them no pretence to beauty
or honour. [22]The arts of amusement are those which aim to
please the eye and the ear. To this class you may assign the
stage-machinists, who invent scaffolding that goes aloft of its
own accord, or floors that rise silently into the air, and many
other surprising devices, as when objects that fit together then
fall apart, or objects which are separate then join together
automatically, or objects which stand erect then gradually
collapse. The eye of the inexperienced is struck with amazement by these things; for such persons marvel at everything
that takes place without warning, because they do not know
the causes. [23]The arts which belong to the education of boys,
and are somewhat similar to the liberal arts, are those which
the Greeks call the "cycle of studies,"[d] but which we Romans

---

[a] In a strict sense; not, as in § 2, as Seneca thinks that the term should
really be defined – the "liberal" study, i.e. the pursuit of wisdom.

[b] For the πρώτη ἀγωγή see Quintilian, ii. [1]4.

[c] From what work of Posidonius Seneca is here quoting we do not know;
it may be from the Προτρεπτικά, or *Exhortations*, indicating the training
preliminary to philosophy.

[d] See § 1 note.

call the "liberal." However, those alone are really liberal – or rather, to give them a truer name, "free" – whose concern is virtue.

[24]"But," one will say, "just as there is a part of philosophy which has to do with nature, and a part which has to do with ethics, and a part which has to do with reasoning, so this group of liberal arts also claims for itself a place in philosophy. When one approaches questions that deal with nature, a decision is reached by means of a word from the mathematician. Therefore mathematics is a department of that branch which it aids."[a] [25]But many things aid us and yet are not parts of ourselves. Nay, if they were, they would not aid us. Food is an aid to the body, but is not a part of it. We get some help from the service which mathematics renders; and mathematics is as indispensable to philosophy as the carpenter is to the mathematician. But carpentering is not a part of mathematics, nor is mathematics a part of philosophy. [26]Moreover, each has its own limits; for the wise man investigates and learns the causes of natural phenomena, while the mathematician follows up and computes their numbers and their measurements.[b] The wise man knows the laws by which the heavenly bodies persist, what powers belong to them, and what attributes; the astronomer merely notes their comings and goings, the rules which govern their settings and their risings, and the occasional periods during which they seem to stand still, although as a matter of fact no heavenly body can stand still. [27]The wise man will know what causes the reflection in a mirror; but, the mathematician can merely tell you how far the body should be from the reflection, and what

[a] i.e., mathematics is a department of *philosophia naturalis*.

[b] This line of argument inversely resembles the criticism by Seneca of Posidonius in Ep. xc. – that the inventions of early science cannot be properly termed a part of philosophy.

shape of mirror will produce a given reflection.[a] The philosopher will demonstrate that the sun is a large body, while the astronomer will compute just how large, progressing in knowledge by his method of trial and experiment; but in order to progress, he must summon to his aid certain principles. No art, however, is sufficient unto itself, if the foundation upon which it rests depends upon mere favour. [28]Now philosophy asks no favours from any other source; it builds everything on its own soil; but the science of numbers is, so to speak, a structure built on another man's land – it builds on everything on alien soil;[b] It accepts first principles, and by their favour arrives at further conclusions. If it could march unassisted to the truth, if it were able to understand the nature of the universe, I should say that it would offer much assistance to our minds; for the mind grows by contact with things heavenly and draws into itself something from on high. There is but one thing that brings the soul to perfection – the unalterable knowledge of good and evil. But there is no other art[c] which investigates good and evil.

I should like to pass in review the several virtues. [29]Bravery is a scorner of things which inspire fear; it looks down upon, challenges, and crushes the powers of terror and all that would drive our freedom under the yoke. But do "liberal studies"[d] strengthen this virtue? Loyalty is the holiest good in the human heart; it is forced into betrayal by no constraint, and it is bribed by no rewards. Loyalty cries: "Burn me, slay me, kill me! I shall not betray my trust; and the more urgently torture shall seek to find my secret, the deeper in my heart will I bury it!" Can the "liberal arts" produce such

[a] See *N. Q.* i. 4 ff.

[b] According to Roman law, *superficies solo cedit*, "the building goes with the ground."

[c] Except philosophy.

[d] i.e., in the more commonly accepted sense of the term.

a spirit within us? Temperance controls our desires; some it hates and routs, others it regulates and restores to a healthy measure, nor does it ever approach our desires for their own sake. Temperance knows that the best measure of the appetites is not what you want to take, but what you ought to take. [30]Kindliness forbids you to be over-bearing towards your associates, and it forbids you to be grasping. In words and in deeds and in feelings it shows itself gentle and courteous to all men. It counts no evil as another's solely. And the reason why it loves its own good is chiefly because it will some day be the good of another. Do "liberal studies" teach a man such character as this? No; no more than they teach simplicity, moderation and self-restraint, thrift and economy, and that kindliness which spares a neighbour's life as if it were one's own and knows that it is not for man to make wasteful use of his fellow-man.

[31]"But," one says, "since you declare that virtue cannot be attained without the 'liberal studies,' how is it that you deny that they offer any assistance to virtue?"[a] Because you cannot attain virtue without food, either; and yet food has nothing to do with virtue. Wood does not offer assistance to a ship, although a ship cannot be built except of wood. There is no reason, I say, why you should think that anything is made by the assistance of that without which it cannot be made. [32]We might even make the statement that it is possible to attain wisdom without the "liberal studies"; for although virtue is a thing that must be learned, yet it is not learned by means of these studies.

What reason have I, however, for supposing that one who is ignorant of letters will never be a wise man, since wisdom is not to be found in letters? Wisdom communicates

[a] This usage is a not infrequent one in Latin; cf. Petronius, *Sat.* [42]*neminem nihil boni facere oportet*; *id. ib.* 58; Verg. *Ecl.* v. 25, etc. See Draeger, *Hist. Syn.* ii. 75, and Roby, ii. 2246 ff.

facts[a] and not words; and it may be true that the memory is more to be depended upon when it has no support outside itself. [33]Wisdom is a large and spacious thing. It needs plenty of free room. One must learn about things divine and human, the past and the future, the ephemeral and the eternal; and one must learn about Time.[b] See how many questions arise concerning time alone: in the first place, whether it is anything in and by itself; in the second place, whether anything exists prior to time and without time; and again, did time begin along with the universe, or, because there was something even before the universe began, did time also exist then? [34]There are countless questions concerning the soul alone: whence it comes, what is its nature, when it begins to exist, and how long it exists; whether it passes from one place to another and changes its habitation, being transferred successively from one animal shape to another, or whether it is a slave but once, roaming the universe after it is set free; whether it is corporeal or not; what will become of it when it ceases to use us as its medium; how it will employ its freedom when it has escaped from this present prison; whether it will forget all its past, and at that moment begin to know itself when, released from the body, it has withdrawn to the skies.

[35]Thus, whatever phase of things human and divine you have apprehended, you will be wearied by the vast number of things to be answered and things to be learned. And in order that these manifold and mighty subjects may have free entertainment in your soul, you must remove there from all superfluous things. Virtue will not surrender herself to these

[a] Cf. Epp. xxxi. 6 and lxxxi. [29]*aestimare res, de quibus . . . cum rerum natura deliberandum est.*

[b] The ancient Stoics defined Time as "extension of the world's motion." The seasons were said to be "alive" because they depended on material conditions. But the Stoics really acknowledged Time to be immaterial. The same problem of corporeality was discussed with regard to the "good."

narrow bounds of ours; a great subject needs wide space in which to move. Let all other things be driven out, and let the breast be emptied to receive virtue.

[36]"But it is a pleasure to be acquainted with many arts." Therefore let us keep only as much of them as is essential. Do you regard that man as blameworthy who puts superfluous things on the same footing with useful things, and in his house makes a lavish display of costly objects, but do not deem him blameworthy who has allowed himself to become engrossed with the useless furniture of learning? This desire to know more than is sufficient is a sort of intemperance. [37]Why? Because this unseemly pursuit of the liberal arts makes men troublesome, wordy, tactless, self-satisfied bores, who fail to learn the essentials just because they have learned the non-essentials. Didymus the scholar wrote four thousand books. I should feel pity for him if he had only read the same number of superfluous volumes. In these books he investigates Homer's birthplace,[a] who was really the mother of Aeneas, whether Anacreon was more of a rake or more of a drunkard, whether Sappho was a bad lot[b] and other problems the answers to which, if found, were forthwith to be forgotten. Come now, do not tell me that life is long! [38]Nay, when you come to consider our own countrymen also, I can show you many works which ought to be cut down with the axe.

It is at the cost of a vast outlay of time and of vast discomfort to the ears of others that we win such praise as this: "What a learned man you are!" Let us be content with

---

[a] Compare the schoolmaster of Juvenal (vii. 234 ff.), who must know

> *Nutricem Anchisae, nomen patriamque novercae*
> *Anchemoli, dicat quot Acestes vixerit annis*, etc.,

and Friedländer's note.

[b] A tradition, probably begun by the Greek comic-writers, and explained by Professor Smyth (*Greek Melic Poets*, pp. 227 f.) as due to the more independent position of women among the Aeolians.

this recommendation, less citified though it be: "What a good man you are!" [39]Do I mean this? Well, would you have me unroll the annals of the world's history and try to find out who first wrote poetry? Or, in the absence of written records, shall I make an estimate of the number of years which lie between Orpheus and Homer? Or shall I make a study of the absurd writings of Aristarchus, wherein he branded the text[a] of other men's verses, and wear my life away upon syllables? Shall I then wallow in the geometrician's dust?[b] Have I so far forgotten that useful saw "Save your time"? Must I know these things? And what may I choose not to know?

[40]Apion, the scholar, who drew crowds to his lectures all over Greece in the days of Gaius Caesar and was acclaimed a Homerid[c] by every state, used to maintain that Homer, when he had finished his two poems, the Iliad and the Odyssey, added a preliminary poem to his work, wherein he embraced the whole Trojan war.[d] The argument which Apion adduced to prove this statement was that Homer had purposely inserted in the opening line two letters which contained a key to the number of his books. [41]A man who wishes to know many things must know such things as these, and must take no thought of all the time which one loses by ill-health, public duties, private duties, daily duties, and sleep. Apply the measure to the years of your life; they have no room for all these things.

[a] Marking supposedly spurious lines by the *obelus*, and using other signs to indicate variations, repetitions, and interpolations. He paid special attention to Homer, Pindar, Hesiod, and the tragedians.

[b] The geometricians drew their figures in the dust or sand.

[c] Originally, rhapsodists who recited from Homer; in general, "interpreters and admirers – in short, the whole 'spiritual kindred' – of Homer" (D. B. Monro)

[d] An ancient explanation of the (now disproved) authorship by Homer of such poems as the *Cypria, Little Iliad, Sack of Troy*, etc.

[42]I have been speaking so far of liberal studies; but think how much superfluous and unpractical matter the philosophers contain! Of their own accord they also have descended to establishing nice divisions of syllables, to determining the true meaning of conjunctions and prepositions; they have been envious of the scholars, envious of the mathematicians. They have taken over into their own art all the superfluities of these other arts; the result is that they know more about careful speaking than about careful living. [43]Let me tell you what evils are due to over-nice exactness, and what an enemy it is of truth! Protagoras declares that one can take either side on any question and debate it with equal success – even on this very question, whether every subject can be debated from either point of view. Nausiphanes holds that in things which seem to exist, there is no difference between existence and non-existence. [44]Parmenides maintains that nothing exists of all this which seems to exist, except the universe alone.[a] Zeno of Elea removed all the difficulties by removing one; for he declares that nothing exists. The Pyrrhonean, Megarian, Eretrian, and Academic schools are all engaged in practically the same task; they have introduced a new knowledge, non-knowledge. [45]You may sweep all these theories in with the superfluous troops of "liberal" studies; the one class of men give me a knowledge that will be of no use to me, the other class do away with any hope of attaining knowledge. It is better, of course, to know useless things than to know nothing. One set of philosophers offers no light by which I may direct my gaze toward the truth; the other digs out my very eyes and leaves me blind. If I cleave to Protagoras, there is nothing in the scheme of nature that is not doubtful; if I hold with Nausiphanes, I am sure only of this – that everything is unsure; if with Parmenides, there

[a] In other words, the unchangeable, perfect Being of the universe is contrasted with the mutable Non-Being of opinion and unreality.

is nothing except the One;[a] if with Zeno, there is not even the One.

[46]What are we, then? What becomes of all these things that surround us, support us, sustain us? The whole universe is then a vain or deceptive shadow. I cannot readily say whether I am more vexed at those who would have it that we know nothing, or with those who would not leave us even this privilege. Farewell.

[a] i.e., the universe.

XC. ON THE PART
PLAYED BY PHILOSOPHY
IN THE PROGRESS
OF MAN

[1]Who can doubt, my dear Lucilius, that life is the gift of the immortal gods, but that living well[a] is the gift of philosophy? Hence the idea that our debt to philosophy is greater than our debt to the gods, in proportion as a good life is more of a benefit than mere life, would be regarded as correct, were not philosophy itself a boon which the gods have bestowed upon us. They have given the knowledge thereof to none, but the faculty of acquiring it they have given to all. [2]For if they had made philosophy also a general good, and if we were gifted with understanding at our birth, wisdom would have lost her best attribute – that she is not one of the gifts of fortune. For as it is, the precious and noble characteristic of wisdom is that she does not advance to meet us, that each man is indebted to himself for her, and that we do not seek her at the hands of others.

What would there be in philosophy worthy of your respect, if she were a thing that came by bounty? [3]Her sole function is to discover the truth about things divine and things human. From her side religion never departs, nor duty, nor justice, nor any of the whole company of virtues which cling

---

[a] Cf. Plato, *Crito* 48, "not life itself, but a good life, is chiefly to be desired."

together in close-united fellowship. Philosophy has taught us to worship that which is divine, to love that which is human;[a] she has told us that with the gods lies dominion, and among men, fellowship. This fellowship remained unspoiled for a long time, until avarice tore the community asunder and became the cause of poverty, even in the case of those whom she herself had most enriched. For men cease to possess all things the moment they desire all things for their own.

[4]But the first men and those who sprang from them, still unspoiled, followed nature, having one man as both their leader and their law, entrusting themselves to the control of one better than themselves. For nature has the habit of subjecting the weaker to the stronger. Even among the dumb animals those which are either biggest or fiercest hold sway. It is no weakling bull that leads the herd; it is one that has beaten the other males by his might and his muscle. In the case of elephants, the tallest goes first; among men, the best is regarded as the highest. That is why it was to the mind that a ruler was assigned; and for that reason the greatest happiness rested with those peoples among whom a man could not be the more powerful unless he were the better. For that man can safely accomplish what he will who thinks he can do nothing except what he ought to do.

[5]Accordingly, in that age which is maintained to be the golden age,[b] Posidonius[c] holds that the government was under

---

[a] Compare the "knowledge of things divine and things human" of lxxxix. 5.

[b] The "Golden Age" motif was a frequent one in Latin literature. Compare, e.g., Tibullus, i. [3]35 ff., the passage beginning:

> Quam bene Saturno vivebant rege, priusquam
> Tellus in longas est patefacta vias!

Cf. § 46, summing up the message of Seneca's letter.

[c] While modern philosophy would probably side with Seneca rather than Posidonius, it is interesting to know the opinion of Macaulay, who holds (*Essay on Bacon*) that there is much in common between Posidonius and

the jurisdiction of the wise. They kept their hands under control, and protected the weaker from the stronger. They gave advice, both to do and not to do; they showed what was useful and what was useless. Their forethought provided that their subjects should lack nothing; their bravery warded off dangers; their kindness enriched and adorned their subjects. For them ruling was a service, not an exercise of royalty. No ruler tried his power against those to whom he owed the beginnings of his power; and no one had the inclination, or the excuse, to do wrong, since the ruler ruled well and the subject obeyed well, and the king could utter no greater threat against disobedient subjects than that they should depart from the kingdom.

[6]But when once vice stole in and kingdoms were transformed into tyrannies, a need arose for laws and these very laws were in turn framed by the wise. Solon, who established Athens upon a firm basis by just laws, was one of the seven men renowned for their wisdom.[a] Had Lycurgus lived in the same period, an eighth would have been added to that hallowed number seven. The laws of Zaleucus and Charondas are praised; it was not in the forum or in the offices of skilled counsellors, but in the silent and holy retreat of Pythagoras, that these two men learned the principles of justice which they were to establish in Sicily (which at that time was prosperous) and throughout Grecian Italy.

[7]Up to this point I agree with Posidonius; but that philosophy discovered the arts of which life makes use in its daily round[b] I refuse to admit. Nor will I ascribe to it an

---

the English inductive philosopher, and thinks but little of Seneca's ideas on the subject. Cf. W. C. Summers, *Select letters of Seneca*, p. 312.

[a] Cleobulus of Rhodes, Periander of Corinth, Pittacus of Mitylene, Bias of Priene, Thales of Miletus, Chilon of Sparta, and Solon of Athens. For some of these substitutions are made in certain lists.

[b] Cf. Ep. lxxxviii. [20]*ad alia multum, ad virtutem nihil.*

artisan's glory. Posidonius says: "When men were scattered over the earth, protected by eaves or by the dug-out shelter of a cliff or by the trunk of a hollow tree, it was philosophy that taught them to build houses." But I, for my part, do not hold that philosophy devised these shrewdly-contrived dwellings of ours which rise story upon story, where city crowds against city, any more than that she invented the fish-preserves, which are enclosed for the purpose of saving men's gluttony from having to run the risk of storms, and in order that, no matter how wildly the sea is raging, luxury may have its safe harbours in which to fatten fancy breeds of fish. [8]What! Was it philosophy that taught the use of keys and bolts? Nay, what was that except giving a hint to avarice? Was it philosophy that erected all these towering tenements, so dangerous to the persons who dwell in them? Was it not enough for man to provide himself a roof of any chance covering, and to contrive for himself some natural retreat without the help of art and without trouble? Believe me, that was a happy age, before the days of architects, before the days of builders! [9]All this sort of thing was born when luxury was being born, – this matter of cutting timbers square and cleaving a beam with unerring hand as the saw made its way over the marked-out line.

The primal man with wedges split his wood.[a]

For they were not preparing a roof for a future banquet-ball; for no such use did they carry the pine trees or the firs along the trembling streets[b] with a long row of drays – merely

[a] Vergil, *Georg.* i. 144.
[b] Cf. Juvenal, iii. 254 ff.:
> *Longa coruscat*
> *Serraco veniente abies, atque altera pinum*
> *Plaustra vehunt, nutant alte populoque minantur.*

to fasten thereon panelled ceilings heavy with gold. [10]Forked poles erected at either end propped up their houses. With close-packed branches and with leaves heaped up and laid sloping they contrived a drainage for even the heaviest rains. Beneath such dwellings, they lived, but they lived in peace. A thatched roof once covered free men; under marble and gold dwells slavery.

[11]On another point also I differ from Posidonius, when he holds that mechanical tools were the invention of wise men. For on that basis one might maintain that those were wise who taught the arts

> Of setting traps for game, and liming twigs
> For birds, and girdling mighty woods with dogs.[a]

It was man's ingenuity, not his wisdom, that discovered all these devices. [12]And I also differ from him when he says that wise men discovered our mines of iron and copper, "when the earth, scorched by forest fires, melted the veins of ore which lay near the surface and caused the metal to gush forth."[b] Nay, the sort of men who discover such things are the sort of men who are busied with them. [13]Nor do I consider this question so subtle as Posidonius thinks, namely, whether the hammer or the tongs came first into use. They were both invented by some man whose mind was nimble and keen, but not great or exalted; and the same holds true of any other discovery which can only be made by means of a bent body and of a mind whose gaze is upon the ground.

The wise man was easy-going in his way of living. And why not? Even in our own times he would prefer to be as

---

Compare also the "towering tenements" of § 8.

[a] Vergil, *Georg.* i. 139 f.

[b] Cf. T. Rice Holmes, *Ancient Britain*, pp. 121 f., who concludes that the discovery of ore-smelting was accidental.

little cumbered as possible. [14]How, I ask, can you consistently admire both Diogenes and Daedalus? Which of these two seems to you a wise man – the one who devised the saw, or the one who, on seeing a boy drink water from the hollow of his hand, forthwith took his cup from his wallet and broke it, upbraiding himself with these words:[a] "Fool that I am, to have been carrying superfluous baggage all this time!" and then curled himself up in his tub and lay down to sleep? [15]In these our own times, which man, pray, do you deem the wiser – the one who invents a process for spraying saffron perfumes to a tremendous height from hidden pipes, who fills or empties canals by a sudden rush of waters, who so cleverly constructs a dining-room with a ceiling of movable panels that it presents one pattern after another, the roof changing as often as the courses,[b] – or the one who proves to others, as well as to himself, that nature has laid upon us no stern and difficult law when she tells us that we can live without the marble-cutter and the engineer, that we can clothe ourselves without traffic in silk fabrics, that we can have everything that is indispensable to our use, provided only that we are content with what the earth has placed on its surface? If mankind were willing to listen to this sage, they would know that the cook is as superfluous to them as the soldier. [16]Those were wise men, or at any rate like the wise, who found the care of the body a problem easy to solve. The things that are indispensable require no elaborate pains for their acquisition; it is only the luxuries that call for labour. Follow nature, and you will need no skilled craftsmen.

---

[a] Cf. Diog. Laert. vi. 37 θεασάμενός ποτε παιδίον ταῖς χερσὶ ἐξέρριψε τῆς πήρας τὴν κοτύλην, εἰπών, Παιδίον με νενίκηκεν εὐτελείᾳ.

[b] Compare the halls of Nero which Seneca may easily have had in mind: (Suet. *Nero* 31) *cenationes laqueatae tabulis eburneis versatilibus . . . prae-cipua cenationum rotunda, quae perpetuo diebus ac noctibus vice mundi circumageretur.*

Nature did not wish us to be harassed. For whatever she forced upon us, she equipped us. "But cold cannot be endured by the naked body." What then? Are there not the skins of wild beasts and other animals, which can protect us well enough, and more than enough, from the cold? Do not many tribes cover their bodies with the bark of trees? Are not the feathers of birds sewn together to serve for clothing? Even at the present day does not a large portion of the Scythian tribe garb itself in the skins of foxes and mice, soft to the touch and impervious to the winds? [17]"For all that, men must have some thicker protection than the skin, in order to keep off the heat of the sun in summer." What then? Has not antiquity produced many retreats which, hollowed out either by the damage wrought by time or by any other occurrence you will, have opened into caverns? What then? Did not the very first-comers take twigs[a] and weave them by hand into wicker mats, smear them with common mud, and then with stubble and other wild grasses construct a roof, and thus pass their winters secure, the rains carried off by means of the sloping gables? What then? Do not the peoples on the edge of the Syrtes dwell in dug-out houses and indeed all the tribes who, because of the too fierce blaze of the sun, possess no protection sufficient to keep off the heat except the parched soil itself?

[18]Nature was not so hostile to man that, when she gave all the other animals an easy rôle in life, she made it impossible for him alone to live without all these artifices. None of these was imposed upon us by her; none of them had to be painfully sought out that our lives might be prolonged. All things were ready for us at our birth; it is we that have made

[a] Cf. Ovid, *Met.* i. 121 f.:

> *Domus antra fuerunt*
> *Et densi frutices et vinctae cortice virgae.*

Among many accounts by Roman writers of early man, compare this passage of Ovid, and that in the fifth book of Lucretius.

everything difficult for ourselves, through our disdain for
what is easy. Houses, shelter, creature comforts, food, and all
that has now become the source of vast trouble, were ready
at hand, free to all, and obtainable for trifling pains. For the
limit everywhere corresponded to the need; it is we that have
made all those things valuable, we that have made them
admired, we that have caused them to be sought for by extensive and manifold devices. [19]Nature suffices for what she
demands. Luxury has turned her back upon nature; each day
she expands herself, in all the ages she has been gathering
strength, and by her wit promoting the vices. At first, luxury
began to lust for what nature regarded as superfluous, then
for that which was contrary to nature; and finally she made
the soul a bondsman to the body, and bade it be an utter slave
to the body's lusts. All these crafts by which the city is
patrolled – or shall I say kept in uproar – are but engaged in
the body's business; time was when all things were offered
to the body as to a slave, but now they are made ready for it
as for a master. Accordingly, hence have come the work-
shops of the weavers and the carpenters; hence the savoury
smells of the professional cooks; hence the wantonness of
those who teach wanton postures, and wanton and affected
singing. For that moderation which nature prescribes, which
limits our desires by resources restricted to our needs, has
abandoned the field; it has now come to this – that to want
only what is enough is a sign both of boorishness and of
utter destitution.

[20]It is hard to believe, my dear Lucilius, how easily the
charm of eloquence wins even great men away from the truth.
Take, for example, Posidonius – who, in my estimation, is of
the number of those who have contributed most to philosophy
– when he wishes to describe the art of weaving. He tells
how, first, some threads are twisted and some drawn out
from the soft, loose mass of wool; next, how the upright warp
keeps the threads stretched by means of hanging weights;

then, how the inserted thread of the woof, which softens the hard texture of the web which holds it fast on either side, is forced by the batten to make a compact union with the warp. He maintains that even the weaver's art was discovered by wise men, forgetting that the more complicated art which he describes was invented in later days – the art wherein

> The web is bound to frame; asunder now
> The reed doth part the warp. Between the threads
> Is shot the woof by pointed shuttles borne;
> The broad comb's well-notched teeth then drive it home.[a]

Suppose he had had the opportunity of seeing the weaving of our own day, which produces the clothing that will conceal nothing, the clothing which affords – I will not say no protection to the body, but none even to modesty!

[21]Posidonius then passes on to the farmer. With no less eloquence he describes the ground which is broken up and crossed again by the plough, so that the earth, thus loosened, may allow freer play to the roots; then the seed is sown, and the weeds plucked out by hand, lest any chance growth or wild plant spring up and spoil the crop. This trade also, he declares, is the creation of the wise, – just as if cultivators of the soil were not even at the present day discovering countless new methods of increasing the soil's fertility! [22]Furthermore, not confining his attention to these arts, he even degrades the wise man by sending him to the mill. For he tells us how the sage, by imitating the processes of nature, began to make bread. "The grain,"[b] he says, "once taken into the mouth, is crushed by the flinty teeth, which meet in hostile encounter,

[a] Ovid, *Met.* vi. 55 ff.

[b] Professor Summers calls attention to the similarity of this passage and Cicero, *De Nat. Deor.* ii. 134 ff. *dentibus manditur . . . a lingua adiuvari videtur . . . in alvo . . . calore . . . in reliquum corpus dividantur.*

and whatever grain slips out the tongue turns back to the selfsame teeth. Then it is blended into a mass, that it may the more easily pass down the slippery throat. When this has readied the stomach, it is digested by the stomach's equable heat; then, and not till then, it is assimilated with the body. [23]Following this pattern," he goes on, "someone placed two rough stones, the one above the other, in imitation of the teeth, one set of which is stationary and awaits the motion of the other set. Then by the rubbing of the one stone against the other, the grain is crushed and brought back again and again, until by frequent rubbing it is reduced to powder. Then this man sprinkled the meal with water, and by continued manipulation subdued the mass and moulded the loaf. This loaf was, at first, baked by hot ashes or by an earthen vessel glowing hot; later on ovens were gradually discovered and the other devices whose heat will render obedience to the sage's will." Posidonius came very near declaring that even the cobbler's trade was the discovery of the wise man.

[24]Reason did indeed devise all these things, but it was not right reason. It was man, but not the wise man, that discovered them; just as they invented ships, in which we cross rivers and seas – ships fitted with sails for the purpose of catching the force of the winds, ships with rudders added at the stern in order to turn the vessel's course in one direction or another. The model followed was the fish, which steers itself by its tail, and by its slightest motion on this side or on that bends its swift course. [25]"But," says Posidonius, "the wise man did indeed discover all these things; they were, however, too petty for him to deal with himself and so he entrusted them to his meaner assistants." Not so; these early inventions were thought out by no other class of men than those who have them in charge today. We know that certain devices have come to light only within our own memory – such as the use of windows which admit the clear light through transparent

tiles,[a] and such as the vaulted baths, with pipes let into their walls for the purpose of diffusing the heat which maintains an even temperature in their lowest as well as in their highest spaces. Why need I mention the marble with which our temples and our private houses are resplendent? Or the rounded and polished masses of stone by means of which we erect colonnades and buildings roomy enough for nations? Or our signs[b] for whole words, which enable us to take down a speech, however rapidly uttered, matching speed of tongue by speed of hand? All this sort of thing has been devised by the lowest grade of slaves. [26]Wisdom's seat is higher; she trains not the hands, but is mistress of our minds.

Would you know what wisdom has brought forth to light, what she has accomplished? It is not the graceful poses of the body, or the varied notes produced by horn and flute, whereby the breath is received and, as it passes out or through, is transformed into voice. It is not wisdom that contrives arms, or walls, or instruments useful in war; nay, her voice is for peace, and she summons all mankind to concord. [27]It is not she, I maintain, who is the artisan of our indispensable implements of daily use. Why do you assign to her such petty things? You see in her the skilled artisan of life. The other arts, it is true, wisdom has under her control; for he whom life serves is also served by the things which equip life. But wisdom's course is toward the state of happiness; thither she guides us, thither she opens the way for us. [28]She shows us what things are evil and what things are seemingly evil; she strips our minds of vain illusion. She bestows upon us a

[a] Besides *lapis specularis* (window-glass) the Romans used alabaster, mica, and shells for this purpose.

[b] Suetonius tells us that a certain Ennius, a grammarian of the Augustan age, was the first to develop shorthand on a scientific basis, and that Tiro, Cicero's freedman, had invented the process. He also mentions Seneca as the most scientific and encyclopaedic authority on the subject.

greatness which is substantial, but she represses the greatness which is inflated, and showy but filled with emptiness; and she does not permit us to be ignorant of the difference between what is great and what is but swollen; nay, she delivers to us the knowledge of the whole of nature and of her own nature. She discloses to us what the gods are and of what sort they are; what are the nether gods, the household deities, and the protecting spirits; what are the souls which have been endowed with lasting life and have been admitted to the second class of divinities,[a] where is their abode and what their activities, powers, and will.

Such are wisdom's rites of initiation, by means of which is unlocked, not a village shrine, but the vast temple of all the gods – the universe itself, whose true apparitions and true aspects she offers to the gaze of our minds. For the vision of our eyes is too dull for sights so great. [29]Then she goes back to the beginnings of things, to the eternal Reason[b] which was imparted to the whole, and to the force which inheres in all the seeds of things, giving them the power to fashion each thing according to its kind. Then wisdom begins to inquire about the soul, whence it comes, where it dwells, how long it abides, into how many divisions it falls. Finally, she has turned her attention from the corporeal to the incorporeal, and has closely examined truth and the marks whereby truth is known, inquiring next how that which is equivocal can be distinguished from the truth, whether in life or in language; for in both are elements of the false mingled with the true.

[30]It is my opinion that the wise man has not withdrawn himself, as Posidonius thinks, from those arts which we were discussing, but that he never took them up at all.[c] For he

---

[a] Possibly either the *manes* or the *indigitamenta* of the early Roman religion.

[b] i.e., λόγος.

[c] Seneca, himself one of the keenest scientific observers in history (witness *Nat. Quaest.*, Epp. lvii., lxxix., etc.), is pushing his argument very far in

would have judged that nothing was worth discovering that he would not afterwards judge to be worth using always. He would not take up things which would have to be laid aside.

[31]"But Anacharsis," says Posidonius, "invented the potter's wheel, whose whirling gives shape to vessels."[a] Then because the potter's wheel is mentioned in Homer, people prefer to believe that Homer's verses are false rather than the story of Posidonius! But I maintain that Anacharsis was not the creator of this wheel; and even if he was, although he was a wise man when he invented it, yet he did not invent it qua "wise man" – just as there are a great many things which wise men do as men, not as wise men. Suppose, for example, that a wise man is exceedingly fleet of foot; he will outstrip all the runners in the race by virtue of being fleet, not by virtue of his wisdom. I should like to show Posidonius some glass-blower who by his breath moulds the glass into manifold shapes which could scarcely be fashioned by the most skilful hand. Nay, these discoveries have been made since we men have ceased to discover wisdom.

[32]But Posidonius again remarks. "Democritus is said to have discovered the arch,[b] whose effect was that the curving line of stones, which gradually lean toward each other, is

---

this letter. His message is clear enough; but the modern combination of natural science, psychology, and philosophy shows that Posidonius had some justification for his theories. Cf. also Lucretius, v. 1105-7 ff.

[a] This Scythian prince and friend of Solon, who visited Athens in the sixth century B.C., is also said to have invented the bellows and the anchor. Cf., however, *Iliad* xviii. 600 f. ὡς ὅτε τις τροχὸν ἄρμενον ἐν παλάμῃσιν ἑζόμενος κεραμεὺς πειρήσεται, and Leaf's comment: "The potter's wheel was known in pre-Mycenean times, and was a very ancient invention to the oldest Epic poets." Seneca is right.

[b] Seneca (see next sentence) is right again. The arch was known in Chaldaea and in Egypt before 3000 B.C. Greek bee-hive tombs, Etruscan gateways, and early Roman remains, testify to its immemorial use.

bound together by the keystone." I am inclined to pronounce this statement false. For there must have been, before Democritus, bridges and gateways in which the curvature did not begin until about the top. [33]It seems to have quite slipped your memory that this same Democritus discovered how ivory could be softened, how, by boiling, a pebble could be transformed into an emerald,[a] – the same process used even today for colouring stones which are found to be amenable to this treatment! It may have been a wise man who discovered all such things, but he did not discover them by virtue of being a wise man; for he does many things which we see done just as well, or even more skilfully and dexterously, by men who are utterly lacking in sagacity.

[34]Do you ask what, then, the wise man has found out and what he has brought to light? First of all there is truth, and nature; and nature he has not followed as the other animals do, with eyes too dull to perceive the divine in it. In the second place, there is the law of life, and life he has made to conform to universal principles; and he has taught us, not merely to know the gods, but to follow them, and to welcome the gifts of chance precisely as if they were divine commands. He has forbidden us to give heed to false opinions, and has weighed the value of each thing by a true standard of appraisement. He has condemned those pleasures with which remorse is intermingled, and has praised those goods which will always satisfy; and he has published the truth abroad that he is most happy who has no need of happiness, and that he is most powerful who has power over himself.

---

[a] The ancients judged precious stones merely by their colour; their *smaragdus* included also malachite, jade, and several kinds of quartz. Exposure to heat alters the colour of some stones; and the alchemists believed that the "angelic stone" changed common flints into diamonds, rubies, emeralds, etc. See G. F. Kunz, *The Magic of Jewels and Charms*, p. 1[6] It was also an ancient superstition that emeralds were produced from jasper.

[35]I am not speaking of that philosophy which has placed the citizen outside his country and the gods outside the universe, and which has bestowed virtue upon pleasure,[a] but rather of that philosophy which counts nothing good except what is honourable, – one which cannot be cajoled by the gifts either of man or fortune, one whose value is that it cannot be bought for any value. That this philosophy existed in such a rude age, when the arts and crafts were still unknown and when useful things could only be learned by use, – this I refuse to believe.

[36]Next there came the fortune-favoured period when the bounties of nature lay open to all, for men's indiscriminate use, before avarice and luxury had broken the bonds which held mortals together, and they, abandoning their communal existence, had separated and turned to plunder. The men of the second age were not wise men, even though they did what wise men should do.[b] [37]Indeed, there is no other condition of the human race that anyone would regard more highly; and if God should commission a man to fashion earthly creatures and to bestow institutions upon peoples, this man would approve of no other system than that which obtained among the men of that age, when

> No ploughman tilled the soil, nor was it right
> To portion off or bound one's property.
> Men shared their gains, and earth more freely gave
> Her riches to her sons who sought them not.[c]

[38]What race of men was ever more blest than that race? They enjoyed all nature in partnership. Nature sufficed for

[a] i.e., the Epicureans, who withdraw from civil life and regarded the gods as taking no part in the affairs of men.

[b] i.e., live according to nature.

[c] Verg. *Georg.* i. 125 ff.

them, now the guardian, as before she was the parent, of all; and this her gift consisted of the assured possession by each man of the common resources. Why should I not even call that race the richest among mortals, since you could not find a poor person among them?

But avarice broke in upon a condition so happily ordained, and, by its eagerness to lay something away and to turn it to its own private use, made all things the property of others, and reduced itself from boundless wealth to straitened need. It was avarice that introduced poverty and, by craving much, lost all. [39]And so, although she now tries to make good her loss, although she adds one estate to another, evicting a neighbour either by buying him out or by wronging him, although she extends her country-seats to the size of provinces and defines ownership as meaning extensive travel through one's own property, – in spite of all these efforts of hers no enlargement of our boundaries will bring us back to the condition from which we have departed.

When there is no more that we can do, we shall possess much; but we once possessed the whole world! [40]The very soil was more productive when untilled, and yielded more than enough for peoples who refrained from despoiling one another. Whatever gift nature had produced, men found as much pleasure in revealing it to another as in having discovered it. It was possible for no man either to surpass another or to fall short of him; what there was, was divided among unquarrelling friends. Not yet had the stronger begun to lay hands upon the weaker; not yet had the miser, by hiding away what lay before him, begun to shut off his neighbour from even the necessities of life; each cared as much for his neighbour as for himself. [41]Armour lay unused, and the hand, unstained by human blood, had turned all its hatred against wild beasts. The men of that day, who had found in some dense grove protection against the sun, and security against the severity of winter or of rain in their mean hiding-places, spent their lives under the branches of the trees and passed tranquil nights without a sigh. Care vexes us in our purple, and routs us from our beds with the sharpest of goads; but how soft was the sleep the hard earth bestowed upon the men of that day! [42]No fretted and panelled ceilings hung over them, but as they lay beneath the open sky the stars glided quietly above them, and the firmament, night's noble pageant, marched swiftly by, conducting its mighty task in silence. For them by day, as well as by night, the visions of this most glorious abode were free and open. It was their joy to watch the constellations as they sank from mid-heaven and others, again, as they rose from their hidden abodes. [43]What else but joy could it be to wander among the marvels which dotted the heavens far and wide? But you of the present day shudder at every sound your houses make, and as you sit among your frescoes the slightest creak makes you shrink in terror. They had no houses as big as cities. The air, the breezes blowing free through the open spaces, the flitting shade of crag or tree, springs crystal-clear and streams not spoiled by man's work, whether by water-pipe[a] or by any confinement of the channel, but running at will, and meadows beautiful without the use of art, – amid such scenes were their rude homes, adorned with rustic hand. Such a dwelling was in accordance with nature; therein it was a joy to live, fearing neither the dwelling itself nor for its safety. In these days, however, our houses constitute a large portion of our dread.

[44]But no matter how excellent and guileless was the life of the men of that age, they were not wise men; for that title is reserved for the highest achievement. Still, I would not deny that they were men of lofty spirit and – I may use the phrase – fresh from the gods. For there is no doubt that

[a] Cf. Horace, *Ep.* i. 1⁰ 20 f.:

> *Purior in vicis aqua tendit rumpere plumbum*
> *Quam quae per pronum trepidat cum murmure rivum?*

the world produced a better progeny before it was yet worn out. However, not all were endowed with mental faculties of highest perfection, though in all cases their native powers were more sturdy than ours and more fitted for toil. For nature does not bestow virtue; it is an art to become good. [45]They, at least, searched not in the lowest dregs of the earth for gold, nor yet for silver or transparent stones; and they still were merciful even to the dumb animals – so far removed was that epoch from the custom of slaying man by man, not in anger or through fear, but just to make a show! They had as yet no embroidered garments nor did they weave cloth of gold; gold was not yet even mined.

[46]What, then, is the conclusion of the matter? It was by reason of their ignorance of things that the men of those days were innocent; and it makes a great deal of difference whether one wills not to sin or has not the knowledge to sin.[a] Justice was unknown to them, unknown prudence, unknown also self-control and bravery; but their rude life possessed certain qualities akin to all these virtues. Virtue is not vouchsafed to a soul unless that soul has been trained and taught, and by unremitting practice brought to perfection. For the attainment of this boon, but not in the possession of it, were we born; and even in the best of men, before you refine them by instruction, there is but the stuff of virtue, not virtue itself. Farewell.

[a] Because virtue depends upon reason, and none but voluntary acts should meet with praise or blame.

XCI. ON THE LESSON TO BE DRAWN FROM THE BURNING OF LYONS[a]

[1]Our friend Liberalis[b] is now downcast; for he has just heard of the fire which has wiped out the colony of Lyons. Such a calamity might upset anyone at all, not to speak of a man who dearly loves his country. But this incident has served to make him inquire about the strength of his own character, which he has trained, I suppose, just to meet situations that he thought might cause him fear. I do not wonder, however, that he was free from apprehension touching an evil so unexpected and practically unheard of as this, since it is without precedent. For fire has damaged many a city, but has annihilated none. Even when fire has been hurled against the walls by the hand of a foe, the flame dies out in many places, and although continually renewed, rarely devours so wholly as to leave nothing for the sword. Even an earthquake has scarcely

[a] In spite of the *centesimus annus* of § 14 (q.v.), the most probable date of this letter, based on Tac. *Ann.* xvi. 13 and other general evidence, is July-September 64 A.D. 58 A.D. would be too early for many reasons – among them that "peace all over the world" would not be a true statement until January of 6[2] (See the monograph of Jonas, O. Binder, Peiper, and Schultess.)

[b] Probably Aebutius Liberalis, to whom the treatise De Beneficiis was dedicated.

ever been so violent and destructive as to overthrow whole cities. Finally, no conflagration has ever before blazed forth so savagely in any town that nothing was left for a second. [2]So many beautiful buildings, any single one of which would make a single town famous, were wrecked in one night. In time of such deep peace an event has taken place worse than men can possibly fear even in time of war. Who can believe it? When weapons are everywhere at rest and when peace prevails throughout the world, Lyons, the pride of Gaul,[a] is missing!

Fortune has usually allowed all men, when she has assailed them collectively, to have a foreboding of that which they were destined to suffer. Every great creation has had granted to it a period of reprieve before its fall; but in this case, only a single night elapsed between the city at its greatest and the city non-existent. In short, it takes me longer to tell you it has perished than it took for the city to perish.

[3]All this has affected our friend Liberalis, bending his will, which is usually so steadfast and erect in the face of his own trials. And not without reason has he been shaken; for it is the unexpected that puts the heaviest load upon us. Strangeness adds to the weight of calamities, and every mortal feels the greater pain as a result of that which also brings surprise.

[4]Therefore, nothing ought to be unexpected by us. Our minds should be sent forward in advance to meet all problems, and we should consider, not what is wont to happen, but what can happen. For what is there in existence that Fortune, when she has so willed, does not drag down from the very height

---

[a] That Lyons, situated at the junction of the Arar and the Rhone, was of especial prominence in Gaul, may be also gathered from the fact that it boasted a government mint and the *Ara Augusti* – a shrine established for the annual worship of all the Gallic states. Moreover, the emperor Claudius delivered his famous address in that city (see Tac. *Ann.* xi. 23 f.).

of its prosperity? And what is there that she does not the more violently assail the more brilliantly it shines? What is laborious or difficult for her? [5]She does not always attack in one way or even with her full strength; at one time she summons our own hands against us; at another time, content with her own powers, she makes use of no agent in devising perils for us. No time is exempt; in the midst of our very pleasures there spring up causes of suffering. War arises in the midst of peace, and that which we depended upon for protection is transformed into a cause of fear; friend becomes enemy, ally becomes foeman. The summer calm is stirred into sudden storms, wilder than the storms of winter.[a] With no foe in sight we are victims of such fates as foes inflict, and if other causes of disaster fail, excessive good fortune finds them for itself. The most temperate are assailed by illness, the strongest by wasting disease, the most innocent by chastisement, the most secluded by the noisy mob.

Chance chooses some new weapon by which to bring her strength to bear against us, thinking we have forgotten her. [6]Whatever structure has been reared by a long sequence of years, at the cost of great toil and through the great kindness of the gods, is scattered and dispersed by a single day. Nay, he who has said "a day" has granted too long a postponement to swift-coming misfortune; an hour, an instant of time, suffices for the overthrow of empires! It would be some consolation for the feebleness of our selves and our works, if all things should perish as slowly as they come into being; but as it is, increases are of sluggish growth, but the way to ruin is rapid. [7]Nothing, whether public or private, is stable; the destinies of men, no less than those of cities, are in a whirl. Amid the greatest calm terror arises, and though no external agencies stir up commotion, yet evils burst forth from sources

[a] Cf. Ep. iv. 7, esp. the words *noli huic tranquillitati confidere; momento mare evertitur.*

whence they were least expected. Thrones which have stood the shock of civil and foreign wars crash to the ground though no one sets them tottering. How few the states which have carried their good fortune through to the end!

We should therefore reflect upon all contingencies, and should fortify our minds against the evils which may possibly come. [8]Exile, the torture of disease, wars, shipwreck, – we must think on these.[a] Chance may tear you from your country or your country from you, or may banish you to the desert; this very place, where throngs are stifling, may become a desert. Let us place before our eyes in its entirety the nature of man's lot, and if we would not be overwhelmed, or even dazed, by those unwonted evils, as if they were novel, let us summon to our minds beforehand, not as great an evil as oftentimes happens, but the very greatest evil that possibly can happen. We must reflect upon fortune fully and completely.

[9]How often have cities in Asia, how often in Achaia, been laid low by a single shock of earthquake! How many towns in Syria, how many in Macedonia, have been swallowed up! How often has this kind of devastation laid Cyprus[b] in ruins! How often has Paphos collapsed! Not infrequently are tidings brought to us of the utter destruction of entire cities; yet how small a part of the world are we, to whom such tidings often come!

Let us rise, therefore, to confront the operations of Fortune, and whatever happens, let us have the assurance

---

[a] The passage bears a striking resemblance to the words of Theseus in an unknown play of Euripides (Nauck. Frag. 964) quoted by Cicero, *Tusc.* iii. 1[4] 29, and by Plutarch, *Consolation to Apollonius*, 112d.

[b] Seneca (*N. Q.* vi. 26) speaks of Paphos (on the island of Cyprus) as having been more than once devastated. We know of two such accidents – one under Augustus and another under Vespasian. See the same passage for other earthquake shocks in various places.

that it is not so great as rumour advertises it to be. [10]A rich city has been laid in ashes, the jewel of the provinces, counted as one of them and yet not included with them;[a] rich though it was, nevertheless it was set upon a single hill,[b] and that not very large in extent. But of all those cities, of whose magnificence and grandeur you hear today, the very traces will be blotted out by time. Do you not see how, in Achaia, the foundations of the most famous cities have already crumbled to nothing, so that no trace is left to show that they ever even existed?[c] [11]Not only does that which has been made with hands totter to the ground, not only is that which has been set in place by man's art and man's efforts overthrown by the passing days; nay, the peaks of mountains dissolve, whole tracts have settled, and places which once stood far from the sight of the sea are now covered by the waves. The mighty power of fires has eaten away the hills through whose sides they used to glow, and has levelled to the ground peaks which were once most lofty – the sailor's solace and his beacon. The works of nature herself are harassed; hence we ought to bear with untroubled minds the destruction of cities. [12]They stand but to fall! This doom awaits them, one and all; it may be that some internal force, and blasts of violence which are tremendous because their way is blocked, will throw off the weight which holds then down; or that a whirlpool of raging currents, mightier because they are hidden in the bosom of the earth, will break through that which resists its power; or that the vehemence of flames will burst asunder the framework of the earth's crust; or that time, from which nothing is safe, will reduce them little by little; or that a pestilential

[a] Lyons held an exceptional position in relation to the three Gallic provinces; it was a free town, belonging to none and yet their capital, much like the city of Washington in relation to the United States.

[b] A fact mentioned merely to suggest Rome with her seven hills.

[c] For example, Mycenae and Tiryns.

climate will drive their inhabitants away and the mould will corrode their deserted walls. It would be tedious to recount all the ways by which fate may come; but this one thing I know: all the works of mortal man have been doomed to mortality, and in the midst of things which have been destined to die, we live!

[13]Hence it is thoughts like these, and of this kind, which I am offering as consolation to our friend Liberalis, who burns with a love for his country that is beyond belief. Perhaps its destruction has been brought about only that it may be raised up again to a better destiny. Oftentimes a reverse has but made room for more prosperous fortune. Many structures have fallen only to rise to a greater height. Timagenes,[a] who had a grudge against Rome and her prosperity, used to say that the only reason he was grieved when conflagrations occurred in Rome was his knowledge that better buildings would arise than those which had gone down in the flames. [14]And probably in this city of Lyons, too, all its citizens will earnestly strive that everything shall be rebuilt better in size and security than what they have lost. May it be built to endure and, under happier auspices, for a longer existence! This is indeed but the hundredth year since this colony was founded – not the limit even of a man's lifetime.[b] Led forth by Plancus, the natural advantages of its site have caused it to wax strong and reach the

[a] Probably the writer, and intimate friend of Augustus, who began life in Rome as a captive from Egypt. Falling into disfavour with the Emperor, he took refuge with the malcontent Asinius Pollio at Tusculum, and subsequently died in the East. Cf. Seneca, *De Ira*, iii. 23.

[b] It was in 43 B.C. that Plancus led out the colonists who were chiefly Roman citizens driven from Vienna. Seneca would have been more accurate had he said "one hundred and eighth (or seventh)." Buecheler and Schultess would (unnecessarily) emend to read *centesimus septimus*. But Seneca was using round numbers.

numbers which it contains today; and yet how many calamities of the greatest severity has it endured within the space of an old man's life!

[15]Therefore let the mind be disciplined to understand and to endure its own lot, and let it have the knowledge that there is nothing which fortune does not dare – that she has the same jurisdiction over empires as over emperors, the same power over cities as over the citizens who dwell therein. We must not cry out at any of these calamities. Into such a world have we entered, and under such laws do we live. If you like it, obey; if not, depart whithersoever you wish. Cry out in anger if any unfair measures are taken with reference to you individually; but if this inevitable law is binding upon the highest and the lowest alike, be reconciled to fate, by which all things are dissolved. [16]You should not estimate our worth by our funeral mounds or by these monuments of unequal size which line the road; their ashes level all men! We are unequal at birth, but are equal in death. What I say about cities I say also about their inhabitants. Ardea was captured as well as Rome.[a] The great founder of human law has not made distinctions between us on the basis of high lineage or of illustrious names, except while we live. When, however, we come to the end which awaits mortals, he says: "Depart, ambition! To all creatures that burden the earth let one and the same[b] law apply!" For enduring all things, we are equal;

---

[a] Ardea, the earliest capital of Latium, and Rome, the present capital of the empire. Seneca probably refers to Ardea's capture and destruction by the Samnites in the fourth century; Rome was captured by the Celts in 390 B.C. The former greatness of Ardea was celebrated by Vergil, *Aeneid*, vii. 411 ff.:

> *et nunc magnum manet Ardea nomen,*
> *Sed fortuna fuit.*

[b] *Siremps* (or *sirempse* – Plaut. *Amph.* 73), an ancient legal term, is derived by Festus from *similis re ipsa*; but Corssen explains it as from *sic rem pse*.

no one is more frail than another, no one more certain of his own life on the morrow.

[17]Alexander, king of Macedon, began to study geometry;[a] unhappy man, because he would thereby learn how puny was that earth of which he had seized but a fraction! Unhappy man, I repeat, because he was bound to understand that he was bearing a false title. For who can be "great" in that which is puny? The lessons which were being taught him were intricate and could be learned only by assiduous application; they were not the kind to be comprehended by a madman, who let his thoughts range beyond the ocean.[b] "Teach me something easy!" he cries; but his teacher answers: "These things are the same for all, as hard for one as for another." [18]Imagine that nature is saying to us: "Those things of which you complain are the same for all. I cannot give anything easier to any man, but whoever wishes will make things easier for himself." In what way? By equanimity. You must suffer pain, and thirst, and hunger, and old age too, if a longer stay among men shall be granted you; you must be sick, and you must suffer loss and death. [19]Nevertheless, you should not believe those whose noisy clamour surrounds you; none of these things is an evil, none is beyond your power to bear, or is burdensome. It is only by common opinion that there is anything formidable in them. Your fearing death is therefore like your fear of gossip. But what is more foolish than a man afraid of words? Our friend Demetrius[c] is wont to put it cleverly when he says: "For me the talk of ignorant men is like the rumblings which issue from the belly. For," he adds, "what difference does it make to me whether such rumblings

---

[a] i.e., surveying. See Ep. lxxxviii. 10.

[b] i.e., Ὠκεανός, the stream which encircles the earth.

[c] This plain-living, plain-speaking philosopher appears also in Epp. xx. 9 and lxii. [3]Seneca refers to him as *seminudum, quanto minus quam stramentis incubantem.*

come from above or from below?" [20]What madness it is to be afraid of disrepute in the judgment of the disreputable! Just as you have had no cause for shrinking in terror from the talk of men, so you have no cause now to shrink from these things, which you would never fear had not their talk forced fear upon you. Does it do any harm to a good man to be besmirched by unjust gossip? [21]Then let not this sort of thing damage death, either, in our estimation; death also is in bad odour. But no one of those who malign death has made trial of it.

Meanwhile it is foolhardy to condemn that of which you are ignorant. This one thing, however, you do know – that death is helpful to many, that it sets many free from tortures, want, ailments, sufferings, and weariness. We are in the power of nothing when once we have death in our own power! Farewell.

CIV. ON CARE OF HEALTH AND PEACE OF MIND

[1]I have run off to my villa at Nomentum, for what purpose, do you suppose? To escape the city? No; to shake off a fever which was surely working its way into my system. It had already got a grip upon me. My physician kept insisting that when the circulation was upset and irregular, disturbing the natural poise, the disease was under way. I therefore ordered my carriage to be made ready at once, and insisted on departing in spite of my wife Paulina's[a] efforts to stop me; for I remembered master Gallio's[b] words, when he began to develop a fever in Achaia and took ship at once, insisting that the disease was not of the body but of the place. [2]That is what I remarked to my dear Paulina, who always urges me to take care of my health. I know that her very life-breath comes and goes with my own, and I am beginning, in my solicitude for

---

[a] Pompeia Paulina, the second wife of Seneca; cf. Tac. *Ann.* xv. 6⁰ Though much younger than her husband, she was a model of devotion, and remained loyal to him through all the Neronian persecution.

[b] Elder brother of Seneca, whose name before his adoption by Lucius Iunius Gallio was Annaeus Novatus. He was governor of Achaia from A.D. July 1, 51 to July 1, 5² See *Acts* xviii. 11 ff., and Duff, *Three Dialogues of Seneca*, p. xliii.

her, to be solicitous for myself. And although old age has made me braver to bear many things, I am gradually losing this boon that old age bestows. For it comes into my mind that in this old man there is a youth also, and youth needs tenderness. Therefore, since I cannot prevail upon her to love me any more heroically, she prevails upon me to cherish myself more carefully. ³For one must indulge genuine emotions; sometimes, even in spite of weighty reasons, the breath of life must be called back and kept at our very lips even at the price of great suffering, for the sake of those whom we hold dear; because the good man should not live as long as it pleases him, but as long as he ought. He who does not value his wife, or his friend, highly enough to linger longer in life – he who obstinately persists in dying is a voluptuary.

The soul should also enforce this command upon itself whenever the needs of one's relatives require; it should pause and humour those near and dear, not only when it desires, but even when it has begun, to die. ⁴It gives proof of a great heart to return to life for the sake of others; and noble men have often done this. But this procedure also, I believe, indicates the highest type of kindness: that although the greatest advantage of old age is the opportunity to be more negligent regarding self-preservation and to use life more adventurously, one should watch over one's old age with still greater care if one knows that such action is pleasing, useful, or desirable in the eyes of a person whom one holds dear. ⁵This is also a source of no mean joy and profit; for what is sweeter than to be so valued by one's wife that one becomes more valuable to oneself for this reason? Hence my dear Paulina is able to make me responsible, not only for her fears, but also for my own.

⁶So you are curious to know the outcome of this prescription of travel? As soon as I escaped from the oppressive atmosphere of the city, and from that awful odour of reeking kitchens which, when in use, pour forth a ruinous mess of

steam and soot, I perceived at once that my health was mending. And how much stronger do you think I felt when I reached my vineyards! Being, so to speak, let out to pasture, I regularly walked into my meals! So I am my old self again, feeling now no wavering languor in my system, and no sluggishness in my brain. I am beginning to work with all my energy.

[7]But the mere place avails little for this purpose, unless the mind is fully master of itself, and can, at its pleasure, find seclusion even in the midst of business; the man, however, who is always selecting resorts and hunting for leisure, will find something to distract his mind in every place. Socrates is reported to have replied, when a certain person complained of having received no benefit from his travels: "It serves you right! You travelled in your own company!"[a] [8]O what a blessing it would be for some men to wander away from themselves! As it is, they cause themselves vexation, worry, demoralization, and fear! What profit is there in crossing the sea and in going from one city to another? If you would escape your troubles, you need not another place but another personality. Perhaps you have reached Athens, or perhaps Rhodes; choose any state you fancy, how does it matter what its character may be? You will be bringing to it your own.

[9]Suppose that you hold wealth to be a good: poverty will then distress you, and, – which is most pitiable, – it will be an imaginary poverty. For you may be rich, and nevertheless, because your neighbour is richer, you suppose yourself to be poor exactly by the same amount in which you fall short of your neighbour. You may deem official position a good; you will be vexed at another's appointment or re-appointment to the consulship; you will be jealous whenever you see a name several times in the state records. Your ambition will be so

---

[a] Cf. Ep. x. 1 *"Mecum loquor." "Cave, rogo, et diligenter adtende; cum homine malo loqueris."*

frenzied that you will regard yourself last in the race if there is anyone in front of you. [10]Or you may rate death as the worst of evils, although there is really no evil therein except that which precedes death's coming – fear. You will be frightened out of your wits, not only by real, but by fancied dangers, and will be tossed for ever on the sea of illusion. What benefit will it be to

> Have threaded all the towns of Argolis,
> A fugitive through midmost press of foes?[a]

For peace itself will furnish further apprehension. Even in the midst of safety you will have no confidence if your mind has once been given a shock; once it has acquired the habit of blind panic, it is incapable of providing even for its own safety. For it does not avoid danger, but runs away. Yet we are more exposed to danger when we turn our backs.

[11]You may judge it the most grievous of ills to lose any of those you love; while all the same this would be no less foolish than weeping because the trees which charm your eye and adorn your home lose their foliage. Regard everything that pleases you as if it were a flourishing plant; make the most of it while it is in leaf, for different plants at different seasons must fall and die. But just as the loss of leaves is a light thing, because they are born afresh, so it is with the loss of those whom you love and regard as the delight of your life; for they can be replaced even though they cannot be born afresh. [12]"New friends, however, will not be the same." No, nor will you yourself remain the same; you change with every day and every hour. But in other men you more readily see what time plunders; in your own case the change is hidden, because it will not take place visibly. Others are snatched from sight; we ourselves are being stealthily filched away from

[a] Vergil, *Aen.* iii. 282 f.

ourselves. You will not think about any of these problems, nor will you apply remedies to these wounds. You will of your own volition be sowing a crop of trouble by alternate hoping and despairing. If you are wise, mingle these two elements: do not hope without despair, or despair without hope.

[13]What benefit has travel of itself ever been able to give anyone? No restraint upon pleasure, no bridling of desire, no checking of bad temper, no crushing of the wild assaults of passion, no opportunity to rid the soul of evil. Travelling cannot give us judgment, or shake off our errors; it merely holds our attention for a moment by a certain novelty, as children pause to wonder at something unfamiliar. [14]Besides, it irritates us, through the wavering of a mind which is suffering from an acute attack of sickness; the very motion makes it more fitful and nervous. Hence the spots we had sought most eagerly we quit still more eagerly, like birds that flit and are off as soon as they have alighted. [15]What travel will give is familiarity with other nations: it will reveal to you mountains of strange shape, or unfamiliar tracts of plain, or valleys that are watered by everflowing springs, or the characteristics of some river that comes to our attention. We observe how the Nile rises and swells in summer, or how the Tigris disappears, runs underground through hidden spaces, and then appears with unabated sweep; or how the Maeander,[a] that oft-rehearsed theme and plaything of the poets, turns in frequent bendings, and often in winding comes close to its own channel before resuming its course. But this sort of information will not make better or sounder men of us.[b]

[16]We ought rather to spend our time in study, and to cultivate those who are masters of wisdom, learning

[a] See Index of Proper Names.

[b] Although Seneca was deeply interested in such matters, as is proved by Ep. lxxix., the *Naturales Quaestiones*, and an early work on the geography of Egypt.

something which has been investigated, but not settled; by this means the mind can be relieved of a most wretched serfdom, and won over to freedom. Indeed, as long as you are ignorant of what you should avoid or seek, or of what is necessary or superfluous, or of what is right or wrong, you will not be travelling, but merely wandering. [17]There will be no benefit to you in this hurrying to and fro; for you are travelling with your emotions and are followed by your afflictions. Would that they were indeed following you! In that case, they would be farther away; as it is, you are carrying and not leading them. Hence they press about you on all sides, continually chafing and annoying you. It is medicine, not scenery, for which the sick man must go a-searching. [18]Suppose that someone has broken a leg or dislocated a joint: he does not take carriage or ship for other regions, but he calls in the physician to set the fractured limb, or to move it back to its proper place in the socket. What then? When the spirit is broken or wrenched in so many places, do you think that change of place can heal it? The complaint is too deep-seated to be cured by a journey. [19]Travel does not make a physician or an orator; no art is acquired by merely living in a certain place.

Where lies the truth, then? Can wisdom, the greatest of all the arts, be picked up on a journey? I assure you, travel as far as you like, you can never establish yourself beyond the reach of desire, beyond the reach of bad temper, or beyond the reach of fear; had it been so, the human race would long ago have banded together and made a pilgrimage to the spot. Such ills, as long as you carry with you their causes, will load you down and worry you to skin and bone in your wanderings over land and sea. [20]Do you wonder that it is of no use to run away from them? That from which you are running, is within you. Accordingly, reform your own self, get the burden off your own shoulders, and keep within safe limits the cravings which ought to be removed. Wipe out from your soul all trace of sin. If you would enjoy your travels, make healthy the companion of your travels. As long as this companion is avaricious and mean, greed will stick to you; and while you consort with an overbearing man, your puffed-up ways will also stick close. Live with a hangman, and you will never be rid of your cruelty. If an adulterer be your club-mate, he will kindle the baser passions. [21]If you would be stripped of your faults leave far behind you the patterns of the faults. The miser, the swindler, the bully, the cheat, who will do you much harm merely by being near you, are within you.

Change therefore to better associations: live with the Catos, with Laelius, with Tubero. Or, if you enjoy living with Greeks also, spend your time with Socrates and with Zeno: the former will show you how to die if it be necessary; the latter how to die before it is necessary. [22]Live with Chrysippus, with Posidonius:[a] they will make you acquainted with things earthly and things heavenly; they will bid you work hard over something more than neat turns of language and phrases mouthed forth for the entertainment of listeners; they will bid you be stout of heart and rise superior to threats. The only harbour safe from the seething storms of this life is scorn of the future, a firm stand, a readiness to receive Fortune's missiles full in the breast, neither skulking nor turning the back. [23]Nature has brought us forth brave of spirit, and, as she has implanted in certain animals a spirit of ferocity, in others craft, in others terror, so she has gifted us with an aspiring and lofty spirit, which prompts us to seek a life of the greatest honour, and not of the greatest security, that most resembles the soul of the universe, which it follows and imitates as far as our mortal steps permit. This spirit thrusts

[a] These men are patterns or interpreters of the virtues. The first-named three represent courage, justice, and self-restraint respectively. Socrates is the ideal wise man, Zeno, Chrysippus, and Posidonus are in turn the founder, the classifier, and the modernizer of Stoicism.

itself forward, confident of commendation and esteem. [24]It is superior to all, monarch of all it surveys; hence it should be subservient to nothing, finding no task too heavy, and nothing strong enough to weigh down the shoulders of a man.

Shapes dread to look upon, of toil or death[a]

are not in the least dreadful, if one is able to look upon them with unflinching gaze, and is able to pierce the shadows. Many a sight that is held a terror in the night-time, is turned to ridicule by day. "Shapes dread to look upon, of toil or death": our Vergil has excellently said that these shapes are dread, not in reality, but only "to look upon" – in other words, they seem terrible, but are not. [25]And in these visions what is there, I say, as fear-inspiring as rumour has proclaimed? Why, pray, my dear Lucilius, should a man fear toil, or a mortal death? Countless cases occur to my mind of men who think that what they themselves are unable to do is impossible, who maintain that we utter words which are too big for man's nature to carry out. [26]But how much more highly do I think of these men! They can do these things, but decline to do them. To whom that ever tried have these tasks proved false? To what man did they not seem easier in the doing? Our lack of confidence is not the result of difficulty. The difficulty comes from our lack of confidence.

[27]If, however, you desire a pattern, take Socrates, a long-suffering old man, who was sea-tossed amid every hardship and yet was unconquered both by poverty (which his troubles at home made more burdensome) and by toil, including the drudgery of military service. He was much tried at home, whether we think of his wife, a woman of rough manners and shrewish tongue, or of the children whose intractability

[a] *Aeneid*, vi. 277.

showed them to be more like their mother than their father.[a]
And if you consider the facts, he lived either in time of war,
or under tyrants, or under a democracy, which is more cruel
than wars and tyrants. [28]The war lasted for twenty-
seven years;[b] then the state became the victim of the Thirty
Tyrants, of whom many were his personal enemies. At the
last came that climax of condemnation under the gravest of
charges: they accused him of disturbing the state religion
and corrupting the youth,[c] for they declared that he had
influenced the youth to defy the gods, to defy the council,
and to defy the state in general. Next came the prison, and
the cup of poison.[d] But all these measures changed the soul
of Socrates so little that they did not even change his features.
What wonderful and rare distinction! He maintained this
attitude up to the very end, and no man ever saw Socrates
too much elated or too much depressed. Amid all the
disturbance of Fortune, he was undisturbed.

[29]Do you desire another case? Take that of the younger
Marcus Cato, with whom Fortune dealt in a more hostile and
more persistent fashion. But he withstood her, on all occasions, and in his last moments, at the point of death, showed
that a brave man can live in spite of Fortune, can die in spite
of her. His whole life was passed either in civil warfare, or
under a political regime which was soon to breed civil war.
And you may say that he, just as much as Socrates, declared
allegiance to liberty in the midst of slavery – unless perchance

[a] At first a sculptor, then an independent seeker after truth, whose wants
were reduced to a minimum. Husband of the shrewish Xanthippe and
father of the dull and worthless Lamprocles. Brave soldier at Potidaea,
Delium, and Amphipolis.

[b] 431-404 B.C. (the Peloponnesian War).

[c] See Plato's *Apology*, 23 D. They had previously aimed at him a law forbidding the teaching of dialectic.

[d] 399 B.C.

you think that Pompey, Caesar, and Crassus[a] were the allies of liberty! [30]No one ever saw Cato change, no matter how often the state changed: he kept himself the same in all circumstances – in the praetorship,[b] in defeat, under accusation,[c] in his province, on the platform, in the army, in death. Furthermore, when the republic was in a crisis of terror, when Caesar was on one side with ten embattled legions at his call, aided by so many foreign nations. and when Pompey was on the other, satisfied to stand alone against all comers, and when the citizens were leaning towards either Caesar or Pompey, Cato alone established a definite party for the Republic. [31]If you would obtain a mental picture of that period, you may imagine on one side the people and the whole proletariat eager for revolution – on the other the senators and knights, the chosen and honoured men of the commonwealth; and there were left between them but these two – the Republic and Cato.

I tell you, you will marvel when you see
Atreus' son, and Priam, and Achilles, wroth at both.[d]

Like Achilles, he scorns and disarms each faction. [32]And this is the vote which he casts concerning them both: "If Caesar wins, I slay myself; if Pompey, I go into exile." What was there for a man to fear who, whether in defeat or in victory, had assigned to himself a doom which might have been assigned to him by his enemies in their utmost rage? So he died by his own decision.

[33]You see that man can endure toil: Cato, on foot, led an

---

[a] Triumvirs in 60 B.C. and rivals in acquiring unconstitutional power.

[b] 54 B.C.

[c] Perhaps a reference to his mission in Cyprus (58-56 B.C.), and his subsequent arraignment by Clodius.

[d] Vergil, *Aen.* i. 458.

army through African deserts. You see that thirst can be endured: he marched over sun-baked hills, dragging the remains of a beaten army and with no train of supplies, undergoing lack of water and wearing a heavy suit of armour; always the last to drink of the few springs which they chanced to find. You see that honour, and dishonour too, can be despised: for they report that on the very day when Cato was defeated at the elections, he played a game of ball. You see also that man can be free from fear of those above him in rank: for Cato attacked Caesar and Pompey simultaneously, at a time when none dared fall foul of the one without endeavouring to oblige the other. You see that death can be scorned as well as exile: Cato inflicted exile upon himself and finally death,[a] and war all the while.

[34]And so, if only we are willing to withdraw our necks from the yoke, we can keep as stout a heart against such terrors as these. But first and foremost, we must reject pleasures; they render us weak and womanish; they make great demands upon us, and, moreover, cause us to make great demands upon Fortune. Second, we must spurn wealth: wealth is the diploma of slavery. Abandon gold and silver, and whatever else is a burden upon our richly-furnished homes; liberty cannot be gained for nothing. If you set a high value on liberty, you must set a low value on everything else. Farewell.

[a] At Utica, in 46 B.C.

CV. ON FACING THE WORLD WITH CONFIDENCE

[1]I shall now tell you certain things to which you should pay attention in order to live more safely. Do you however, – such is my judgment, – hearken to my precepts just as if I were counselling you to keep safe your health in your country-place at Ardea.

Reflect on the things which goad man into destroying man: you will find that they are hope, envy, hatred, fear, and contempt. [2]Now, of all these, contempt is the least harmful, so much so that many have skulked behind it as a sort of cure. When a man despises you, he works you injury, to be sure, but he passes on; and no one persistently or of set purpose does hurt to a person whom he despises. Even in battle, prostrate soldiers are neglected: men fight with those who stand their ground. [3]And you can avoid the envious hopes of the wicked so long as you have nothing which can stir the evil desires of others, and so long as you possess nothing remarkable. For people crave even little things, if these catch the attention or are of rare occurrence.

You will escape envy if you do not force yourself upon the public view, if you do not boast your possessions, if you understand how to enjoy things privately. Hatred comes either from running foul of others: and this can be avoided by never provoking anyone; or else it is uncalled for: and commonsense[a] will keep you safe from it. Yet it has been dangerous to many; some people have been hated without having had an enemy. [4]As to not being feared, a moderate fortune and an easy disposition will guarantee you that; men should know that you are the sort of person who can be offended without danger; and your reconciliation should be easy and sure. Moreover, it is as troublesome to be feared at home as abroad; it is as bad to be feared by a slave as by a gentleman. For every one has strength enough to do you some harm. Besides, he who is feared, fears also; no one has been able to arouse terror and live in peace of mind.

[5]Contempt remains to be discussed. He who has made this quality an adjunct of his own personality, who is despised because he wishes to be despised and not because he must be despised, has the measure of contempt under his control. Any inconveniences in this respect can be dispelled by honourable occupations and by friendships with men who have influence with an influential person; with these men it will profit you to engage but not to entangle yourself, lest the cure may cost you more than the risk. [6]Nothing, however, will help you so much as keeping still – talking very little with others, and as much as may be with yourself. For there is a sort of charm about conversation, something very subtle and coaxing, which, like intoxication or love, draws secrets from us. No man will keep to himself what he hears. No one will tell another only as much as he has heard. And he who tells tales will tell names, too. Everyone has someone to whom he entrusts exactly what has been entrusted to him. Though he checks his own garrulity, and is content with one hearer, he will bring about him a nation, if that which was a secret shortly before becomes common talk.

[7]The most important contribution to peace of mind is

[a] i.e., tact.

never to do wrong. Those who lack self-control lead disturbed and tumultuous lives; their crimes are balanced by their fears, and they are never at ease. For they tremble after the deed, and they are embarrassed; their consciences do not allow them to busy themselves with other matters, and continually compel them to give an answer. Whoever expects punishment, receives it, but whoever deserves it, expects it. [8]Where there is an evil conscience something may bring safety, but nothing can bring ease; for a man imagines that, even if he is not under arrest, he may soon be arrested. His sleep is troubled; when he speaks of another man's crime, he reflects upon his own, which seems to him not sufficiently blotted out, not sufficiently hidden from view. A wrongdoer sometimes has the luck to escape notice but never the assurance thereof. Farewell.

CVII. ON OBEDIENCE TO THE UNIVERSAL WILL

[1]Where is that common-sense of yours? Where that deftness in examining things? That greatness of soul? Have you come to be tormented by a trifle? Your slaves regarded your absorption in business as an opportunity for them to run away. Well, if your friends deceived you (for by all means let them have the name which we mistakenly bestowed upon them, and so call them, that they may incur more shame by not being such friends) – if your friends, I repeat, deceived you, all your affairs would lack something; as it is, you merely lack men who damaged your own endeavours and considered you burdensome to your neighbours. [2]None of these things is unusual or unexpected. It is as nonsensical to be put out by such events as to complain of being spattered in the street or at getting befouled in the mud. The programme of life is the same as that of a bathing establishment, a crowd, or a journey: sometimes things will be thrown at you, and sometimes they will strike you by accident. Life is not a dainty business. You have started on a long journey; you are bound to slip, collide, fall, become weary, and cry out: "O for Death!" – or in other words, tell lies. At one stage you will leave a comrade behind you, at another you will bury someone, at another you will be

apprehensive. It is amid stumblings of this sort that you must travel out this rugged journey.

[3]Does one wish to die? Let the mind be prepared to meet everything; let it know that it has reached the heights round which the thunder plays. Let it know that it has arrived where –

> Grief and avenging Care have set their couch,
> And pallid sickness dwells, and drear Old Age.[a]

With such messmates must you spend your days. Avoid them you cannot, but despise them you can. And you will despise them, if you often take thought and anticipate the future. [4]Everyone approaches courageously a danger which he has prepared himself to meet long before, and withstands even hardships if he has previously practised how to meet them. But, contrariwise, the unprepared are panic-stricken even at the most trifling things. We must see to it that nothing shall come upon us unforeseen. And since things are all the more serious when they are unfamiliar, continual reflection will give you the power, no matter what the evil may be, not to play the unschooled boy.

[5]"My slaves have run away from me!" Yes, other men have been robbed, blackmailed, slain, betrayed, stamped under foot, attacked by poison or by slander; no matter what trouble you mention, it has happened to many. Again, there are manifold kinds of missiles which are hurled at us. Some are planted in us, some are being brandished and at this very moment are on the way, some which were destined for other men graze us instead. [6]We should not manifest surprise at any sort of condition into which we are born, and which should be lamented by no one, simply because it is equally ordained for all. Yes, I say, equally

---

[a] Vergil, *Aen.* vi. 274 f.

ordained; for a man might have experienced even that which he has escaped. And an equal law consists, not of that which all have experienced, but of that which is laid down for all. Be sure to prescribe for your mind this sense of equity; we should pay without complaint the tax of our mortality.

[7]Winter brings on cold weather; and we must shiver. Summer returns, with its heat; and we must sweat. Unseasonable weather upsets the health; and we must fall ill. In certain places we may meet with wild beasts, or with men who are more destructive than any beasts. Floods, or fires, will cause us loss. And we cannot change this order of things; but what we can do is to acquire stout hearts, worthy of good men, thereby courageously enduring chance and placing ourselves in harmony with Nature. [8]And Nature moderates this world-kingdom which you see, by her changing seasons: clear weather follows cloudy; after a calm, comes the storm; the winds blow by turns; day succeeds night; some of the heavenly bodies rise, and some set. Eternity consists of opposites.

[9]It is to this law that our souls must adjust themselves, this they should follow, this they should obey. Whatever happens, assume that it was bound to happen, and do not be willing to rail at Nature. That which you cannot reform, it is best to endure, and to attend uncomplainingly upon the God under whose guidance everything progresses; for it is a bad soldier who grumbles when following his commander. [10]For this reason we should welcome our orders with energy and vigour, nor should we cease to follow the natural course of this most beautiful universe, into which all our future sufferings are woven.

Let us address Jupiter, the pilot of this world-mass, as did our great Cleanthes in those most eloquent lines – lines which I shall allow myself to render in Latin, after the example of the eloquent Cicero. If you like them, make the most of them; if they displease you, you will understand that I have simply been following the practise of Cicero:

> [11]Lead me, O Master of the lofty heavens,
> My Father, whithersoever thou shalt wish.
> I shall not falter, but obey with speed.
> And though I would not, I shall go, and suffer,
> In sin and sorrow what I might have done
> In noble virtue. Aye, the willing soul
> Fate leads, but the unwilling drags along.[a]

[12]Let us live thus, and speak thus; let Fate find us ready and alert. Here is your great soul – the man who has given himself over to Fate; on the other hand, that man is a weakling and a degenerate who struggles and maligns the order of the universe and would rather reform the gods than reform himself. Farewell.

---

[a] Cleanthes, Frag. 527 von Arnim. In Epictetus (*Ench.* 53) these verses are assigned to Cleanthes (omitting the last line); while St. Augustine (*Civ. Dei.* v. 8) quotes them as Seneca's: *Annaei Senecae sunt, nisi fallor, hi versus.* Wilamowitz and others follow the latter view.

CVIII. ON THE APPROACHES TO PHILOSOPHY

[1]The topic about which you ask me is one of those where our only concern with knowledge is to have the knowledge. Nevertheless, because it does so far concern us, you are in a hurry; you are not willing to wait for the books which I am at this moment arranging for you, and which embrace the whole department of moral philosophy.[a] I shall send you the books at once; but I shall, before doing that, write and tell you how this eagerness to learn, with which I see you are aflame, should be regulated, so that it may not get in its own way. [2]Things are not to be gathered at random; nor should they be greedily attacked in the mass; one will arrive at a knowledge of the whole by studying the parts. The burden should be suited to your strength, nor should you tackle more than you can adequately handle. Absorb not all that you wish, but all that you can hold. Only be of a sound mind, and then you will be able to hold all that you wish. For the more the mind receives, the more does it expand.

[3]This was the advice, I remember, which Attalus[b] gave

[a] Cf. Ep. cvi. 2 *scis enim me moralem philosophiam velle conplecti*, etc.

[b] Seneca's first and most convincing teacher of Stoicism, to whom this letter is a tribute. The ablest of contemporary philosophers, he was banished

me in the days when I practically laid siege to his class-room, the first to arrive and the last to leave. Even as he paced up and down, I would challenge him to various discussions; for he not only kept himself accessible to his pupils, but met them half-way. His words were: "The same purpose should possess both master and scholar – an ambition in the one case to promote, and in the other to progress." [4]He who studies with a philosopher should take away with him some one good thing every day: he should daily return home a sounder man, or in the way to become sounder. And he will thus return; for it is one of the functions of philosophy to help not only those who study her, but those also who associate with her. He that walks in the sun, though he walk not for that purpose, must needs become sunburned. He who frequents the perfumer's shop and lingers even for a short time, will carry with him the scent of the place. And he who follows a philosopher is bound to derive some benefit therefrom, which will help him even though he be remiss. Mark what I say: "remiss," not "recalcitrant."

[5]"What then?" you say, "do we not know certain men who have sat for many years at the feet of a philosopher and yet have not acquired the slightest tinge of wisdom?" Of course I know such men. There are indeed persevering gentlemen who stick at it; I do not call them pupils of the wise, but merely "squatters."[a] [6]Certain of them come to hear and not to learn, just as we are attracted to the theatre to satisfy the pleasures of the ear, whether by a speech, or by a song, or by a play. This class, as you will see, constitutes a large part of the listeners, who regard the philosopher's lecture-room merely as a sort of lounging-place for their leisure. They do not set about to lay aside any faults there, or to receive a rule of life, by which they may test their characters; they merely wish to enjoy to the full the delights of the ear. And yet some arrive

---

during the reign of Tiberius. See Index of Proper Names.

[a] Literally "tenants," "lodgers," of a temporary sort.

even with notebooks, not to take down the matter, but only the words,[a] that they may presently repeat them to others with as little profit to these as they themselves received when they heard them. [7]A certain number are stirred by high-sounding phrases, and adapt themselves to the emotions of the speaker with lively change of face and mind – just like the emasculated Phrygian priests[b] who are wont to be roused by the sound of the flute and go mad to order. But the true hearer is ravished and stirred by the beauty of the subject matter, not by the jingle of empty words. When a bold word has been uttered in defiance of death, or a saucy fling in defiance of Fortune, we take delight in acting straightway upon that which we have heard. Men are impressed by such words, and become what they are bidden to be, should but the impression abide in the mind, and should the populace, who discourage honourable things, not immediately lie in wait to rob them of this noble impulse; only a few can carry home the mental attitude with which they were inspired. [8]It is easy to rouse a listener so that he will crave righteousness; for Nature has laid the foundations and planted the seeds of virtue in us all. And we are all born to these general privileges; hence, when the stimulus is added, the good spirit is stirred as if it were freed from bonds. Have you not noticed how the theatre re-echoes whenever any words are spoken whose truth we appreciate generally and confirm unanimously.

[9]The poor lack much; the greedy man lacks all.[c]

A greedy man does good to none; he does
Most evil to himself.[d]

---

[a] Cf. the dangers of such *lusoria* (Ep. xlviii. 8) and *a rebus studium transferendum est ad verba* (Ep. xl. 14).

[b] i.e., mendicant Galli, worshippers of Cybele, the Magna Mater.

[c] *Syri Sententiae*, Frag. 236 Ribbeck.

[d] *Ib.*, Frag. 234 R.

At such verses as these, your meanest miser claps applause and rejoices to hear his own sins reviled. How much more do you think this holds true, when such things are uttered by a philosopher, when he introduces verses among his wholesome precepts, that he may thus make those verses sink more effectively into the mind of the neophyte! [10]Cleanthes used to say:[a] "As our breath produces a louder sound when it passes through the long and narrow opening of the trumpet and escapes by a hole which widens at the end, even so the fettering rules of poetry clarify our meaning." The very same words are more carelessly received and make less impression upon us, when they are spoken in prose; but when metre is added and when regular prosody has compressed a noble idea, then the selfsame thought comes, as it were, hurtling with a fuller fling. [11]We talk much about despising money, and we give advice on this subject in the lengthiest of speeches, that mankind may believe true riches to exist in the mind and not in one's bank account, and that the man who adapts himself to his slender means and makes himself wealthy on a little sum, is the truly rich man; but our minds are struck more effectively when a verse like this is repeated:

He needs but little who desires but little.

or,

He hath his wish, whose wish includeth naught
Save that which is enough.[b]

[12]When we hear such words as these, we are led towards a confession of the truth.

Even men in whose opinion nothing is enough, wonder

---

[a] Frag. 487 von Arnim.

[b] Pall. Incert. Fab. 65 and 66 Ribbeck.

and applaud when they hear such words, and swear eternal hatred against money. When you see them thus disposed, strike home, keep at them, and charge them with this duty, dropping all double meanings, syllogisms, hair-splitting, and the other side-shows of ineffective smartness. Preach against greed, preach against high living; and when you notice that you have made progress and impressed the minds of your hearers, lay on still harder. You cannot imagine how much progress can be brought about by an address of that nature, when you are bent on curing your hearers and are absolutely devoted to their best interests. For when the mind is young, it may most easily be won over to desire what is honourable and upright; truth, if she can obtain a suitable pleader, will lay strong hands upon those who can still be taught, those who have been but superficially spoiled.

[13]At any rate, when I used to hear Attalus denouncing sin, error, and the evils of life, I often felt sorry for mankind and regarded Attalus as a noble and majestic being – above our mortal heights. He called himself a king,[a] but I thought him more than a king, because he was entitled to pass judgment on kings. [14]And in truth, when he began to uphold poverty, and to show what a useless and dangerous burden was everything that passed the measure of our need, I often desired to leave his lecture-room a poor man. Whenever he castigated our pleasure-seeking lives, and extolled personal purity, moderation in diet, and a mind free from unnecessary, not to speak of unlawful, pleasures, the desire came upon me to limit my food and drink. [15]And that is why some of these habits have stayed with me, Lucilius. For I had planned my whole life with great resolves. And later, when I returned to the duties of a citizen, I did indeed keep a few of these good resolutions. That is why I have forsaken oysters and mushrooms for ever: since they are not really food, but are relishes

[a] A characteristic Stoic paradox.

to bully the sated stomach into further eating, as is the fancy of gourmands and those who stuff themselves beyond their powers of digestion: down with it quickly, and up with it quickly! [16]That is why I have also throughout my life avoided perfumes; because the best scent for the person is no scent at all.[a] That is why my stomach is unacquainted with wine. That is why throughout my life I have shunned the bath, and have believed that to emaciate the body and sweat it into thinness is at once unprofitable and effeminate. Other resolutions have been broken, but after all in such a way that, in cases where I ceased to practice abstinence, I have observed a limit which is indeed next door to abstinence; perhaps it is even a little more difficult, because it is easier for the will to cut off certain things utterly than to use them with restraint.

[17]Inasmuch as I have begun to explain to you how much greater was my impulse to approach philosophy in my youth than to continue it in my old age, I shall not be ashamed to tell you what ardent zeal Pythagoras inspired in me. Sotion[b] used to tell me why Pythagoras abstained from animal food, and why, in later times, Sextius did also. In each case, the reason was different, but it was in each case a noble reason. [18]Sextius believed that man had enough sustenance without resorting to blood, and that a habit of cruelty is formed whenever butchery is practised for pleasure. Moreover, he thought we should curtail the sources of our luxury; he argued that a varied diet was contrary to the laws of health, and was unsuited to our constitutions. [19]Pythagoras, on the other hand, held that all beings were inter-related, and that there was a system of exchange between souls which transmigrated from one bodily shape into another. If one may believe him, no

[a] An almost proverbial saying; cf. the *recte olet ubi nil olet* of Plautus (*Most.* 273), Cicero, and Martial.

[b] Pythagorean philosopher of the Augustine age, and one of Seneca's early teachers.

soul perishes or ceases from its functions at all, except for a tiny interval – when it is being poured from one body into another. We may question at what time and after what seasons of change the soul returns to man, when it has wandered through many a dwelling-place; but meantime, he made men fearful of guilt and parricide, since they might be, without knowing it, attacking the soul of a parent and injuring it with knife or with teeth – if, as is possible, the related spirit be dwelling temporarily in this bit of flesh! [20]When Sotion had set forth this doctrine, supplementing it with his own proofs, he would say: "You do not believe that souls are assigned, first to one body and then to another, and that our so-called death is merely a change of abode? You do not believe that in cattle, or in wild beasts, or in creatures of the deep, the soul of him who was once a man may linger? You do not believe that nothing on this earth is annihilated, but only changes its haunts? And that animals also have cycles of progress and, so to speak, an orbit for their souls, no less than the heavenly bodies, which revolve in fixed circuits? Great men have put faith in this idea; [21]therefore, while holding to your own view, keep the whole question in abeyance in your mind. If the theory is true, it is a mark of purity to refrain from eating flesh; if it be false, it is economy. And what harm does it do to you to give such credence? I am merely depriving you of food which sustains lions and vultures."

[22]I was imbued with this teaching, and began to abstain from animal food; at the end of a year the habit was as pleasant as it was easy. I was beginning to feel that my mind was more active; though I would not today positively state whether it really was or not. Do you ask how I came to abandon the practice? It was this way: The days of my youth coincided with the early part of the reign of Tiberius Caesar. Some foreign rites were at that time[a] being inaugurated, and

---

[a] A.D. 1[9] Cf. Tacitus, *Ann.* ii. 85 *actum de sacris Aegyptiis Iudaicisque pellendis.*

abstinence from certain kinds of animal food was set down as a proof of interest in the strange cult. So at the request of my father, who did not fear prosecution, but who detested philosophy, I returned to my previous habits; and it was no very hard matter to induce me to dine more comfortably.

[23]Attalus used to recommend a pillow which did not give in to the body; and now, old as I am, I use one so hard that it leaves no trace after pressure. I have mentioned all this in order to show you how zealous neophytes are with regard to their first impulses towards the highest ideals, provided that some one does his part in exhorting them and in kindling their ardour. There are indeed mistakes made, through the fault of our advisers, who teach us how to debate and not how to live; there are also mistakes made by the pupils, who come to their teachers to develop, not their souls, but their wits. Thus the study of wisdom has become the study of words.

[24]Now it makes a great deal of difference what you have in mind when you approach a given subject. If a man is to be a scholar,[a] and is examining the works of Vergil, he does not interpret the noble passage

Time flies away, and cannot be restored[b]

in the following sense: "We must wake up; unless we hasten, we shall be left behind. Time rolls swiftly ahead, and rolls us with it. We are hurried along ignorant of our destiny; we arrange all our plans for the future, and on the edge of a precipice are at our ease." Instead of this, he brings to our

[a] In this passage Seneca differs (as also in Ep. lxxxviii. § 3) from the earlier Roman idea of *grammaticus* as *poetarum interpres*: he is thinking of one who deals with verbal expressions and the meaning of words. Cf. Sandys, *Hist. Class. Schol.* i. 8 ff.

[b] *Georg.* iii. 284.

attention how often Vergil, in speaking of the rapidity of time, uses the word "flies" (*fugit*).

> The choicest days of hapless human life
> Fly first; disease and bitter eld succeed,
> And toil, till harsh death rudely snatches all.[a]

[25]He who considers these lines in the spirit of a philosopher comments on the words in their proper sense: "Vergil never says, 'Time goes,' but 'Time flies,' because the latter is the quickest kind of movement, and in every case our best days are the first to be snatched away; why, then, do we hesitate to bestir ourselves so that we may be able to keep pace with this swiftest of all swift things?" The good flies past and the bad takes its place. [26]Just as the purest wine flows from the top of the jar and the thickest dregs settle at the bottom; so in our human life, that which is best comes first. Shall we allow other men to quaff the best, and keep the dregs for ourselves? Let this phrase cleave to your soul; you should be satisfied thereby as if it were uttered by an oracle:

> Each choicest day of hapless human life
> Flies first.

[27]Why "choicest day?" Because what's to come is unsure. Why "choicest day"? Because in our youth we are able to learn; we can bend to nobler purposes minds that are ready and still pliable; because this is the time for work, the time for keeping our minds busied in study and in exercising our bodies with useful effort; for that which remains is more sluggish and lacking in spirit – nearer the end.

Let us therefore strive with all courage, omitting attractions by the way; let us struggle with a single purpose,

[a] *Georg.* iii. 66 ff.

lest, when we are left behind, we comprehend too late the speed of quick-flying time, whose course we cannot stay. Let every day, as soon as it comes, be welcome as being the choicest, and let it be made our own possession. [28]We must catch that which flees. Now he who scans with a scholar's eye the lines I have just quoted, does not reflect that our first days are the best because disease is approaching and old age weighs upon us and hangs over our heads while we are still thinking about our youth. He thinks rather of Vergil's usual collocation of *disease and eld*; and indeed rightly. For old age is a disease which we cannot cure. [29]"Besides," he says to himself, "think of the epithet that accompanies *eld*; Vergil calls it *bitter*," –

> Disease and bitter eld succeed.
> And elsewhere Vergil says:
> There dwelleth pale disease and bitter eld.[a]

There is no reason why you should marvel that each man can collect from the same source suitable matter for his own studies; for in the same meadow the cow grazes, the dog hunts the hare, and the stork the lizard. [30]When Cicero's book *On the State* is opened by a philologist, a scholar, or a follower of philosophy, each man pursues his investigation in his own way. The philosopher wonders that so much could have been said therein against justice. The philologist takes up the same book and comments on the text as follows: There were two Roman kings – one without a father and one without a mother. For we cannot settle who was Servius's mother, and Ancus, the grandson of Numa, has no father on record.[b] [31]The

---

[a] *Aen.* vi. 275.

[b] Cicero, *De re publica*, ii. 18 *Numae Pompili nepos ex filia rex a populo est Ancus Marcius constitutus . . . siquidem istius regis matrem habemus, ignoramus patrem.*

philologist also notes that the officer whom we call dictator, and about whom we read in our histories under that title, was named in old times the *magister populi*; such is the name existing today in the augural records, proved by the fact that he whom the dictator chose as second in command was called *magister equitum*. He will remark, too, that Romulus met his end during an eclipse; that there was an appeal to the people even from the kings (this is so stated in the pontiffs' register and is the opinion of others, including Fenestella[a]). [32]When the scholar unrolls this same volume, he puts down in his notebook the forms of words, noting that *reapse*, equivalent to *re ipsa*, is used by Cicero, and *sepse* [b] just as frequently, which means *se ipse*. Then he turns his attention to changes in current usage. Cicero, for example, says: "Inasmuch as we are summoned back from the very calx by his interruption." Now the line in the circus which we call the *creta*[c] was called the calx by men of old time. [33]Again, he puts together some verses by Ennius, especially those which referred to Africanus:

A man to whom nor friend nor foe could give
Due meed for all his efforts and his deed.[d]

From this passage the scholar declares that he infers the word *opem* to have meant formerly not merely *assistance*, but *efforts*. For Ennius must mean that neither friend nor foe could pay Scipio a reward worthy of his efforts. [34]Next, he congratulates himself on finding the source of Vergil's words:

[a] Fl. in the Augustan Age. *Provocatio* is defined by Greenidge (*Rom. Pub. Life.* p. 64) as "a challenge by an accused to a magistrate to appear before another tribunal."

[b] A suffix, probably related to the intensive *-pte*

[c] Literally, the chalk-marked, or lime-marked, goal-line.

[d] Vahlen's *Ennius*, p. 215.

> Over whose head the mighty gate of Heaven
> Thunders,[a]

remarking that Ennius stole the idea from Homer, and Vergil from Ennius. For there is a couplet by Ennius, preserved in this same book of Cicero's, *On the State*:[b]

> If it be right for a mortal to scale the regions of Heaven,
> Then the huge gate of the sky opens in glory to *me*.

[35]But that I, too, while engaged upon another task, may not slip into the department of the philologist or the scholar, my advice is this – that all study of philosophy and all reading should be applied to the idea of living the happy life, that we should not hunt out archaic or far-fetched words and eccentric metaphors and figures of speech, but that we should seek precepts which will help us, utterances of courage and spirit which may at once be turned into facts. We should so learn them that words may become deeds. [36]And I hold that no man has treated mankind worse than he who has studied philosophy as if it were some marketable trade, who lives in a different manner from that which he advises. For those who are liable to every fault which they castigate advertise themselves as patterns of useless training. [37]A teacher like that can help me no more than a sea-sick pilot can be efficient in a storm. He must hold the tiller when the waves are tossing him; he must wrestle, as it were, with the sea; he must furl his sails when the storm rages; what good is a frightened and vomiting steersman to *me*? And how much greater, think you, is the storm of life than that which tosses any ship! One must steer, not talk.

All the words that these men utter and juggle before a

[a] *Georg.* iii. 260 f.

[b] Vahlen's *Ennius*, p. 216.

listening crowd, belong to others. [38]They have been spoken by Plato, spoken by Zeno, spoken by Chrysippus or by Posidonius, and by a whole host of Stoics as numerous as excellent. I shall show you how men can prove their words to be their own: it is by doing what they have been talking about. Since therefore I have given you the message I wished to pass on to you, I shall now satisfy your craving and shall reserve for a new letter a complete answer to your summons; so that you may not approach in a condition of weariness a subject which is thorny and which should be followed with an attentive and painstaking ear. Farewell.

CXIV. ON STYLE AS A MIRROR OF CHARACTER

[1]You have been asking me why, during certain periods, a degenerate style of speech comes to the fore, and how it is that men's wits have gone downhill into certain vices – in such a way that exposition at one time has taken on a kind of puffed-up strength, and at another has become mincing and modulated like the music of a concert piece. You wonder why sometimes bold ideas – bolder than one could believe – have been held in favour, and why at other times one meets with phrases that are disconnected and full of innuendo, into which one must read more meaning than was intended to meet the ear. Or why there have been epochs which maintained the right to a shameless use of metaphor. For answer, here is a phrase which you are wont to notice in the popular speech – one which the Greeks have made into a proverb: "Man's speech is just like his life."[a] [2]Exactly as each individual man's actions seem to speak, so people's style of speaking often reproduces the general character of the time, if the morale of the public has relaxed and has given itself over to effeminacy. Wantonness in speech is proof of public luxury,

[a] οἷος ὁ βίος, τοιοῦτος καὶ ὁ λόγος. The saying is referred to Socrates by Cicero (*Tusc.* v. 47).

if it is popular and fashionable, and not confined to one or two individual instances. [3]A man's ability[a] cannot possibly be of one sort and his soul of another. If his soul be wholesome, well-ordered, serious, and restrained, his ability also is sound and sober. Conversely, when the one degenerates, the other is also contaminated. Do you not see that if a man's soul has become sluggish, his limbs drag and his feet move indolently? If it is womanish, that one can detect the effeminacy by his very gait? That a keen and confident soul quickens the step? That madness in the soul, or anger (which resembles madness), hastens our bodily movements from walking to rushing?

And how much more do you think that this affects one's ability, which is entirely interwoven with the soul, – being moulded thereby, obeying its commands, and deriving therefrom its laws! [4]How Maecenas lived is too well-known for present comment. We know how he walked, how effeminate he was, and how he desired to display himself; also, how unwilling he was that his vices should escape notice. What, then? Does not the looseness of his speech match his ungirt attire?[b] Are his habits, his attendants, his house, his wife,[c] any less clearly marked than his words? He would have been a man of great powers, had he set himself to his task by a straight path, had he not shrunk from making himself understood, had he not been so loose in his style of speech also. You will therefore see that his eloquence was that of an intoxicated man – twisting, turning, unlimited in its slackness.

[a] i.e., that inborn quality which is compounded of character and intelligence.

[b] Cf. Suetonius, *Aug.* 86, where the Emperor *Maecenatem suum, cuius "myrobrechis," ut ait, "cincinnos"* ("unguent-dripping curls" (Rolfe)) *usque quaque persequitur et imitando per iocum irridet.* Augustus here refers especially to the style of Maecenas as a writer.

[c] Terentia. For her charms see Horace, *Od.* ii. 12; for her faults see *De prov.* iii. 10, where Seneca calls her "petulant."

[5]What is more unbecoming than the words: Maecenas, Frag. 11 Lunderstedt.[a] "A stream and a bank covered with long-tressed woods"? And see how "men plough the channel with boats and, turning up the shallows, leave gardens behind them." Or, "He curls his lady-locks, and bills and coos, and starts a-sighing, like a forest lord who offers prayers with down-bent neck." Or, "An unregenerate crew, they search out people at feasts, and assail households with the wine-cup, and, by hope, exact death." Or, "A Genius could hardly bear witness to his own festival"; or "threads of tiny tapers and crackling meal"; "mothers or wives clothing the hearth."

[6]Can you not at once imagine, on reading through these words, that this was the man who always paraded through the city with a flowing[b] tunic? For even if he was discharging the absent emperor's duties, he was always in undress when they asked him for the countersign. Or that this was the man who, as judge on the bench, or as an orator, or at any public function, appeared with his cloak wrapped about his head, leaving only the ears exposed,[c] like the millionaire's runaway slaves in the farce? Or that this was the man who, at the very time when the state was embroiled in civil strife, when the city was in difficulties and under martial law, was attended in public by two eunuchs – both of them more men than himself? Or that this was the man who had but one wife, and yet was married countless times?[d] [7]These words of his, put together so faultily, thrown off so carelessly, and arranged in such marked contrast to the usual practice, declare that the character of their writer was equally unusual, unsound, and eccentric. To be sure, we bestow upon him the highest praise for

[a] Maecenas, Frag. 11 Lunderstedt.

[b] Instead of properly girt up – a mark of slackness.

[c] For a similar mark of slovenliness, in Pompey's freedman Demetrius, see Plutarch, *Pompey*, xl. 4.

[d] i.e., often repulsed by his wife Terentia, and then restored to grace.

his humanity; he was sparing with the sword and refrained
from bloodshed;[a] and he made a show of his power only in
the course of his loose living; but he spoiled, by such prepos-
terous finickiness of style, this genuine praise, which was his
due. [8]For it is evident that he was not really gentle, but
effeminate, as is proved by his misleading word-order, his
inverted expressions, and the surprising thoughts which
frequently contain something great, but in finding expression
have become nerveless. One would say that his head was
turned by too great success.

This fault is due sometimes to the man, and sometimes
to his epoch. [9]When prosperity has spread luxury far and
wide, men begin by paying closer attention to their personal
appearance. Then they go crazy over furniture. Next, they
devote attention to their houses – how to take up more space
with them, as if they were country-houses, how to make the
walls glitter with marble that has been imported over seas,
how to adorn a roof with gold, so that it may match the
brightness of the inlaid floors. After that, they transfer their
exquisite taste to the dinner-table, attempting to court
approval by novelty and by departures from the customary
order of dishes, so that the courses which we are accustomed
to serve at the end of the meal may be served first, and so
that the departing guests may partake of the kind of food
which in former days was set before them on their arrival.

[10]When the mind has acquired the habit of scorning the
usual things of life, and regarding as mean that which was
once customary, it begins to hunt for novelties in speech also;
now it summons and displays obsolete and old-fashioned
words; now it coins even unknown words or misshapes them;
and now a bold and frequent metaphorical usage is made a
special feature of style, according to the fashion which has

[a] e.g., in the Treaty of Brundisium (37 B.C.), and often during the
Triumvirate.

just become prevalent. [11]Some cut the thoughts short, hoping to make a good impression by leaving the meaning in doubt and causing the hearer to suspect his own lack of wit. Some dwell upon them and lengthen them out. Others, too, approach just short of a fault – for a man must really do this if he hopes to attain an imposing effect – but actually love the fault for its own sake. In short, whenever you notice that a degenerate style pleases the critics, you may be sure that character also has deviated from the right standard.

Just as luxurious banquets and elaborate dress are indications of disease in the state, similarly a lax style, if it be popular, shows that the mind (which is the source of the word) has lost its balance. Indeed you ought not to wonder that corrupt speech is welcomed not merely by the more squalid mob[a] but also by our more cultured throng; for it is only in their dress and not in their judgments that they differ. [12]You may rather wonder that not only the effects of vices, but even vices themselves, meet with approval. For it has ever been thus: no man's ability has ever been approved without something being pardoned. Show me any man, however famous; I can tell you what it was that his age forgave in him, and what it was that his age purposely overlooked. I can show you many men whose vices have caused them no harm, and not a few who have been even helped by these vices. Yes, I will show you persons of the highest reputation, set up as models for our admiration; and yet if you seek to correct their errors, you destroy them; for vices are so intertwined with virtues that they drag the virtues along with them. [13]Moreover, style has no fixed laws; it is changed by the usage of the people, never the same for any length of time. Many orators hark back to earlier epochs for their vocabulary, speaking in the language of the Twelve Tables.[b] Gracchus, Crassus, and Curio, in their

[a] i.e., the "ring" of onlookers, the "pit."

[b] Fifth century B.C.

eyes, are too refined and too modern; so back to Appius and Coruncanius![a] Conversely, certain men, in their endeavour to maintain nothing but well-worn and common usages, fall into a humdrum style. [14]These two classes, each in its own way, are degenerate; and it is no less degenerate to use no words except those which are conspicuous, high-sounding, and poetical, avoiding what is familiar and in ordinary usage. One is, I believe, as faulty as the other: the one class are unreasonably elaborate, the other are unreasonably negligent; the former depilate the leg, the latter not even the armpit.[b]

[15]Let us now turn to the arrangement of words. In this department, what countless varieties of fault I can show you! Some are all for abruptness and unevenness of style, purposely disarranging anything which seems to have a smooth flow of language. They would have jolts in all their transitions; they regard as strong and manly whatever makes an uneven impression on the ear. With some others it is not so much an "arrangement" of words as it is a setting to music; so wheedling and soft is their gliding style. [16]And what shall I say of that arrangement in which words are put off and, after being long waited for, just manage to come in at the end of a period? Or again of that softly-concluding style, Cicero-fashion,[c] with a gradual and gently poised descent always the same and always with the customary arrangement of the rhythm! Nor is the fault only in the style of the sentences, if they are either petty and childish, or debasing, with more daring than modesty should allow, or if they are flowery and cloying, or if they end in emptiness, accomplishing mere sound and nothing more.

[a] i.e., from the second and first centuries B.C., back to the third century.

[b] The latter a reasonable mark of good breeding, the former an ostentatious bit of effeminacy. Summers cites Ovid, *A. A.* i. 506 "don't rub your legs smooth with the tight-scraping pumice stone."

[c] As Cicero (see Ep. xl. 11) was an example of the rhythmical in style, so Pollio is the representative of the "bumpy" (*salebrosa*) manner (Ep. c. 7).

[17]Some individual makes these vices fashionable – some person who controls the eloquence of the day; the rest follow his lead and communicate the habit to each other. Thus when Sallust[a] was in his glory, phrases were lopped off, words came to a close unexpectedly, and obscure conciseness was equivalent to elegance. L. Arruntius, a man of rare simplicity, author of a historical work on the Punic War, was a member and a strong supporter of the Sallust school. There is a phrase in Sallust: exercitum argento fecit,[b] meaning thereby that he recruited[c] an army by means of money. Arruntius began to like this idea; he therefore inserted the verb facio all through his book. Hence, in one passage, fugam nostris fecere;[d] in another, Hiero, rex Syracusanorum, bellum fecit;[e] and in another, quae audita Panhormitanos dedere Romanis fecere.[f] [18]I merely desired to give you a taste; his whole book is interwoven with such stuff as this. What Sallust reserved for occasional use, Arruntius makes into a frequent and almost continual habit – and there was a reason: for Sallust used the words as they occurred to his mind, while the other writer went afield in search of them. So you see the results of copying another man's vices. [19]Again, Sallust said: aquis hiemantibus.[g] Arruntius, in his first book on the Punic War, uses the words: repente hiemavit tempestas.[h] And elsewhere, wishing to

---

[a] Flor. 40 B.C.

[b] For these Sallust fragments see the edition of Kritz, Nos. 33, *Jug.* 37 4, and 42; for Arruntius see H. Peter, *Frag. Hist. Rom.* ii. pp. 41 f.

[c] Literally, "created," "made."

[d] "Brought to pass flight for our men"

[e] "Hiero, king of the Syracusans brought about war"

[f] "The news brought the men of Panormus" (now Palermo, Sicily) "to the point of surrendering to the Romans."

[g] "Amid the wintry waters"

[h] "The storm suddenly grew wintry"

describe an exceptionally cold year, he says: lotus hiemavit annus.[a] And in another passage: inde sexaginta onerarias leves praeter militem et necessarios nautarum hiemante aquilone misit;[b] and he continues to bolster many passages with this metaphor. In a certain place, Sallust gives the words: inter arma civilia aequi bonique famas[c] petit; and Arruntius cannot restrain himself from mentioning at once, in the first book, that there were extensive "reminders" concerning Regulus.

[20]These and similar faults, which imitation stamps upon one's style, are not necessarily indications of loose standards or of debased mind; for they are bound to be personal and peculiar to the writer, enabling one to judge thereby of a particular author's temperament; just as an angry man will talk in an angry way, an excitable man in a flurried way, and an effeminate man in a style that is soft and unresisting. [21]You note this tendency in those who pluck out, or thin out, their beards, or who closely shear and shave the upper lip while preserving the rest of the hair and allowing it to grow, or in those who wear cloaks of outlandish colours, who wear transparent togas, and who never deign to do anything which will escape general notice; they endeavour to excite and attract men's attention, and they put up even with censure, provided that they can advertise themselves. That is the style of Maecenas and all the others who stray from the path, not by hazard, but consciously and voluntarily. [22]This is the result of great evil in the soul. As in the case of drink, the tongue does not trip until the mind is overcome beneath its load and gives way or betrays itself; so that intoxication of style – for what else than this can I call it? – never gives trouble to

[a] "The whole year was like winter"

[b] "Then he dispatched sixty transports of light draught besides the soldiers and the necessary sailors amid a wintry storm."

[c] The peculiarity here is the use of the plural instead of the singular form. "Amid civil war he seeks reminders of justice and virtue."

anyone unless the soul begins to totter. Therefore, I say, take care of the soul; for from the soul issue our thoughts, from the soul our words, from the soul our dispositions, our expressions, and our very gait. When the soul is sound and strong, the style too is vigorous, energetic, manly; but if the soul lose its balance, down comes all the rest in ruins.

> [23]If but the king be safe, your swarm will live
> Harmonious; if he die, the bees revolt.[a]

The soul is our king. If it be safe, the other functions remain on duty and serve with obedience; but the slightest lack of equilibrium in the soul causes them to waver along with it. And when the soul has yielded to pleasure, its functions and actions grow weak, and any undertaking comes from a nerveless and unsteady source. [24]To persist in my use of this simile – our soul is at one time a king, at another a tyrant. The king, in that he respects things honourable, watches over the welfare of the body which is entrusted to his charge, and gives that body no base, no ignoble commands. But an uncontrolled, passionate, and effeminate soul changes kingship into that most dread and detestable quality – tyranny; then it becomes a prey to the uncontrolled emotions, which dog its steps, elated at first, to be sure, like a populace idly sated with a largess which will ultimately be its undoing, and spoiling what it cannot consume. [25]But when the disease has gradually eaten away the strength, and luxurious habits have penetrated the marrow and the sinews, such a soul exults at the sight of limbs which, through its overindulgence, it has made useless; instead of its own pleasures, it views those of others; it becomes the go-between and witness of the passions which, as the result of self-gratification, it can no longer feel. Abundance of delights is not so pleasing a thing to that soul as it is bitter,

---

[a] Vergil, *Georg.* iv. 212 f.

because it cannot send all the dainties of yore down through the over-worked throat and stomach, because it can no longer whirl in the maze of eunuchs and mistresses, and it is melancholy because a great part of its happiness is shut off, through the limitations of the body.

[26]Now is it not madness, Lucilius, for none of us to reflect that he is mortal? Or frail? Or again that he is but one individual? Look at our kitchens, and the cooks, who bustle about over so many fires; is it, think you, for a single belly that all this bustle and preparation of food takes place? Look at the old brands of wine and store-houses filled with the vintages of many ages; is it, think you, a single belly that is to receive the stored wine, sealed with the names of so many consuls, and gathered from so many vineyards? Look, and mark in how many regions men plough the earth, and how many thousands of farmers are tilling and digging; is it, think you, for a single belly that crops are planted in Sicily and Africa? [27]We should be sensible, and our wants more reasonable, if each of us were to take stock of himself, and to measure his bodily needs also, and understand how little he can consume, and for how short a time! But nothing will give you so much help toward moderation as the frequent thought that life is short and uncertain here below; whatever you are doing, have regard to death. Farewell.

CXXII. ON DARKNESS AS A VEIL FOR WICKEDNESS

[1]The day has already begun to lessen. It has shrunk considerably, but yet will still allow a goodly space of time if one rises, so to speak, with the day itself. We are more industrious, and we are better men if we anticipate the day and welcome the dawn; but we are base churls if we lie dozing when the sun is high in the heavens, or if we wake up only when noon arrives; and even then to many it seems not yet dawn. [2]Some have reversed the functions of light and darkness; they open eyes sodden with yesterday's debauch only at the approach of night. It is just like the condition of those peoples whom, according to Vergil, Nature has hidden away and placed in an abode directly opposite to our own:

> When in our face the Dawn with panting steeds
> Breathes down, for them the ruddy evening kindles
> Her late-lit fires.[a]

It is not the country of these men, so much as it is their life, that is "directly opposite" to our own. [3]There may be Antipodes dwelling in this same city of ours who, in Cato's

[a] Vergil, *Georg.* i. 250 ff.

words,[a] "have never seen the sun rise or set." Do you think that these men know how to live, if they do not know when to live? Do these men fear death, if they have buried themselves alive? They are as weird as the birds of night.[b] Although they pass their hours of darkness amid wine and perfumes, although they spend the whole extent of their unnatural waking hours in eating dinners – and those too cooked separately to make up many courses – they are not really banqueting; they are conducting their own funeral services. And the dead at least have their banquets by daylight.[c]

But indeed to one who is active no day is long. So let us lengthen our lives; for the duty and the proof of life consist in action. Cut short the night: use some of it for the day's business. [4]Birds that are being prepared for the banquet, that they may be easily fattened through lack of exercise, are kept in darkness; and similarly, if men vegetate without physical activity, their idle bodies are overwhelmed with flesh, and in their self-satisfied retirement the fat of indolence grows upon them. Moreover, the bodies of those who have sworn allegiance to the hours of darkness have a loathsome appearance. Their complexions are more alarming than those of anaemic invalids; they are lackadaisical and flabby with dropsy; though still alive, they are already carrion. But this, to my thinking, would be among the least of their evils. How much more darkness there is in their souls! Such a man is internally dazed; his vision is darkened; he envies the blind. And what man ever had eyes for the purpose of seeing in the dark?

[5]You ask me how this depravity comes upon the soul – this habit of reversing the daylight and giving over one's whole existence to the night? All vices rebel against Nature; they all

[a] Cato, Frag. p. 110 Jordan.

[b] i.e., owls, of ill omen.

[c] n connexion with the *Parentalia*, Feb. 13-21, and at other anniversary observations, the ceremonies were held in the daytime.

abandon the appointed order. It is the motto of luxury to enjoy what is unusual, and not only to depart from that which is right, but to leave it as far behind as possible, and finally even take a stand in opposition thereto. [6]Do you not believe that men live contrary to Nature who drink fasting,[a] who take wine into empty veins, and pass to their food in a state of intoxication? And yet this is one of youth's popular vices – to perfect their strength in order to drink on the very threshold of the bath, amid the unclad bathers; nay even to soak in wine and then immediately to rub off the sweat which they have promoted by many a hot glass of liquor! To them, a glass after lunch or one after dinner is bourgeois; it is what the country squires do, who are not connoisseurs in pleasure. This unmixed wine delights them just because there is no food to float in it, because it readily makes its way into their muscles; this boozing pleases them just because the stomach is empty.

[7]Do you not believe that men live contrary to Nature who exchange the fashion of their attire with women?[b] Do not men live contrary to Nature who endeavour to look fresh and boyish at an age unsuitable for such an attempt? What could be more cruel or more wretched? Cannot time and man's estate ever carry such a person beyond an artificial boyhood?[c] [8]Do not men live contrary to Nature who crave roses in winter, or seek to raise a spring flower like the lily by means of hot-water heaters and artificial changes of

[a] A vice which Seneca especially abhors; cf. Ep. xv. 3 *multum potionis altius ieiunio iturae.*

[b] By wearing silk gowns of transparent material.

[c] Not literally translated. For the same thought see Ep. xlvii. 7, etc. *Transcriber's note: The Latin which Gummere refused to translate literally is "Numquam vir erit, ut diu virum pati possit? Et cum illum contumeliae sexus eripuisse debuerat, non ne aetas quidem eripiet?" or roughly: "Will he never become a man, so that he can continue to be screwed by men? And though his sex ought to spare him this insult, won't even his age spare him?"*

temperature? Do not men live contrary to Nature who grow fruit-trees on the top of a wall? Or raise waving forests upon the roofs and battlements of their houses – the roots starting at a point to which it would be outlandish for the tree-tops to reach? Do not men live contrary to Nature who lay the foundations of bathrooms in the sea and do not imagine that they can enjoy their swim unless the heated pool is lashed as with the waves of a storm?

⁹When men have begun to desire all things in opposition to the ways of Nature, they end by entirely abandoning the ways of Nature. They cry: "It is daytime – let us go to sleep! It is the time when men rest: now for exercise, now for our drive, now for our lunch! Lo, the dawn approaches: it is dinner-time! We should not do as mankind do. It is low and mean to live in the usual and conventional way. Let us abandon the ordinary sort of day. Let us have a morning that is a special feature of ours, peculiar to ourselves!" ¹⁰Such men are, in my opinion, as good as dead. Are they not all but present at a funeral – and before their time too – when they live amid torches and tapers?ᵃ I remember that this sort of life was very fashionable at one time: among such men as Acilius Buta, a person of praetorian rank, who ran through a tremendous estate and on confessing his bankruptcy to Tiberius, received the answer: "You have waked up too late!" ¹¹Julius Montanus was once reading a poem aloud he was a middling good poet, noted for his friendship with Tiberius, as well as his fall from favour. He always used to fill his poems with a generous sprinkling of sunrises and sunsets. Hence, when a certain person was complaining that Montanus had read all day long, and declared that no man should attend any of his readings, Natta Pinariusᵇ remarked: "I couldn't

---

ᵃ The symbols of a Roman funeral. For the same practice, purposely performed, see Ep. xii. 8 (and the note of W. C. Summers).

ᵇ Called by Tacitus, *Ann.* iv. 34, a *Seiani cliens.*

make a fairer bargain than this: I am ready to listen to him from sunrise to sunset!" [12]Montanus was reading, and had reached the words:[a]

> 'Gins the bright morning to spread forth his flames clear-burning; the red dawn
> Scatters its light; and the sad-eyed swallow[b] returns to her nestlings,
> Bringing the chatterers' food, and with sweet bill sharing and serving.

Then Varus, a Roman knight, the hanger-on of Marcus Vinicius,[c] and a sponger at elegant dinners which he earned by his degenerate wit, shouted: "Bed-time for Buta!" [13]And later, when Montanus declaimed

> Lo, now the shepherds have folded their flocks, and the slow-moving darkness
> 'Gins to spread silence o'er lands that are drowsily lulled into slumber,

this same Varus remarked: "What? Night already? I'll go and pay my morning call on Buta!" You see, nothing was more notorious than Buta's upside-down manner of life. But this life, as I said, was fashionable at one time. [14]And the reason why some men live thus is not because they think that night in itself offers any greater attractions, but because that which is normal gives them no particular pleasure; light being a bitter enemy of the evil conscience, and, when one craves or scorns all things in proportion as they have cost

[a] Baehrens, *Frag. Poet. Rom.* p. 355.

[b] i.e., Procne, in the well-known nightingale myth.

[c] Son of the P. Vinicius ridiculed in Ep. xl. 9. He was husband of Julia, youngest daughter of Germanicus, and was poisoned by Messalina.

one much or little, illumination for which one does not pay is an object of contempt. Moreover, the luxurious person wishes to be an object of gossip his whole life; if people are silent about him, he thinks that he is wasting his time. Hence he is uncomfortable whenever any of his actions escape notoriety.

Many men eat up their property, and many men keep mistresses. If you would win a reputation among such persons, you must make your programme not only one of luxury but one of notoriety; for in such a busy community wickedness does not discover the ordinary sort of scandal. [15]I heard Pedo Albinovanus, that most attractive story-teller, speaking of his residence above the town-house of Sextus Papinius. Papinius belonged to the tribe of those who shun the light. "About nine o'clock at night I hear the sound of whips. I ask what is going on, and they tell me that Papinius is going over his accounts.[a] About twelve there is a strenuous shouting; I ask what the matter is, and they say he is exercising his voice. About two A.M. I ask the significance of the sound of wheels; they tell me that he is off for a drive. [16]And at dawn there is a tremendous flurry-calling of slaves and butlers, and pandemonium among the cooks. I ask the meaning of this also, and they tell me that he has called for his cordial and his appetizer, after leaving the bath. His dinner," said Pedo, "never went beyond the day,[b] for he lived very sparingly; he was lavish with nothing but the night. Accordingly, if you believe those who call him tight-fisted and mean, you will call him also a 'slave of the lamp.'"[c]

[17]You should not be surprised at finding so many special

[a] i.e., is punishing his slaves for errors in the day's work.

[b] i.e., balancing the custom of the ordinary Roman, whose dinner never continued beyond nightfall.

[c] "'A liver by candle-light,' with a play on the word λίχνος, 'luxurious'" (Summers).

manifestations of the vices; for vices vary, and there are countless phases of them, nor can all their various kinds be classified. The method of maintaining righteousness is simple; the method of maintaining wickedness is complicated, and has infinite opportunity to swerve. And the same holds true of character; if you follow nature, character is easy to manage, free, and with very slight shades of difference; but the sort of person I have mentioned possesses badly warped character, out of harmony with all things, including himself. [18]The chief cause, however, of this disease seems to me to be a squeamish revolt from the normal existence. Just as such persons mark themselves off from others in their dress, or in the elaborate arrangement of their dinners, or in the elegance of their carriages; even so they desire to make themselves peculiar by their way of dividing up the hours of their day. They are unwilling to be wicked in the conventional way, because notoriety is the reward of their sort of wickedness. Notoriety is what all such men seek – men who are, so to speak, *living* backwards.

[19]For this reason, Lucilius, let us keep to the way which Nature has mapped out for us, and let us not swerve therefrom. If we follow Nature, all is easy and unobstructed; but if we combat Nature, our life differs not a whit from that of men who row against the current. Farewell.

CXXIII. ON THE CONFLICT BETWEEN PLEASURE AND VIRTUE

[1]Wearied with the discomfort rather than with the length of my journey, I have reached my Alban villa late at night, and I find nothing in readiness except myself. So I am getting rid of fatigue at my writing-table: I derive some good from this tardiness on the part of my cook and my baker. For I am communing with myself on this very topic – that nothing is heavy if one accepts it with a light heart, and that nothing need provoke one's anger if one does not add to one's pile of troubles by getting angry. [2]My baker is out of bread; but the overseer, or the house-steward, or one of my tenants can supply me therewith. "Bad bread!" you say. But just wait for it; it will become good. Hunger will make even such bread delicate and of the finest flavour. For that reason I must not eat until hunger bids me; so I shall wait and shall not eat until I can either get good bread or else cease to be squeamish about it. [3]It is necessary that one grow accustomed to slender fare: because there are many problems of time and place which will cross the path even of the rich man and one equipped for pleasure, and bring him up with a round turn. To have whatsoever he wishes is in no man's power; it is in his power not to wish for what he has not, but cheerfully to employ what comes to him. A great step towards independence is a

good-humoured stomach, one that is willing to endure rough treatment.

[4]You cannot imagine how much pleasure I derive from the fact that my weariness is becoming reconciled to itself; I am asking for no slaves to rub me down, no bath, and no other restorative except time. For that which toil has accumulated, rest can lighten. This repast, whatever it may be, will give me more pleasure than an inaugural banquet.[a] [5]For I have made trial of my spirit on a sudden – a simpler and a truer test. Indeed, when a man has made preparations and given himself a formal summons to be patient, it is not equally clear just how much real strength of mind he possesses; the surest proofs are those which one exhibits off-hand, viewing one's own troubles not only fairly but calmly, not flying into fits of temper or wordy wranglings, supplying one's own needs by not craving something which was really due, and reflecting that our habits may be unsatisfied, but never our own real selves. [6]How many things are superfluous we fail to realize until they begin to be wanting; we merely used them not because we needed them but because we had them. And how much do we acquire simply because our neighbours have acquired such things, or because most men possess them! Many of our troubles may be explained from the fact that we live according to a pattern, and, instead of arranging our lives according to reason, are led astray by convention.

There are things which, if done by the few, we should refuse to imitate; yet when the majority have begun to do them, we follow along – just as if anything were more honourable because it is more frequent! Furthermore, wrong views, when they have become prevalent, reach, in our eyes, the standard of righteousness. [7]Everyone now travels with Numidian outriders preceding him, with a troop of slave-runners to clear the way; we deem it disgraceful to have no

---

[a] i.e., a dinner given by an official when he entered upon (*adeo*) his office.

attendants who will elbow crowds from the road, or will prove, by a great cloud of dust, that a high dignitary is approaching! Everyone now possesses mules that are laden with crystal and myrrhine cups carved by skilled artists of great renown; it is disgraceful for all your baggage to be made up of that which can be rattled along without danger. Everyone has pages who ride along with ointment-covered faces so that the heat or the cold will not harm their tender complexions; it is disgraceful that none of your attendant slave-boys should show a healthy cheek, not covered with cosmetics.

[8]You should avoid conversation with all such persons: they are the sort that communicate and engraft their bad habits from one to another. We used to think that the very worst variety of these men were those who vaunted their words; but there are certain men who vaunt their wickedness. Their talk is very harmful; for even though it is not at once convincing, yet they leave the seeds of trouble in the soul, and the evil which is sure to spring into new strength follows us about even when we have parted from them. [9]Just as those who have attended a concert carry about in their heads the melodies and the charm of the songs they have heard – a proceeding which interferes with their thinking and does not allow them to concentrate upon serious subjects, – even so the speech of flatterers and enthusiasts over that which is depraved sticks in our minds long after we have heard them talk. It is not easy to rid the memory of a catching tune; it stays with us, lasts on, and comes back from time to time. Accordingly, you should close your ears against evil talk, and right at the outset, too; for when such talk has gained an entrance and the words are admitted and are in our minds, they become more shameless. [10]And then we begin to speak as follows: "Virtue, Philosophy, Justice – this is a jargon of empty words. The only way to be happy is to do yourself well. To eat, drink, and spend your money is the only real life, the only way to remind yourself that you are mortal. Our days

flow on, and life – which we cannot restore – hastens away from us. Why hesitate to come to our senses? This life of ours will not always admit pleasures; meantime, while it can do so, while it clamours for them, what profit lies in imposing thereupon frugality? Therefore get ahead of death, and let anything that death will filch from you be squandered now upon yourself. You have no mistress, no favourite slave to make your mistress envious; you are sober when you make your daily appearance in public; you dine as if you had to show your account-book to 'Papa'; but that is not living, it is merely going shares in someone else's existence. [11]And what madness it is to be looking out for the interests of your heir, and to deny yourself everything, with the result that you turn friends into enemies by the vast amount of the fortune you intend to leave! For the more the heir is to get from you, the more he will rejoice in your taking-off! All those sour fellows who criticize other men's lives in a spirit of priggishness and are real enemies to their own lives, playing schoolmaster to the world – you should not consider them as worth a farthing, nor should you hesitate to prefer good living to a good reputation."

[12]These are voices which you ought to shun just as Ulysses did; he would not sail past them until he was lashed to the mast. They are no less potent; they lure men from country, parents, friends, and virtuous ways; and by a hope that, if not base, is ill-starred, they wreck them upon a life of baseness. How much better to follow a straight course and attain a goal where the words "pleasant" and "honourable" have the same meaning![a] [13]This end will be possible for us if we understand that there are two classes of objects which either attract us or repel us. We are attracted by such things as riches, pleasures, beauty, ambition, and other such coaxing and pleasing objects; we are repelled by toil, death, pain,

[a] i.e., to live by Stoicism rather than by Epicureanism.

disgrace, or lives of greater frugality. We ought therefore to train ourselves so that we may avoid a fear of the one or a desire for the other. Let us fight in the opposite fashion: let us retreat from the objects that allure, and rouse ourselves to meet the objects that attack.

[14]Do you not see how different is the method of descending a mountain from that employed in climbing upwards? Men coming down a slope bend backwards; men ascending a steep place lean forward. For, my dear Lucilius, to allow yourself to put your body's weight ahead when coming down, or, when climbing up, to throw it backward is to comply with vice. The pleasures take one down hill but one must work upwards toward that which is rough and hard to climb; in the one case let us throw our bodies forward, in the others let us put the check-rein on them.

[15]Do you believe me to be stating now that only those men bring ruin to our ears, who praise pleasure, who inspire us with fear of pain – that element which is in itself provocative of fear? I believe that we are also in injured by those who masquerade under the disguise of the Stoic school and at the same time urge us on into vice. They boast that only the wise man and the learned is a lover.[a] "He alone has wisdom in this art; the wise man too is best skilled in drinking and feasting. Our study ought to be this alone: up to what age the bloom of love can endure!" [16]All this may be regarded as a concession to the ways of Greece; we ourselves should preferably turn our attention to words like these: "No man is good by chance. Virtue is something which must be learned. Pleasure is low, petty, to be deemed worthless, shared even by dumb animals – the tiniest and meanest of whom fly towards pleasure. Glory is an empty and fleeting thing, lighter than air. Poverty is an evil to no man unless he kick against the

[a] Meaning, in line with the Stoic paradoxes, that only the sage knows how to be rightly in love.

goads.[a] Death is not an evil; why need you ask? Death alone is the equal privilege of mankind. Superstition is the misguided idea of a lunatic; it fears those whom it ought to love; it is an outrage upon those whom it worships. For what difference is there between denying the gods and dishonouring them?"

[17]You should learn such principles as these, nay rather you should learn them by heart; philosophy ought not to try to explain away vice. For a sick man, when his physician bids him live recklessly, is doomed beyond recall. Farewell.

---

[a] *Transcriber's note: The Latin is "Paupertas nulli malum est nisi repugnanti,"* *i.e. "Poverty is an evil to noone unless they resist." Gummere's odd phrase* *"kick against the goads" is actually from the Bible (Acts 26:14)*

CXXIV. ON THE TRUE GOOD AS ATTAINED BY REASON

[1]Full many an ancient precept could I give,
Didst thou not shrink, and feel it shame to learn
Such lowly duties.[a]

But you do not shrink, nor are you deterred by any subtleties of study. For your cultivated mind is not wont to investigate such important subjects in a free-and-easy manner. I approve your method in that you make everything count towards a certain degree of progress, and in that you are disgruntled only when nothing can be accomplished by the greatest degree of subtlety. And I shall take pains to show that this is the case now also. Our question is, whether the Good is grasped by the senses or by the understanding; and the corollary thereto is that it does not exist in dumb animals or little children.

[2]Those who rate pleasure as the supreme ideal hold that the Good is a matter of the senses; but we Stoics maintain that it is a matter of the understanding, and we assign it to the mind. If the senses were to pass judgment on what is good, we should never reject any pleasure; for there is no pleasure that does not attract, no pleasure that does not please.

[a] Vergil, *Georg.* i. 176 f.

Conversely, we should undergo no pain voluntarily; for there is no pain that does not clash with the senses. [3]Besides, those who are too fond of pleasure and those who fear pain to the greatest degree would in that case not deserve reproof. But we condemn men who are slaves to their appetites and their lusts, and we scorn men who, through fear of pain, will dare no manly deed. But what wrong could such men be committing if they looked merely to the senses as arbiters of good and evil? For it is to the senses that you and yours have entrusted the test of things to be sought and things to be avoided!

[4]Reason, however, is surely the governing element in such a matter as this; as reason has made the decision concerning the happy life, and concerning virtue and honour also, so she has made the decision with regard to good and evil. For with them[a] the vilest part is allowed to give sentence about the better, so that the senses – dense as they are, and dull, and even more sluggish in man than in the other animals, – pass judgment on the Good. [5]Just suppose that one should desire to distinguish tiny objects by the touch rather than by the eyesight! There is no special faculty more subtle and acute than the eye, that would enable us to distinguish between good and evil. You see, therefore, in what ignorance of truth a man spends his days and how abjectly he has overthrown lofty and divine ideals, if he thinks that the sense of touch can pass judgment upon the nature of the Supreme Good and the Supreme Evil! [6]He[b] says: "Just as every science and every art should possess an element that is palpable and capable of being grasped by the senses (their source of origin and growth), even so the happy life derives its foundation and its beginnings from things that are palpable, and from that which falls within the scope

[a] i.e., the Epicureans.

[b] i.e., the advocate of the "touch" theory.

of the senses. Surely you admit that the happy life takes its beginnings from things palpable to the senses." [7]But we define as "happy" those things that are in accord with Nature. And that which is in accord with Nature is obvious and can be seen at once – just as easily as that which is complete. That which is according to Nature, that which is given us as a gift immediately at our birth, is, I maintain, not a Good, but the beginning of a Good. You, however, assign the Supreme Good, pleasure, to mere babies, so that the child at its birth begins at the point whither the perfected man arrives. You are placing the tree-top where the root ought to be. [8]If anyone should say that the child, hidden in its mother's womb, of unknown sex too, delicate, unformed, and shapeless – if one should say that this child is already in a state of goodness, he would clearly seem to be astray in his ideas. And yet how little difference is there between one who has just lately received the gift of life, and one who is still a hidden burden in the bowels of the mother! They are equally developed, as far as their understanding of good or evil is concerned; and a child is as yet no more capable of comprehending the Good than is a tree or any dumb beast.

But why is the Good non-existent in a tree or in a dumb beast? Because there is no reason there, either. For the same cause, then, the Good is non-existent in a child, for the child also has no reason; the child will reach the Good only when he reaches reason.[a] [9]There are animals without reason, there are animals not yet endowed with reason, and there are animals who possess reason, but only incompletely;[b] in none of these does the Good exist, for it is reason that brings the Good in its company. What, then,

---

[a] According to the Stoics (and other schools also), the "innate notions," or groundwork of knowledge, begin to be subject to reason after the attainment of a child's seventh year.

[b] i.e., they are limited to "practical judgment."

is the distinction between the classes which I have mentioned? In that which does not possess reason, the Good will never exist. In that which is not yet endowed with reason, the Good cannot be existent at the time. And in that which possesses reason but only incompletely, the Good is capable of existing, but does not yet exist. [10]This is what I mean, Lucilius: the Good cannot be discovered in any random person, or at any random age; and it is as far removed from infancy as last is from first, or as that which is complete from that which has just sprung into being. Therefore, it cannot exist in the delicate body, when the little frame has only just begun to knit together. Of course not – no more than in the seed. [11]Granting the truth of this, we understand that there is a certain kind of Good of a tree or in a plant; but this is not true of its first growth, when the plant has just begun to spring forth out of the ground. There is a certain Good of wheat: it is not yet existent, however, in the swelling stalk, nor when the soft ear is pushing itself out of the husk, but only when summer days and its appointed maturity have ripened the wheat. Just as Nature in general does not produce her Good until she is brought to perfection, even so man's Good does not exist in man until both reason and man are perfected. [12]And what is this Good? I shall tell you: it is a free mind, an upright mind, subjecting other things to itself and itself to nothing. So far is infancy from admitting this Good that boyhood has no hope of it, and even young manhood cherishes the hope without justification; even our old age is very fortunate if it has reached this Good after long and concentrated study. If this, then, is the Good, the good is a matter of the understanding.

[13]"But," comes the retort, "you admitted that there is a certain Good of trees and of grass; then surely there can be a certain Good of a child also." But the true Good is not found in trees or in dumb animals the Good which exists in them

is called good only by courtesy.[a] "Then what is it?" you say. Simply that which is in accord with the nature of each. The real Good cannot find a place in dumb animals – not by any means; its nature is more blest and is of a higher class. And where there is no place for reason, the Good does not exist. [14]There are four natures which we should mention here: of the tree, animal, man, and God. The last two, having reasoning power, are of the same nature, distinct only by virtue of the immortality of the one and the mortality of the other. Of one of these, then – to wit God – it is Nature that perfects the Good; of the other – to wit man – pains and study do so. All other things are perfect only in their particular nature, and not truly perfect, since they lack reason.

Indeed, to sum up, that alone is perfect which is perfect according to nature as a whole, and nature as a whole is possessed of reason. Other things can be perfect according to their kind. [15]That which cannot contain the happy life cannot contain that which produces the happy life; and the happy life is produced by Goods alone. In dumb animals there is not a trace of the happy life, nor of the means whereby the happy life is produced; in dumb animals the Good does not exist. [16]The dumb animal comprehends the present world about him through his senses alone. He remembers the past only by meeting with something which reminds his senses; a horse, for example, remembers the right road only when he is placed at the starting-point. In his stall, however, he has no memory of the road, no matter how often he may have stepped along it. The third state – the future – does not come within the ken of dumb beasts.

[17]How, then, can we regard as perfect the nature of those who have no experience of time in its perfection? For time is three-fold, – past, present, and future. Animals perceive only

---

[a] Just as Academic and Peripatetic philosophers sometimes defined as "goods" what the Stoics called "advantages."

the time which is of greatest moment to them within the limits of their coming and going – the present. Rarely do they recollect the past – and that only when they are confronted with present reminders.[18] Therefore the Good of a perfect nature cannot exist in an imperfect nature; for if the latter sort of nature should possess the Good, so also would mere vegetation. I do not indeed deny that dumb animals have strong and swift impulses toward actions which seem according to nature, but such impulses are confused and disordered. The Good however, is never confused or disordered.

[19]"What!" you say, "do dumb animals move in disturbed and ill-ordered fashion?" I should say that they moved in disturbed and ill-ordered fashion, if their nature admitted of order; as it is, they move in accordance with their nature. For that is said to be "disturbed" which can also at some other time be "not disturbed"; so, too, that is said to be in a state of trouble which can be in a state of peace. No man is vicious except one who has the capacity of virtue; in the case of dumb animals their motion is such as results from their nature. [20]But, not to weary you, a certain sort of good will be found in a dumb animal, and a certain sort of virtue, and a certain sort of perfection – but neither the Good, nor virtue, nor perfection in the absolute sense. For this is the privilege of reasoning beings alone, who are permitted to know the cause, the degree, and the means. Therefore, good can exist only in that which possesses reason.

[21]Do you ask now whither our argument is tending, and of what benefit it will be to your mind? I will tell you: it exercises and sharpens the mind, and ensures, by occupying it honourably, that it will accomplish some sort of good. And even that is beneficial which holds men back when they are hurrying into wickedness. However, I will say this also: I can be of no greater benefit to you than by revealing the Good that is rightly yours, by taking you out of the class of dumb animals, and by placing you on a level with God. [22]Why, pray,

do you foster and practise your bodily strength? Nature has granted strength in greater degree to cattle and wild beasts. Why cultivate your beauty? After all your efforts, dumb animals surpass you in comeliness. Why dress your hair with such unending attention? Though you let it down in Parthian fashion, or tie it up in the German style, or, as the Scythians do, let it flow wild – yet you will see a mane of greater thickness tossing upon any horse you choose, and a mane of greater beauty bristling upon the neck of any lion. And even after training yourself for speed, you will be no match for the hare. [23]Are you not willing to abandon all these details – wherein you must acknowledge defeat, striving as you are for something that is not your own and come back to the Good that is really yours?

And what is this Good? It is a clear and flawless mind, which rivals that of God,[a] raised far above mortal concerns, and counting nothing of its own to be outside itself. You are a reasoning animal. What Good, then, lies within you? Perfect reason. Are you willing to develop this to its farthest limits – to its greatest degree of increase? [24]Only consider yourself happy when all your joys are born of reason, and when – having marked all the objects which men clutch at, or pray for, or watch over – you find nothing which you will desire; mind, I do not say *prefer*. Here is a short rule by which to measure yourself, and by the test of which you may feel that you have reached perfection: "You will come to your own when you shall understand that those whom the world calls fortunate are really the most unfortunate of all." Farewell.

---

[a] One of the most conspicuous Stoic paradoxes maintained that "the wise man is a God."

Accoucheur NOUN a male midwife or doctor ❏ *I think my sister must have had some general idea that I was a young offender whom an Accoucheur Policemen had taken up (on my birthday) and delivered over to her* (*Great Expectations* by Charles Dickens)

addled ADJ confused and unable to think properly ❏ *But she counted and counted till she got that addled* (*The Adventures of Huckleberry Finn* by Mark Twain)

admiration NOUN amazement or wonder ❏ *lifting up his hands and eyes by way of admiration* (*Gulliver's Travels* by Jonathan Swift)

afeard ADJ afeard means afraid ❏ *shake it–and don't be afeard* (*The Adventures of Huckleberry Finn* by Mark Twain)

affected VERB affected means to assume the appearance of ❏ *Hadst thou affected sweet divinity* (*Doctor Faustus 5.2* by Christopher Marlowe)

aground ADV when a boat runs aground, it touches the ground in a shallow part of the water and gets stuck ❏ *what kep' you?–boat get aground?* (*The Adventures of Huckleberry Finn* by Mark Twain)

ague NOUN a fever in which the patient has alternate hot and cold shivering fits ❏ *his exposure to the wet and cold had brought on fever and ague* (*Oliver Twist* by Charles Dickens)

alchemy ADJ false or worthless ❏ *all wealth alchemy* (*The Sun Rising* by John Donne)

all alike PHRASE the same all the time ❏ *Love, all alike* (*The Sun Rising* by John Donne)

alow and aloft PHRASE alow means in the lower part or bottom, and aloft means on the top, so alow and aloft means on the top and in the bottom or throughout ❏ *Someone's turned the chest out alow and aloft* (*Treasure Island* by Robert Louis Stevenson)

ambuscade NOUN ambuscade is not a proper word. Tom means an ambush, which is when a group of people attack their enemies, after hiding and waiting for them ❏ *and so we would lie in ambuscade, as he called it* (*The Adventures of Huckleberry Finn* by Mark Twain)

amiable ADJ likeable or pleasant ❏ *Such amiable qualities must speak for themselves* (*Pride and Prejudice* by Jane Austen)

amulet NOUN an amulet is a charm thought to drive away evil spirits. ❏ *uttered phrases at once occult and familiar, like the amulet worn on the heart* (*Silas Marner* by George Eliot)

amusement NOUN here amusement means a strange and disturbing puzzle ❏ *this was an amusement the other way* (*Robinson Crusoe* by Daniel Defoe)

ancient NOUN an ancient was the flag displayed on a ship to show which country it belongs to. It is also called the ensign ❏ *her ancient and pendants out* (*Robinson Crusoe* by Daniel Defoe)

antic ADJ here antic means horrible or grotesque ❏ *armed and dressed after a very antic manner* (*Gulliver's Travels* by Jonathan Swift)

antics NOUN antics is an old word meaning clowns, or people who do silly things to make other people laugh ❏ *And point like antics at his triple crown* (*Doctor Faustus 3.2* by Christopher Marlowe)

appanage NOUN an appanage is a living allowance ❏ *As if loveliness were not the special prerogative of woman–her legitimate appanage and heritage!* (*Jane Eyre* by Charlotte Brontë)

appended VERB appended means attached or added to ❏ *and these words appended* (*Treasure Island* by Robert Louis Stevenson)

approver NOUN an approver is someone who gives evidence against someone he used to work with ❏ *Mr. Noah Claypole: receiving a free pardon from the Crown in consequence of being admitted approver against Fagin* (*Oliver Twist* by Charles Dickens)

areas NOUN the areas is the space, below street level, in front of the basement of a house ❏ *The Dodger had a vicious propensity, too, of pulling the caps from the heads of small boys and tossing them down areas* (*Oliver Twist* by Charles Dickens)

argument NOUN theme or important idea or subject which runs through a piece of writing ❏ *Thrice needful to the argument which now* (*The Prelude* by William Wordsworth)

artificially ADV artfully or cleverly ❏ *and he with a sharp flint sharpened very artificially* (*Gulliver's Travels* by Jonathan Swift)

artist NOUN here artist means a skilled workman ❏ *This man was a most ingenious artist* (*Gulliver's Travels* by Jonathan Swift)

assizes NOUN assizes were regular court sessions which a visiting judge was in charge of ❏ *you shall hang at the next assizes* (*Treasure Island* by Robert Louis Stevenson)

attraction NOUN gravitation, or Newton's theory of gravitation ❏ *he predicted the same fate to attraction* (*Gulliver's Travels* by Jonathan Swift)

aver VERB to aver is to claim something strongly ❏ *for Jem Rodney, the mole catcher, averred that one evening as he was returning homeward* (*Silas Marner* by George Eliot)

baby NOUN here baby means doll, which is a child's toy that looks like a small person ❏ *and skilful dressing her baby* (*Gulliver's Travels* by Jonathan Swift)

bagatelle NOUN bagatelle is a game rather like billiards and pool ❏ *Breakfast had been ordered at a pleasant little tavern, a mile or so away upon the rising ground beyond the green; and there was a bagatelle board in the room, in case we should desire to unbend our minds after the solemnity.* (*Great Expectations* by Charles Dickens)

bah EXCLAM Bah is an exclamation of frustration or anger ❏ *"Bah," said Scrooge.* (*A Christmas Carol* by Charles Dickens)

bairn NOUN a northern word for child ❏ *Who has taught you those fine words, my bairn?* (*Wuthering Heights* by Emily Brontë)

bait VERB to bait means to stop on a journey to take refreshment ❏ *So, when they stopped to bait the horse, and ate and drank and enjoyed themselves, I could touch nothing that they touched, but kept my fast unbroken.* (*David Copperfield* by Charles Dickens)

balustrade NOUN a balustrade is a row of vertical columns that form railings ❏ *but I mean to say you might have got a hearse up that staircase, and taken it broadwise, with the splinter-bar towards the wall, and the door towards the balustrades: and done it easy* (*A Christmas Carol* by Charles Dickens)

bandbox NOUN a large lightweight box for carrying bonnets or hats ❏ *I am glad I bought my bonnet, if it is only for the fun of having another bandbox* (*Pride and Prejudice* by Jane Austen)

barren NOUN a barren here is a stretch or expanse of barren land ❏ *a line of upright stones, continued the* *length of the barren (Wuthering Heights by Emily Brontë)*

basin NOUN a basin was a cup without a handle ❏ *who is drinking his tea out of a basin (Wuthering Heights by Emily Brontë)*

battalia NOUN the order of battle ❏ *till I saw part of his army in battalia (Gulliver's Travels by Jonathan Swift)*

battery NOUN a Battery is a fort or a place where guns are positioned ❏ *You bring the lot to me, at that old Battery over yonder (Great Expectations by Charles Dickens)*

battledore and shuttlecock NOUN The game battledore and shuttlecock was an early version of the game now known as badminton. The aim of the early game was simply to keep the shuttlecock from hitting the ground. ❏ *Battledore and shuttlecock's a wery good game vhen you an't the shuttlecock and two lawyers the battledores, in which case it gets too excitin' to be pleasant (Pickwick Papers by Charles Dickens)*

beadle NOUN a beadle was a local official who had power over the poor ❏ *But these impertinences were speedily checked by the evidence of the surgeon, and the testimony of the beadle (Oliver Twist by Charles Dickens)*

bearings NOUN the bearings of a place are the measurements or directions that are used to find or locate it ❏ *the bearings of the island (Treasure Island by Robert Louis Stevenson)*

beaufet NOUN a beaufet was a sideboard ❏ *and sweet-cake from the beaufet (Emma by Jane Austen)*

beck NOUN a beck is a small stream ❏ *a beck which follows the bend of the glen (Wuthering Heights by Emily Brontë)*

bedight VERB decorated ❏ *and bedight with Christmas holly stuck into the top. (A Christmas Carol by Charles Dickens)*

Bedlam NOUN Bedlam was a lunatic asylum in London which had statues carved by Caius Gabriel Cibber at its entrance ❏ *Bedlam, and those carved maniacs at the gates (The Prelude by William Wordsworth)*

beeves NOUN oxen or castrated bulls which are animals used for pulling vehicles or carrying things ❏ *to deliver in every morning six beeves (Gulliver's Travels by Jonathan Swift)*

begot VERB created or caused ❏ *Begot in thee (On His Mistress by John Donne)*

behoof NOUN behoof means benefit ❏ *"Yes, young man," said he, releasing the handle of the article in question, retiring a step or two from my table, and speaking for the behoof of the landlord and waiter at the door (Great Expectations by Charles Dickens)*

berth NOUN a berth is a bed on a boat ❏ *this is the berth for me (Treasure Island by Robert Louis Stevenson)*

bevers NOUN a bever was a snack, or small portion of food, eaten between main meals ❏ *that buys me thirty meals a day and ten bevers (Doctor Faustus 2.1 by Christopher Marlowe)*

bilge water NOUN the bilge is the widest part of a ship's bottom, and the bilge water is the dirty water that collects there ❏ *no gush of bilge-water had turned it to fetid puddle (Jane Eyre by Charlotte Brontë)*

bills NOUN bills is an old term meaning prescription. A prescription is the piece of paper on which your doctor writes an order for medicine and which you give to a chemist to get the medicine ❏ *Are not thy bills hung up as monuments (Doctor Faustus 1.1 by Christopher Marlowe)*

black cap NOUN a judge wore a black cap when he was about to sentence a prisoner to death ❏ *The judge assumed the black cap, and the prisoner still stood with the same air and gesture.* (*Oliver Twist* by Charles Dickens)

boot-jack NOUN a wooden device to help take boots off ❏ *The speaker appeared to throw a boot-jack, or some such article, at the person he addressed* (*Oliver Twist* by Charles Dickens)

booty NOUN booty means treasure or prizes ❏ *would be inclined to give up their booty in payment of the dead man's debts* (*Treasure Island* by Robert Louis Stevenson)

Bow Street runner PHRASE Bow Street runners were the first British police force, set up by the author Henry Fielding in the eighteenth century ❏ *as would have convinced a judge or a Bow Street runner* (*Treasure Island* by Robert Louis Stevenson)

brawn NOUN brawn is a dish of meat which is set in jelly ❏ *Heaped up upon the floor, to form a kind of throne, were turkeys, geese, game, poultry, brawn, great joints of meat, suckling-pigs* (*A Christmas Carol* by Charles Dickens)

bray VERB when a donkey brays, it makes a loud, harsh sound ❏ *and she doesn't bray like a jackass* (*The Adventures of Huckleberry Finn* by Mark Twain)

break VERB in order to train a horse you first have to break it ❏ *"If a high-mettled creature like this," said he, "can't be broken by fair means, she will never be good for anything"* (*Black Beauty* by Anna Sewell)

bullyragging VERB bullyragging is an old word which means bullying. To bullyrag someone is to threaten or force someone to do something they don't want to do ❏ *and a lot of loafers bullyragging him for sport* (*The Adventures of Huckleberry Finn* by Mark Twain)

but PREP except for (this) ❏ *but this, all pleasures fancies be* (*The Good-Morrow* by John Donne)

by hand PHRASE by hand was a common expression of the time meaning that baby had been fed either using a spoon or a bottle rather than by breast-feeding ❏ *My sister, Mrs. Joe Gargery, was more than twenty years older than I, and had established a great reputation with herself . . . because she had bought me up "by hand"* (*Great Expectations* by Charles Dickens)

bye-spots NOUN bye-spots are lonely places ❏ *and bye-spots of tales rich with indigenous produce* (*The Prelude* by William Wordsworth)

calico NOUN calico is plain white fabric made from cotton ❏ *There was two old dirty calico dresses* (*The Adventures of Huckleberry Finn* by Mark Twain)

camp-fever NOUN camp-fever was another word for the disease typhus ❏ *during a severe camp-fever* (*Emma* by Jane Austen)

cant NOUN cant is insincere or empty talk ❏ *"Man," said the Ghost, "if man you be in heart, not adamant, forbear that wicked cant until you have discovered What the surplus is, and Where it is."* (*A Christmas Carol* by Charles Dickens)

canty ADJ canty means lively, full of life ❏ *My mother lived til eighty, a canty dame to the last* (*Wuthering Heights* by Emily Brontë)

canvas VERB to canvas is to discuss ❏ *We think so very differently on this point Mr Knightley, that there can be no use in canvassing it* (*Emma* by Jane Austen)

capital ADJ capital means excellent or extremely good ❏ *for it's capital, so shady, light, and big* (*Little Women* by Louisa May Alcott)

capstan NOUN a capstan is a device used on a ship to lift sails and anchors ❏ *capstans going, ships going out to sea, and unintelligible sea creatures roaring curses over the* *bulwarks at respondent lightermen* (*Great Expectations* by Charles Dickens)

case-bottle NOUN a square bottle designed to fit with others into a case ❑ *The spirit being set before him in a huge case-bottle, which had originally come out of some ship's locker* (*The Old Curiosity Shop* by Charles Dickens)

casement NOUN casement is a word meaning window. The teacher in *Nicholas Nickleby* misspells window showing what a bad teacher he is ❑ *W-i-n, win, d-e-r, der, winder, a casement.* (*Nicholas Nickleby* by Charles Dickens)

cataleptic ADJ a cataleptic fit is one in which the victim goes into a trancelike state and remains still for a long time ❑ *It was at this point in their history that Silas's cataleptic fit occurred during the prayer-meeting* (*Silas Marner* by George Eliot)

cauldron NOUN a cauldron is a large cooking pot made of metal ❑ *stirring a large cauldron which seemed to be full of soup* (*Alice's Adventures in Wonderland* by Lewis Carroll)

cephalic ADJ cephalic means to do with the head ❑ *with ink composed of a cephalic tincture* (*Gulliver's Travels* by Jonathan Swift)

chaise and four NOUN a closed four-wheel carriage pulled by four horses ❑ *he came down on Monday in a chaise and four to see the place* (*Pride and Prejudice* by Jane Austen)

chamberlain NOUN the main servant in a household ❑ *In those times a bed was always to be got there at any hour of the night, and the chamberlain, letting me in at his ready wicket, lighted the candle next in order on his shelf* (*Great Expectations* by Charles Dickens)

characters NOUN distinguishing marks ❑ *Impressed upon all forms the characters* (*The Prelude* by William Wordsworth)

chary ADJ cautious ❑ *I should have been chary of discussing my guardian too freely even with her* (*Great Expectations* by Charles Dickens)

cherishes VERB here cherishes means cheers or brightens ❑ *some philosophic song of Truth that cherishes our daily life* (*The Prelude* by William Wordsworth)

chickens' meat PHRASE chickens' meat is an old term which means chickens' feed or food ❑ *I had shook a bag of chickens' meat out in that place* (*Robinson Crusoe* by Daniel Defoe)

chimeras NOUN a chimera is an unrealistic idea or a wish which is unlikely to be fulfilled ❑ *with many other wild impossible chimeras* (*Gulliver's Travels* by Jonathan Swift)

chines NOUN chine is a cut of meat that includes part or all of the backbone of the animal ❑ *and they found hams and chines uncut* (*Silas Marner* by George Eliot)

chits NOUN chits is a slang word which means girls ❑ *I hate affected, niminy-piminy chits!* (*Little Women* by Louisa May Alcott)

chopped VERB chopped means come suddenly or accidentally ❑ *if I had chopped upon them* (*Robinson Crusoe* by Daniel Defoe)

chute NOUN a narrow channel ❑ *One morning about day-break, I found a canoe and crossed over a chute to the main shore* (*The Adventures of Huckleberry Finn* by Mark Twain)

circumspection NOUN careful observation of events and circumstances; caution ❑ *I honour your circumspection* (*Pride and Prejudice* by Jane Austen)

clambered VERB clambered means to climb somewhere with difficulty, usually using your hands and your feet ❑ *he clambered up and down stairs* (*Treasure Island* by Robert Louis Stevenson)

clime NOUN climate ❑ *no season knows nor clime* (*The Sun Rising* by John Donne)

clinched VERB clenched ❑ *the tops whereof I could but just reach with my fist clinched* (*Gulliver's Travels* by Jonathan Swift)

close chair NOUN a close chair is a sedan chair, which is an covered chair which has room for one person. The sedan chair is carried on two poles by two men, one in front and one behind ❑ *persuaded even the Empress herself to let me hold her in her close chair* (*Gulliver's Travels* by Jonathan Swift)

clown NOUN clown here means peasant or person who lives off the land ❑ *In ancient days by emperor and clown* (*Ode on a Nightingale* by John Keats)

coalheaver NOUN a coalheaver loaded coal onto ships using a spade ❑ *Good, strong, wholesome medicine, as was given with great success to two Irish labourers and a coalheaver* (*Oliver Twist* by Charles Dickens)

coal-whippers NOUN men who worked at docks using machines to load coal onto ships ❑ *here, were colliers by the score and score, with the coal-whippers plunging off stages on deck* (*Great Expectations* by Charles Dickens)

cobweb NOUN a cobweb is the net which a spider makes for catching insects ❑ *the walls and ceilings were all hung round with cobwebs* (*Gulliver's Travels* by Jonathan Swift)

coddling VERB coddling means to treat someone too kindly or protect them too much ❑ *and I've been coddling the fellow as if I'd been his grandmother* (*Little Women* by Louisa May Alcott)

coil NOUN coil means noise or fuss or disturbance ❑ *What a coil is there?* (*Doctor Faustus 4.7* by Christopher Marlowe)

collared VERB to collar something is a slang term which means to capture.

In this sentence, it means he stole it [the money] ❑ *he collared it* (*The Adventures of Huckleberry Finn* by Mark Twain)

colling VERB colling is an old word which means to embrace and kiss ❑ *and no clasping and colling at all* (*Tess of the D'Urbervilles* by Thomas Hardy)

colloquies NOUN colloquy is a formal conversation or dialogue ❑ *Such colloquies have occupied many a pair of pale-faced weavers* (*Silas Marner* by George Eliot)

comfit NOUN sugar-covered pieces of fruit or nut eaten as sweets ❑ *and pulled out a box of comfits* (*Alice's Adventures in Wonderland* by Lewis Carroll)

coming out VERB when a girl came out in society it meant she was of marriageable age. In order to "come out" girls were expecting to attend balls and other parties during a season ❑ *The younger girls formed hopes of coming out a year or two sooner than they might otherwise have done* (*Pride and Prejudice* by Jane Austen)

commit VERB commit means arrest or stop ❑ *Commit the rascals* (*Doctor Faustus 4.7* by Christopher Marlowe)

commodious ADJ commodious means convenient ❑ *the most commodious and effectual ways* (*Gulliver's Travels* by Jonathan Swift)

commons NOUN commons is an old term meaning food shared with others ❑ *his pauper assistants ranged themselves behind him; the gruel was served out; and a long grace was said over the short commons.* (*Oliver Twist* by Charles Dickens)

complacency NOUN here complacency means a desire to please others. To-day complacency means feeling pleased with oneself without good reason. ❑ *'Twas thy power that raised the first complacency in me* (*The Prelude* by William Wordsworth)

complaisance NOUN complaisance was eagerness to please ❏ *we cannot wonder at his complaisance* (*Pride and Prejudice* by Jane Austen)

complaisant ADJ complaisant means polite ❏ *extremely cheerful and complaisant to their guest* (*Gulliver's Travels* by Jonathan Swift)

conning VERB conning means learning by heart ❏ *Or conning more* (*The Prelude* by William Wordsworth)

consequent NOUN consequence ❏ *as avarice is the necessary consequent of old age* (*Gulliver's Travels* by Jonathan Swift)

consorts NOUN concerts ❏ *The King, who delighted in music, had frequent consorts at Court* (*Gulliver's Travels* by Jonathan Swift)

conversible ADJ conversible meant easy to talk to, companionable ❏ *He can be a conversible companion* (*Pride and Prejudice* by Jane Austen)

copper NOUN a copper is a large pot that can be heated directly over a fire ❏ *He gazed in stupefied astonishment on the small rebel for some seconds, and then clung for support to the copper* (*Oliver Twist* by Charles Dickens)

copper-stick NOUN a copper-stick is the long piece of wood used to stir washing in the copper (or boiler) which was usually the biggest cooking pot in the house ❏ *It was Christmas Eve, and I had to stir the pudding for next day, with a copper-stick, from seven to eight by the Dutch clock* (*Great Expectations* by Charles Dickens)

counting-house NOUN a counting-house is a place where accountants work ❏ *Once upon a time–of all the good days in the year, on Christmas Eve–old Scrooge sat busy in his counting-house* (*A Christmas Carol* by Charles Dickens)

courtier NOUN a courtier is someone who attends the king or queen–a member of the court ❏ *next the ten courtiers;* (*Alice's Adventures in Wonderland* by Lewis Carroll)

covies NOUN covies were flocks of partridges ❏ *and will save all of the best covies for you* (*Pride and Prejudice* by Jane Austen)

cowed VERB cowed means frightened or intimidated ❏ *it cowed me more than the pain* (*Treasure Island* by Robert Louis Stevenson)

cozened VERB cozened means tricked or deceived ❏ *Do you remember, sir, how you cozened me* (*Doctor Faustus 4.7* by Christopher Marlowe)

cravats NOUN a cravat is a folded cloth that a man wears wrapped around his neck as a decorative item of clothing ❏ *we'd 'a' slept in our cravats to-night* (*The Adventures of Huckleberry Finn* by Mark Twain)

crock and dirt PHRASE crock and dirt is an old expression meaning soot and dirt ❏ *and the mare catching cold at the door, and the boy grimed with crock and dirt* (*Great Expectations* by Charles Dickens)

crockery NOUN here crockery means pottery ❏ *By one of the parrots was a cat made of crockery* (*The Adventures of Huckleberry Finn* by Mark Twain)

crooked sixpence PHRASE it was considered unlucky to have a bent sixpence ❏ *You've got the beauty, you see, and I've got the luck, so you must keep me by you for your crooked sixpence* (*Silas Marner* by George Eliot)

croquet NOUN croquet is a traditional English summer game in which players try to hit wooden balls through hoops ❏ *and once she remembered trying to box her own ears for having cheated herself in a game of croquet* (*Alice's Adventures in Wonderland* by Lewis Carroll)

cross PREP across ❏ *The two great streets, which run cross and divide it into four quarters* (*Gulliver's Travels* by Jonathan Swift)

culpable ADJ if you are culpable for something it means you are to blame ❑ *deep are the sorrows that spring from false ideas for which no man is culpable.* (*Silas Marner* by George Eliot)

cultured ADJ cultivated ❑ *Nor less when spring had warmed the cultured Vale* (*The Prelude* by William Wordsworth)

cupidity NOUN cupidity is greed ❑ *These people hated me with the hatred of cupidity and disappointment.* (*Great Expectations* by Charles Dickens)

curricle NOUN an open two-wheeled carriage with one seat for the driver and space for a single passenger ❑ *and they saw a lady and a gentleman in a curricle* (*Pride and Prejudice* by Jane Austen)

cynosure NOUN a cynosure is something that strongly attracts attention or admiration ❑ *Then I thought of Eliza and Georgiana; I beheld one the cynosure of a ballroom, the other the inmate of a convent cell* (*Jane Eyre* by Charlotte Brontë)

dalliance NOUN someone's dalliance with something is a brief involvement with it ❑ *nor sporting in the dalliance of love* (*Doctor Faustus Chorus* by Christopher Marlowe)

darkling ADV darkling is an archaic way of saying in the dark ❑ *Darkling I listen* (*Ode on a Nightingale* by John Keats)

delf-case NOUN a sideboard for holding dishes and crockery ❑ *at the pewter dishes and delf-case* (*Wuthering Heights* by Emily Brontë)

determined ■ VERB here determined means ended ❑ *and be out of vogue when that was determined* (*Gulliver's Travels* by Jonathan Swift) ■ VERB determined can mean to have been learned or found especially by investigation or experience ❑ *All the sensitive feelings it wounded so cruelly, all the shame and misery it kept alive within my breast, became more poignant as I thought of this; and I determined that the life was unendurable* (*David Copperfield* by Charles Dickens)

Deuce NOUN a slang term for the Devil ❑ *Ah, I dare say I did. Deuce take me, he added suddenly, I know I did. I find I am not quite unscrewed yet.* (*Great Expectations* by Charles Dickens)

diabolical ADJ diabolical means devilish or evil ❑ *and with a thousand diabolical expressions* (*Treasure Island* by Robert Louis Stevenson)

direction NOUN here direction means address ❑ *Elizabeth was not surprised at it, as Jane had written the direction remarkably ill* (*Pride and Prejudice* by Jane Austen)

discover VERB to make known or announce ❑ *the Emperor would discover the secret while I was out of his power* (*Gulliver's Travels* by Jonathan Swift)

dissemble VERB hide or conceal ❑ *Dissemble nothing* (*On His Mistress* by John Donne)

dissolve VERB dissolve here means to release from life, to die ❑ *Fade far away, dissolve, and quite forget* (*Ode on a Nightingale* by John Keats)

distrain VERB to distrain is to seize the property of someone who is in debt in compensation for the money owed ❑ *for he's threatening to distrain for it* (*Silas Marner* by George Eliot)

Divan NOUN a Divan was originally a Turkish council of state–the name was transferred to the couches they sat on and is used to mean this in English ❑ *Mr Brass applauded this picture very much, and the bed being soft and comfortable, Mr Quilp determined to use it, both as a sleeping place by night and as a kind of Divan by day.* (*The Old Curiosity Shop* by Charles Dickens)

divorcement NOUN separation ❑ *By all pains which want and divorcement* *hath* (*On His Mistress* by John Donne)

dog in the manger, PHRASE this phrase describes someone who prevents you from enjoying something that they themselves have no need for ❏ *You are a dog in the manger, Cathy, and desire no one to be loved but yourself* (*Wuthering Heights* by Emily Brontë)

dolorifuge NOUN dolorifuge is a word which Thomas Hardy invented. It means pain-killer or comfort ❏ *as a species of dolorifuge* (*Tess of the D'Urbervilles* by Thomas Hardy)

dome NOUN building ❏ *that river and that mouldering dome* (*The Prelude* by William Wordsworth)

domestic NOUN here domestic means a person's management of the house ❏ *to give some account of my domestic* (*Gulliver's Travels* by Jonathan Swift)

dunce NOUN a dunce is another word for idiot ❏ *Do you take me for a dunce? Go on?* (*Alice's Adventures in Wonderland* by Lewis Carroll)

Ecod EXCLAM a slang exclamation meaning "oh God!" ❏ *"Ecod," replied Wemmick, shaking his head, "that's not my trade."* (*Great Expectations* by Charles Dickens)

egg-hot NOUN an egg-hot (see also "flip" and "negus") was a hot drink made from beer and eggs, sweetened with nutmeg ❏ *She fainted when she saw me return, and made a little jug of egg-hot afterwards to console us while we talked it over.* (*David Copperfield* by Charles Dickens)

encores NOUN an encore is a short extra performance at the end of a longer one, which the entertainer gives because the audience has enthusiastically asked for it ❏ *we want a little something to answer encores with, anyway* (*The Adventures of Huckleberry Finn* by Mark Twain)

equipage NOUN an elegant and impressive carriage ❏ *and besides, the equipage did not answer to any of*

their neighbours (*Pride and Prejudice* by Jane Austen)

exordium NOUN an exordium is the opening part of a speech ❏ *"Now, Handel," as if it were the grave beginning of a portentous business exordium, he had suddenly given up that tone* (*Great Expectations* by Charles Dickens)

expect VERB here expect means to wait for ❏ *to expect his farther commands* (*Gulliver's Travels* by Jonathan Swift)

familiars NOUN familiars means spirits or devils who come to someone when they are called ❏ *I'll turn all the lice about thee into familiars* (*Doctor Faustus 1.4* by Christopher Marlowe)

fantods NOUN a fantod is a person who fidgets or can't stop moving nervously ❏ *It most give me the fantods* (*The Adventures of Huckleberry Finn* by Mark Twain)

farthing NOUN a farthing is an old unit of British currency which was worth a quarter of a penny ❏ *Not a farthing less. A great many back-payments are included in it, I assure you.* (*A Christmas Carol* by Charles Dickens)

farthingale NOUN a hoop worn under a skirt to extend it ❏ *A bell with an old voice–which I dare say in its time had often said to the house, Here is the green farthingale* (*Great Expectations* by Charles Dickens)

favours NOUN here favours is an old word which means ribbons ❏ *A group of humble mourners entered the gate: wearing white favours* (*Oliver Twist* by Charles Dickens)

feigned VERB pretend or pretending ❏ *not my feigned page* (*On His Mistress* by John Donne)

fence ■ NOUN a fence is someone who receives and sells stolen goods ❏ *What are you up to? Ill-treating the boys, you covetous, avaricious, in-sa-ti-a-ble old fence?* (*Oliver Twist* by

Charles Dickens) ■ NOUN defence or protection ❑ *but honesty hath no fence against superior cunning* (*Gulliver's Travels* by Jonathan Swift)

fess ADJ fess is an old word which means pleased or proud ❑ *You'll be fess enough, my poppet* (*Tess of the D'Urbervilles* by Thomas Hardy)

fettered ADJ fettered means bound in chains or chained ❑ *"You are fettered," said Scrooge, trembling. "Tell me why?"* (*A Christmas Carol* by Charles Dickens)

fidges VERB fidges means fidgets, which is to keep moving your hands slightly because you are nervous or excited ❑ *Look, Jim, how my fingers fidges* (*Treasure Island* by Robert Louis Stevenson)

finger-post NOUN a finger-post is a sign-post showing the direction to different places ❑ *"The gallows," continued Fagin, "the gallows, my dear, is an ugly finger-post, which points out a very short and sharp turning that has stopped many a bold fellow's career on the broad highway."* (*Oliver Twist* by Charles Dickens)

fire-irons NOUN fire-irons are tools kept by the side of the fire to either cook with or look after the fire ❑ *the fire-irons came first* (*Alice's Adventures in Wonderland* by Lewis Carroll)

fire-plug NOUN a fire-plug is another word for a fire hydrant ❑ *The pony looked with great attention into a fire-plug, which was near him, and appeared to be quite absorbed in contemplating it* (*The Old Curiosity Shop* by Charles Dickens)

flank NOUN flank is the side of an animal ❑ *And all her silken flanks with garlands dressed* (*Ode on a Grecian Urn* by John Keats)

flip NOUN a flip is a drink made from warmed ale, sugar, spice and beaten egg ❑ *The events of the day, in combination with the twins, if not with the flip, had made Mrs.*

Micawber hysterical, and she shed tears as she replied (*David Copperfield* by Charles Dickens)

flit VERB flit means to move quickly ❑ *and if he had meant to flit to Thrushcross Grange* (*Wuthering Heights* by Emily Brontë)

floorcloth NOUN a floorcloth was a hard-wearing piece of canvas used instead of carpet ❑ *This avenging phantom was ordered to be on duty at eight on Tuesday morning in the hall (it was two feet square, as charged for floorcloth)* (*Great Expectations* by Charles Dickens)

fly-driver NOUN a fly-driver is a carriage drawn by a single horse ❑ *The fly-drivers, among whom I inquired next, were equally jocose and equally disrespectful* (*David Copperfield* by Charles Dickens)

fob NOUN a small pocket in which a watch is kept ❑ *"Certain," replied the man, drawing a gold watch from his fob* (*Oliver Twist* by Charles Dickens)

folly NOUN folly means foolishness or stupidity ❑ *the folly of beginning a work* (*Robinson Crusoe* by Daniel Defoe)

fond ADJ fond means foolish ❑ *Fond worldling* (*Doctor Faustus 5.2* by Christopher Marlowe)

fondness NOUN silly or foolish affection ❑ *They have no fondness for their colts or foals* (*Gulliver's Travels* by Jonathan Swift)

for his fancy PHRASE for his fancy means for his liking or as he wanted ❑ *and as I did not obey quick enough for his fancy* (*Treasure Island* by Robert Louis Stevenson)

forlorn ADJ lost or very upset ❑ *you are from that day forlorn* (*Gulliver's Travels* by Jonathan Swift)

foster-sister NOUN a foster-sister was someone brought up by the same nurse or in the same household ❑ *I had been his foster-sister* (*Wuthering Heights* by Emily Brontë)

fox-fire NOUN fox-fire is a weak glow that is given off by decaying, rotten wood ❑ *what we must have was a lot of them rotten chunks that's called fox-fire* (*The Adventures of Huckleberry Finn* by Mark Twain)

frozen sea PHRASE the Arctic Ocean ❑ *into the frozen sea* (*Gulliver's Travels* by Jonathan Swift)

gainsay VERB to gainsay something is to say it isn't true or to deny it ❑ *"So she had," cried Scrooge. "You're right. I'll not gainsay it, Spirit. God forbid!"* (*A Christmas Carol* by Charles Dickens)

gaiters NOUN gaiters were leggings made of a cloth or piece of leather which covered the leg from the knee to the ankle ❑ *Mr Knightley was hard at work upon the lower buttons of his thick leather gaiters* (*Emma* by Jane Austen)

galluses NOUN galluses is an old spelling of gallows, and here means suspenders. Suspenders are straps worn over someone's shoulders and fastened to their trousers to prevent the trousers falling down ❑ *and home-knit galluses* (*The Adventures of Huckleberry Finn* by Mark Twain)

galoot NOUN a sailor but also a clumsy person ❑ *and maybe a galoot on it chopping* (*The Adventures of Huckleberry Finn* by Mark Twain)

gayest ADJ gayest means the most lively and bright or merry ❑ *Beth played her gayest march* (*Little Women* by Louisa May Alcott)

gem NOUN here gem means jewellery ❑ *the mountain shook off turf and flower, had only heath for raiment and crag for gem* (*Jane Eyre* by Charlotte Brontë)

giddy ADJ giddy means dizzy ❑ *and I wish you wouldn't keep appearing and vanishing so suddenly; you make one quite giddy.* (*Alice's Adventures in Wonderland* by Lewis Carroll)

gig NOUN a light two-wheeled carriage ❑ *when a gig drove up to the garden gate: out of which there jumped a fat gentleman* (*Oliver Twist* by Charles Dickens)

gladsome ADJ gladsome is an old word meaning glad or happy ❑ *Nobody ever stopped him in the street to say, with gladsome looks* (*A Christmas Carol* by Charles Dickens)

glen NOUN a glen is a small valley; the word is used commonly in Scotland ❑ *a beck which follows the bend of the glen* (*Wuthering Heights* by Emily Brontë)

gravelled VERB gravelled is an old term which means to baffle or defeat someone ❑ *Gravelled the pastors of the German Church* (*Doctor Faustus 1.1* by Christopher Marlowe)

grinder NOUN a grinder was a private tutor ❑ *but that when he had had the happiness of marrying Mrs Pocket very early in his life, he had impaired his prospects and taken up the calling of a Grinder* (*Great Expectations* by Charles Dickens)

gruel NOUN gruel is a thin, watery cornmeal or oatmeal soup ❑ *and the little saucepan of gruel (Scrooge had a cold in his head) upon the hob.* (*A Christmas Carol* by Charles Dickens)

guinea, half a NOUN half a guinea was ten shillings and sixpence ❑ *but lay out half a guinea at Ford's* (*Emma* by Jane Austen)

gull VERB gull is an old term which means to fool or deceive someone ❑ *Hush, I'll gull him supernaturally* (*Doctor Faustus 3.4* by Christopher Marlowe)

gunnel NOUN the gunnel, or gunwale, is the upper edge of a boat's side ❑ *But he put his foot on the gunnel and rocked her* (*The Adventures of Huckleberry Finn* by Mark Twain)

gunwale NOUN the side of a ship ❑ *He dipped his hand in the water over the boat's gunwale* (*Great Expectations* by Charles Dickens)

Gytrash NOUN a Gytrash is an omen of misfortune to the superstitious, usually taking the form of a hound ❏ *I remembered certain of Bessie's tales, wherein figured a North-of-England spirit, called a "Gytrash"* (*Jane Eyre* by Charlotte Brontë)

hackney-cabriolet NOUN a two-wheeled carriage with four seats for hire and pulled by a horse ❏ *A hackney-cabriolet was in waiting; with the same vehemence which she had exhibited in addressing Oliver, the girl pulled him in with her, and drew the curtains close.* (*Oliver Twist* by Charles Dickens)

hackney-coach NOUN a four-wheeled horse-drawn vehicle for hire ❏ *The twilight was beginning to close in, when Mr. Brownlow alighted from a hackney-coach at his own door, and knocked softly.* (*Oliver Twist* by Charles Dickens)

haggler NOUN a haggler is someone who travels from place to place selling small goods and items ❏ *when I be plain Jack Durbeyfield, the haggler* (*Tess of the D'Urbervilles* by Thomas Hardy)

halter NOUN a halter is a rope or strap used to lead an animal or to tie it up ❏ *I had of course long been used to a halter and a headstall* (*Black Beauty* by Anna Sewell)

hamlet NOUN a hamlet is a small village or a group of houses in the countryside ❏ *down from the hamlet* (*Treasure Island* by Robert Louis Stevenson)

hand-barrow NOUN a hand-barrow is a device for carrying heavy objects. It is like a wheelbarrow except that it has handles, rather than wheels, for moving the barrow ❏ *his sea chest following behind him in a hand-barrow* (*Treasure Island* by Robert Louis Stevenson)

handspike NOUN a handspike was a stick which was used as a lever ❏ *a bit of stick like a handspike* (*Treasure Island* by Robert Louis Stevenson)

haply ADV haply means by chance or perhaps ❏ *And haply the Queen-Moon is on her throne* (*Ode on a Nightingale* by John Keats)

harem NOUN the harem was the part of the house where the women lived ❏ *mostly they hang round the harem* (*The Adventures of Huckleberry Finn* by Mark Twain)

hautboys NOUN hautboys are oboes ❏ *sausages and puddings resembling flutes and hautboys* (*Gulliver's Travels* by Jonathan Swift)

hawker NOUN a hawker is someone who sells goods to people as he travels rather than from a fixed place like a shop ❏ *to buy some stockings from a hawker* (*Treasure Island* by Robert Louis Stevenson)

hawser NOUN a hawser is a rope used to tie up or tow a ship or boat ❏ *Again among the tiers of shipping, in and out, avoiding rusty chain-cables, frayed hempen hawsers* (*Great Expectations* by Charles Dickens)

headstall NOUN the headstall is the part of the bridle or halter that goes around a horse's head ❏ *I had of course long been used to a halter and a headstall* (*Black Beauty* by Anna Sewell)

hearken VERB hearken means to listen ❏ *though we sometimes stopped to lay hold of each other and hearken* (*Treasure Island* by Robert Louis Stevenson)

heartless ADJ here heartless means without heart or dejected ❏ *I am not heartless* (*The Prelude* by William Wordsworth)

hebdomadal ADJ hebdomadal means weekly ❏ *It was the hebdomadal treat to which we all looked forward from Sabbath to Sabbath* (*Jane Eyre* by Charlotte Brontë)

highwaymen NOUN highwaymen were people who stopped travellers and robbed them ❏ *We are high-waymen* (*The Adventures of Huckleberry Finn* by Mark Twain)

hinds NOUN hinds means farm hands, or people who work on a farm ❑ *He called his hinds about him* (*Gulliver's Travels* by Jonathan Swift)

histrionic ADJ if you refer to someone's behaviour as histrionic, you are being critical of it because it is dramatic and exaggerated ❑ *But the histrionic muse is the darling* (*The Adventures of Huckleberry Finn* by Mark Twain)

hogs NOUN hogs is another word for pigs ❑ *Tom called the hogs "ingots"* (*The Adventures of Huckleberry Finn* by Mark Twain)

horrors NOUN the horrors are a fit, called delirium tremens, which is caused by drinking too much alcohol ❑ *I'll have the horrors* (*Treasure Island* by Robert Louis Stevenson)

huffy ADJ huffy means to be obviously annoyed or offended about something ❑ *They will feel that more than angry speeches or huffy actions* (*Little Women* by Louisa May Alcott)

hulks NOUN hulks were prison-ships ❑ *The miserable companion of thieves and ruffians, the fallen outcast of low haunts, the associate of the scourings of the jails and hulks* (*Oliver Twist* by Charles Dickens)

humbug NOUN humbug means nonsense or rubbish ❑ *"Bah," said Scrooge. "Humbug!"* (*A Christmas Carol* by Charles Dickens)

humours NOUN it was believed that there were four fluids in the body called humours which decided the temperament of a person depending on how much of each fluid was present ❑ *other peccant humours* (*Gulliver's Travels* by Jonathan Swift)

husbandry NOUN husbandry is farming animals ❑ *bad husbandry were plentifully anointing their wheels* (*Silas Marner* by George Eliot)

huswife NOUN a huswife was a small sewing kit ❑ *but I had put my huswife on it* (*Emma* by Jane Austen)

ideal ADJ ideal in this context means imaginary ❑ *I discovered the yell was not ideal* (*Wuthering Heights* by Emily Brontë)

If our two PHRASE if both our ❑ *If our two loves be one* (*The Good-Morrow* by John Donne)

ignis-fatuus NOUN ignis-fatuus is the light given out by burning marsh gases, which lead careless travellers into danger ❑ *it is madness in all women to let a secret love kindle within them, which, if unreturned and unknown, must devour the life that feeds it; and, if discovered and responded to, must lead ignis-fatuus-like, into miry wilds whence there is no extrication.* (*Jane Eyre* by Charlotte Brontë)

imaginations NOUN here imaginations means schemes or plans ❑ *soon drove out those imaginations* (*Gulliver's Travels* by Jonathan Swift)

impressible ADJ impressible means open or impressionable ❑ *for Marner had one of those impressible, self-doubting natures* (*Silas Marner* by George Eliot)

in good intelligence PHRASE friendly with each other ❑ *that these two persons were in good intelligence with each other* (*Gulliver's Travels* by Jonathan Swift)

inanity NOUN inanity is silliness or dull stupidity ❑ *Do we not wile away moments of inanity* (*Silas Marner* by George Eliot)

incivility NOUN incivility means rudeness or impoliteness ❑ *if it's only for a piece of incivility like to-night's* (*Treasure Island* by Robert Louis Stevenson)

indigenae NOUN indigenae means natives or people from that area ❑ *an exotic that the surly indigenae will not recognise for kin* (*Wuthering Heights* by Emily Brontë)

indocible ADJ unteachable ❑ *so they were the most restive and indocible* (*Gulliver's Travels* by Jonathan Swift)

ingenuity NOUN inventiveness ❑ *entreated me to give him something as an encouragement to ingenuity* (*Gulliver's Travels* by Jonathan Swift)

ingots NOUN an ingot is a lump of a valuable metal like gold, usually shaped like a brick ❑ *Tom called the hogs "ingots"* (*The Adventures of Huckleberry Finn* by Mark Twain)

inkstand NOUN an inkstand is a pot which was put on a desk to contain either ink or pencils and pens ❑ *throwing an inkstand at the Lizard as she spoke* (*Alice's Adventures in Wonderland* by Lewis Carroll)

inordinate ADJ without order. To-day inordinate means "excessive". ❑ *Though yet untutored and inordinate* (*The Prelude* by William Wordsworth)

intellectuals NOUN here intellectuals means the minds (of the workmen) ❑ *those instructions they give being too refined for the intellectuals of their workmen* (*Gulliver's Travels* by Jonathan Swift)

interview NOUN meeting ❑ *By our first strange and fatal interview* (*On His Mistress* by John Donne)

jacks NOUN jacks are rods for turning a spit over a fire ❑ *It was a small bit of pork suspended from the kettle hanger by a string passed through a large door key, in a way known to primitive housekeepers unpossessed of jacks* (*Silas Marner* by George Eliot)

jews-harp NOUN a jews-harp is a small, metal, musical instrument that is played by the mouth ❑ *A jews-harp's plenty good enough for a rat* (*The Adventures of Huckleberry Finn* by Mark Twain)

jorum NOUN a large bowl ❑ *while Miss Skiffins brewed such a jorum of tea, that the pig in the back premises became strongly excited* (*Great Expectations* by Charles Dickens)

jostled VERB jostled means bumped or pushed by someone or some people *being jostled himself into the kennel* (*Gulliver's Travels* by Jonathan Swift)

keepsake NOUN a keepsake is a gift which reminds someone of an event or of the person who gave it to them. ❑ *books and ornaments they had in their boudoirs at home: keepsakes that different relations had presented to them* (*Jane Eyre* by Charlotte Brontë)

kenned VERB kenned means knew ❑ *though little kenned the lamplighter that he had any company but Christmas!* (*A Christmas Carol* by Charles Dickens)

kennel NOUN kennel means gutter, which is the edge of a road next to the pavement, where rain water collects and flows away ❑ *being jostled himself into the kennel* (*Gulliver's Travels* by Jonathan Swift)

knock-knee ADJ knock-knee means slanted, at an angle. ❑ *LOT 1 was marked in whitewashed knock-knee letters on the brewhouse* (*Great Expectations* by Charles Dickens)

ladylike ADJ to be ladylike is to behave in a polite, dignified and graceful way ❑ *No, winking isn't ladylike* (*Little Women* by Louisa May Alcott)

lapse NOUN flow ❑ *Stealing with silent lapse to join the brook* (*The Prelude* by William Wordsworth)

larry NOUN larry is an old word which means commotion or noisy celebration ❑ *That was all a part of the larry!* (*Tess of the D'Urbervilles* by Thomas Hardy)

laths NOUN laths are strips of wood ❑ *The panels shrunk, the windows cracked; fragments of plaster fell out of the ceiling, and the naked laths were shown instead* (*A Christmas Carol* by Charles Dickens)

leer NOUN a leer is an unpleasant smile ❑ *with a kind of leer* (*Treasure Island* by Robert Louis Stevenson)

lenitives NOUN these are different kinds of drugs or medicines: lenitives and palliatives were pain relievers; aperitives were laxatives; abstersives caused vomiting; corrosives destroyed human tissue; restringents caused constipation; cephalalgics stopped headaches; icterics were used as medicine for jaundice; apophlegmatics were cough medicine, and acoustics were cures for the loss of hearing ❏ *lenitives, aperitives, abstersives, corrosives, restringents, palliatives, laxatives, cephalalgics, icterics, apophlegmatics, acoustics* (*Gulliver's Travels* by Jonathan Swift)

lest CONJ in case. If you do something lest something (usually) unpleasant happens you do it to try to prevent it happening ❏ *She went in without knocking, and hurried upstairs, in great fear lest she should meet the real Mary Ann* (*Alice's Adventures in Wonderland* by Lewis Carroll)

levee NOUN a levee is an old term for a meeting held in the morning, shortly after the person holding the meeting has got out of bed ❏ *I used to attend the King's levee once or twice a week* (*Gulliver's Travels* by Jonathan Swift)

life-preserver NOUN a club which had lead inside it to make it heavier and therefore more dangerous ❏ *and with no more suspicious articles displayed to view than two or three heavy bludgeons which stood in a corner, and a "life-preserver" that hung over the chimney-piece.* (*Oliver Twist* by Charles Dickens)

lighterman NOUN a lighterman is another word for sailor ❏ *in and out, hammers going in ship-builders' yards, saws going at timber, clashing engines going at things unknown, pumps going in leaky ships, capstans going, ships going out to sea, and unintelligible sea creatures roaring curses over the bulwarks at respondent lightermen* (*Great Expectations* by Charles Dickens)

livery NOUN servants often wore a uniform known as a livery ❏ *suddenly a footman in livery came running out of the wood* (*Alice's Adventures in Wonderland* by Lewis Carroll)

livid ADJ livid means pale or ash coloured. Livid also means very angry ❏ *a dirty, livid white* (*Treasure Island* by Robert Louis Stevenson)

lottery-tickets NOUN a popular card game ❏ *and Mrs. Philips protested that they would have a nice comfortable noisy game of lottery tickets* (*Pride and Prejudice* by Jane Austen)

lower and upper world PHRASE the earth and the heavens are the lower and upper worlds ❏ *the changes in the lower and upper world* (*Gulliver's Travels* by Jonathan Swift)

lustres NOUN lustres are chandeliers. A chandelier is a large, decorative frame which holds light bulbs or candles and hangs from the ceiling ❏ *the lustres, lights, the carving and the guilding* (*The Prelude* by William Wordsworth)

lynched VERB killed without a criminal trial by a crowd of people ❏ *He'll never know how nigh he come to getting lynched* (*The Adventures of Huckleberry Finn* by Mark Twain)

malingering VERB if someone is malingering they are pretending to be ill to avoid working ❏ *And you stand there malingering* (*Treasure Island* by Robert Louis Stevenson)

managing PHRASE treating with consideration ❏ *to think the honour of my own kind not worth managing* (*Gulliver's Travels* by Jonathan Swift)

manhood PHRASE manhood means human nature ❏ *concerning the nature of manhood* (*Gulliver's Travels* by Jonathan Swift)

man-trap NOUN a man-trap is a set of steel jaws that snap shut when trodden on and trap a person's leg

❑ *"Don't go to him," I called out of the window, "he's an assassin! A man-trap!"* (*Oliver Twist* by Charles Dickens)

maps NOUN charts of the night sky ❑ *Let maps to others, worlds on worlds have shown* (*The Good-Morrow* by John Donne)

mark VERB look at or notice ❑ *Mark but this flea, and mark in this* (*The Flea* by John Donne)

maroons NOUN A maroon is someone who has been left in a place which it is difficult for them to escape from, like a small island ❑ *if schooners, islands, and maroons* (*Treasure Island* by Robert Louis Stevenson)

mast NOUN here mast means the fruit of forest trees ❑ *a quantity of acorns, dates, chestnuts, and other mast* (*Gulliver's Travels* by Jonathan Swift)

mate VERB defeat ❑ *Where Mars did mate the warlike Carthigens* (*Doctor Faustus Chorus* by Christopher Marlowe)

mealy ADJ Mealy when used to describe a face meant pallid, pale or colourless ❑ *I only know two sorts of boys. Mealy boys, and beef-faced boys* (*Oliver Twist* by Charles Dickens)

middling ADV fairly or moderately ❑ *she worked me middling hard for about an hour* (*The Adventures of Huckleberry Finn* by Mark Twain)

mill NOUN a mill, or treadmill, was a device for hard labour or punishment in prison ❑ *Was you never on the mill?* (*Oliver Twist* by Charles Dickens)

milliner's shop NOUN a milliner's sold fabrics, clothing, lace and accessories; as time went on they specialized more and more in hats ❑ *to pay their duty to their aunt and to a milliner's shop just over the way* (*Pride and Prejudice* by Jane Austen)

minching un' munching PHRASE how people in the north of England used to describe the way people from the south speak ❑ *Minching un' munching!* (*Wuthering Heights* by Emily Brontë)

mine NOUN gold ❑ *Whether both th'Indias of spice and mine* (*The Sun Rising* by John Donne)

mire NOUN mud ❑ *Tis my fate to be always ground into the mire under the iron heel of oppression* (*The Adventures of Huckleberry Finn* by Mark Twain)

miscellany NOUN a miscellany is a collection of many different kinds of things ❑ *under that, the miscellany began* (*Treasure Island* by Robert Louis Stevenson)

mistarshers NOUN mistarshers means moustache, which is the hair that grows on a man's upper lip ❑ *when he put his hand up to his mistarshers* (*Tess of the D'Urbervilles* by Thomas Hardy)

morrow NOUN here good-morrow means tomorrow and a new and better life ❑ *And now good-morrow to our waking souls* (*The Good-Morrow* by John Donne)

mortification NOUN mortification is an old word for gangrene which is when part of the body decays or "dies" because of disease ❑ *Yes, it was a mortification—that was it* (*The Adventures of Huckleberry Finn* by Mark Twain)

mought VERB mought is an old spelling of might ❑ *what you mought call me? You mought call me captain* (*Treasure Island* by Robert Louis Stevenson)

move VERB move me not means do not make me angry ❑ *Move me not, Faustus* (*Doctor Faustus 2.1* by Christopher Marlowe)

muffin-cap NOUN a muffin-cap is a flat cap made from wool ❑ *the old one, remained stationary in the muffin-cap and leathers* (*Oliver Twist* by Charles Dickens)

mulatter NOUN a mulatter was another word for mulatto, which is a person with parents who are from different races ❏ *a mulatter, most as white as a white man* (*The Adventures of Huckleberry Finn* by Mark Twain)

mummery NOUN mummery is an old word that meant meaningless (or pretentious) ceremony ❏ *When they were all gone, and when Trabb and his men—but not his boy: I looked for him—had crammed their mummery into bags, and were gone too, the house felt wholesomer.* (*Great Expectations* by Charles Dickens)

nap NOUN the nap is the woolly surface on a new item of clothing. Here the surface has been worn away so it looks bare ❏ *like an old hat with the nap rubbed off* (*The Adventures of Huckleberry Finn* by Mark Twain)

natural ■ NOUN a natural is a person born with learning difficulties ❏ *though he had been left to his particular care by their deceased father, who thought him almost a natural.* (*David Copperfield* by Charles Dickens) ■ ADJ natural meant illegitimate ❏ *Harriet Smith was the natural daughter of somebody* (*Emma* by Jane Austen)

navigator NOUN a navigator was originally someone employed to dig canals. It is the origin of the word "navvy" meaning a labourer ❏ *She ascertained from me in a few words what it was all about, comforted Dora, and gradually convinced her that I was not a labourer—from my manner of stating the case I believe Dora concluded that I was a navigator, and went balancing myself up and down a plank all day with a wheelbarrow—and so brought us together in peace.* (*David Copperfield* by Charles Dickens)

necromancy NOUN necromancy means a kind of magic where the magician speaks to spirits or ghosts to find out what will happen in the future ❏ *He surfeits upon cursed necromancy* (*Doctor Faustus chorus* by Christopher Marlowe)

negus NOUN a negus is a hot drink made from sweetened wine and water ❏ *He sat placidly perusing the newspaper, with his little head on one side, and a glass of warm sherry negus at his elbow.* (*David Copperfield* by Charles Dickens)

nice ADJ discriminating. Able to make good judgements or choices ❏ *consequently a claim to be nice* (*Emma* by Jane Austen)

nigh ADV nigh means near ❏ *He'll never know how nigh he come to getting lynched* (*The Adventures of Huckleberry Finn* by Mark Twain)

nimbleness NOUN nimbleness means being able to move very quickly or skilfully ❏ *and with incredible accuracy and nimbleness* (*Treasure Island* by Robert Louis Stevenson)

noggin NOUN a noggin is a small mug or a wooden cup ❏ *you'll bring me one noggin of rum* (*Treasure Island* by Robert Louis Stevenson)

none ADJ neither ❏ *none can die* (*The Good-Morrow* by John Donne)

notices NOUN observations ❏ *Arch are his notices* (*The Prelude* by William Wordsworth)

occiput NOUN occiput means the back of the head ❏ *saw off the occiput of each couple* (*Gulliver's Travels* by Jonathan Swift)

officiously ADV kindly ❏ *the governess who attended Glumdalclitch very officiously lifted me up* (*Gulliver's Travels* by Jonathan Swift)

old salt PHRASE old salt is a slang term for an experienced sailor ❏ *a "true sea-dog", and a "real old salt"* (*Treasure Island* by Robert Louis Stevenson)

or ere PHRASE before ❏ *or ere the Hall was built* (*The Prelude* by William Wordsworth)

ostler NOUN one who looks after horses at an inn ❏ *The bill paid, and the waiter remembered, and the ostler not forgotten, and the chambermaid taken into consideration* (*Great Expectations* by Charles Dickens)

ostry NOUN an ostry is an old word for a pub or hotel ❏ *lest I send you into the ostry with a vengeance* (*Doctor Faustus 2.2* by Christopher Marlowe)

outrunning the constable PHRASE outrunning the constable meant spending more than you earn ❏ *but I shall by this means be able to check your bills and to pull you up if I find you outrunning the constable.* (*Great Expectations* by Charles Dickens)

over ADV across ❏ *It is in length six yards, and in the thickest part at least three yards over* (*Gulliver's Travels* by Jonathan Swift)

over the broomstick PHRASE this is a phrase meaning "getting married without a formal ceremony" ❏ *They both led tramping lives, and this woman in Gerrard-street here, had been married very young, over the broomstick (as we say), to a tramping man, and was a perfect fury in point of jealousy.* (*Great Expectations* by Charles Dickens)

own VERB own means to admit or to acknowledge ❏ *It's my old girl that advises. She has the head. But I never own to it before her. Discipline must be maintained* (*Bleak House* by Charles Dickens)

page NOUN here page means a boy employed to run errands ❏ *not my feigned page* (*On His Mistress* by John Donne)

paid pretty dear PHRASE paid pretty dear means paid a high price or suffered quite a lot ❏ *I paid pretty dear for my monthly fourpenny piece* (*Treasure Island* by Robert Louis Stevenson)

pannikins NOUN pannikins were small tin cups ❏ *of lifting light glasses and cups to his lips, as if they were clumsy pannikins* (*Great Expectations* by Charles Dickens)

pards NOUN pards are leopards ❏ *Not charioted by Bacchus and his pards* (*Ode on a Nightingale* by John Keats)

parlour boarder NOUN a pupil who lived with the family ❏ *and somebody had lately raised her from the condition of scholar to parlour boarder* (*Emma* by Jane Austen)

particular, a London PHRASE London in Victorian times and up to the 1950s was famous for having very dense fog–which was a combination of real fog and the smog of pollution from factories ❏ *This is a London particular . . . A fog, miss* (*Bleak House* by Charles Dickens)

patten NOUN pattens were wooden soles which were fixed to shoes by straps to protect the shoes in wet weather ❏ *carrying a basket like the Great Seal of England in plaited straw, a pair of pattens, a spare shawl, and an umbrella, though it was a fine bright day* (*Great Expectations* by Charles Dickens)

paviour NOUN a paviour was a labourer who worked on the street pavement ❏ *the paviour his pickaxe* (*Oliver Twist* by Charles Dickens)

peccant ADJ peccant means unhealthy ❏ *other peccant humours* (*Gulliver's Travels* by Jonathan Swift)

penetralium NOUN penetralium is a word used to describe the inner rooms of the house ❏ *and I had no desire to aggravate his impatience previous to inspecting the penetralium* (*Wuthering Heights* by Emily Brontë)

pensive ADV pensive means deep in thought or thinking seriously about something ❏ *and she was leaning pensive on a tomb-stone on her right elbow* (*The Adventures of Huckleberry Finn* by Mark Twain)

penury NOUN penury is the state of being extremely poor ❏ *Distress, if not penury, loomed in the distance* (*Tess of the D'Urbervilles* by Thomas Hardy)

perspective NOUN telescope ❏ *a pocket perspective* (*Gulliver's Travels* by Jonathan Swift)

phaeton NOUN a phaeton was an open carriage for four people ❏ *often* *condescends to drive by my humble abode in her little phaeton and ponies* (*Pride and Prejudice* by Jane Austen)

phantasm NOUN a phantasm is an illusion, something that is not real. It is sometimes used to mean ghost ❑ *Experience had bred no fancies in him that could raise the phantasm of appetite* (*Silas Marner* by George Eliot)

physic NOUN here physic means medicine ❑ *there I studied physic two years and seven months* (*Gulliver's Travels* by Jonathan Swift)

pinioned VERB to pinion is to hold both arms so that a person cannot move them ❑ *But the relentless Ghost pinioned him in both his arms, and forced him to observe what happened next.* (*A Christmas Carol* by Charles Dickens)

piquet NOUN piquet was a popular card game in the C18th ❑ *Mr Hurst and Mr Bingley were at piquet* (*Pride and Prejudice* by Jane Austen)

plaister NOUN a plaister is a piece of cloth on which an apothecary (or pharmacist) would spread ointment. The cloth is then applied to wounds or bruises to treat them ❑ *Then, she gave the knife a final smart wipe on the edge of the plaister, and then sawed a very thick round off the loaf: which she finally, before separating from the loaf, hewed into two halves, of which Joe got one, and I the other.* (*Great Expectations* by Charles Dickens)

plantations NOUN here plantations means colonies, which are countries controlled by a more powerful country ❑ *besides our plantations in America* (*Gulliver's Travels* by Jonathan Swift)

plastic ADJ here plastic is an old term meaning shaping or a power that was forming ❑ *A plastic power abode with me* (*The Prelude* by William Wordsworth)

players NOUN actors ❑ *of players which upon the world's stage be* (*On His Mistress* by John Donne)

plump ADV all at once, suddenly ❑ *But it took a bit of time to get it well round, the change come so uncommon plump, didn't it? (Great Expectations* by Charles Dickens)

plundered VERB to plunder is to rob or steal from ❑ *These crosses stand for the names of ships or towns that they sank or plundered* (*Treasure Island* by Robert Louis Stevenson)

pommel ■ VERB to pommel someone is to hit them repeatedly with your fists ❑ *hug him round the neck, pommel his back, and kick his legs in irrepressible affection! (A Christmas Carol* by Charles Dickens) ■ NOUN a pommel is the part of a saddle that rises up at the front ❑ *He had his gun across his pommel* (*The Adventures of Huckleberry Finn* by Mark Twain)

poor's rates NOUN poor's rates were property taxes which were used to support the poor ❑ *"Oh!" replied the undertaker; "why, you know, Mr. Bumble, I pay a good deal towards the poor's rates." (Oliver Twist* by Charles Dickens)

popular ADJ popular means ruled by the people, or Republican, rather than ruled by a monarch ❑ *With those of Greece compared and popular Rome* (*The Prelude* by William Wordsworth)

porringer NOUN a porringer is a small bowl ❑ *Of this festive composition each boy had one porringer, and no more* (*Oliver Twist* by Charles Dickens)

postboy NOUN a postboy was the driver of a horse-drawn carriage ❑ *He spoke to a postboy who was dozing under the gateway* (*Oliver Twist* by Charles Dickens)

post-chaise NOUN a fast carriage for two or four passengers ❑ *Looking round, he saw that it was a post-chaise, driven at great speed* (*Oliver Twist* by Charles Dickens)

postern NOUN a small gate usually at the back of a building ❑ *The little servant happening to be entering the* *fortress with two hot rolls, I passed through the postern and crossed the drawbridge, in her company* (*Great Expectations* by Charles Dickens)

pottle NOUN a pottle was a small basket ❑ *He had a paper-bag under each arm and a pottle of strawberries in one hand . . .* (*Great Expectations* by Charles Dickens)

pounce NOUN pounce is a fine powder used to prevent ink spreading on untreated paper ❑ *in that grim atmosphere of pounce and parchment, red-tape, dusty wafers, ink-jars, brief and draft paper, law reports, writs, declarations, and bills of costs* (*David Copperfield* by Charles Dickens)

pox NOUN pox means sexually transmitted diseases like syphilis ❑ *how the pox in all its consequences and denominations* (*Gulliver's Travels* by Jonathan Swift)

prelibation NOUN prelibation means a foretaste of or an example of something to come ❑ *A prelibation to the mower's scythe* (*The Prelude* by William Wordsworth)

prentice NOUN an apprentice ❑ *and Joe, sitting on an old gun, had told me that when I was 'prentice to him regularly bound, we would have such Larks there!* (*Great Expectations* by Charles Dickens)

presently ADV immediately ❑ *I presently knew what they meant* (*Gulliver's Travels* by Jonathan Swift)

pumpion NOUN pumpkin ❑ *for it was almost as large as a small pumpion* (*Gulliver's Travels* by Jonathan Swift)

punctual ADJ kept in one place ❑ *was not a punctual presence, but a spirit* (*The Prelude* by William Wordsworth)

quadrille ■ NOUN a quadrille is a dance invented in France which is usually performed by four couples ❑ *However, Mr Swiveller had Miss Sophy's hand for the first quadrille*

(country-dances being low, were utterly proscribed) (*The Old Curiosity Shop* by Charles Dickens) ■ NOUN quadrille was a card game for four people ❑ *to make up her pool of quadrille in the evening* (*Pride and Prejudice* by Jane Austen)

quality NOUN gentry or upper-class people ❑ *if you are with the quality* (*The Adventures of Huckleberry Finn* by Mark Twain)

quick parts PHRASE quick-witted ❑ *Mr Bennet was so odd a mixture of quick parts* (*Pride and Prejudice* by Jane Austen)

quid NOUN a quid is something chewed or kept in the mouth, like a piece of tobacco ❑ *rolling his quid* (*Treasure Island* by Robert Louis Stevenson)

quit VERB quit means to avenge or to make even ❑ *But Faustus's death shall quit my infamy* (*Doctor Faustus 4.3* by Christopher Marlowe)

rags NOUN divisions ❑ *Nor hours, days, months, which are the rags of time* (*The Sun Rising* by John Donne)

raiment NOUN raiment means clothing ❑ *the mountain shook off turf and flower, had only heath for raiment and crag for gem* (*Jane Eyre* by Charlotte Brontë)

rain cats and dogs PHRASE an expression meaning rain heavily. The origin of the expression is unclear ❑ *But it'll perhaps rain cats and dogs to-morrow* (*Silas Marner* by George Eliot)

raised Cain PHRASE raised Cain means caused a lot of trouble. Cain is a character in the Bible who killed his brother Abel ❑ *and every time he got drunk he raised Cain around town* (*The Adventures of Huckleberry Finn* by Mark Twain)

rambling ADJ rambling means confused and not very clear ❑ *my head began to be filled very early with rambling thoughts* (*Robinson Crusoe* by Daniel Defoe)

raree-show NOUN a raree-show is an old term for a peep-show or a fairground entertainment ❑ *A raree-show is here, with children gathered round* (*The Prelude* by William Wordsworth)

recusants NOUN people who resisted authority ❑ *hardy recusants* (*The Prelude* by William Wordsworth)

redounding VERB eddying. An eddy is a movement in water or air which goes round and round instead of flowing in one direction ❑ *mists and steam-like fogs redounding everywhere* (*The Prelude* by William Wordsworth)

redundant ADJ here redundant means overflowing but Wordsworth also uses it to mean excessively large or too big ❑ *A tempest, a redundant energy* (*The Prelude* by William Wordsworth)

reflex NOUN reflex is a shortened version of reflexion, which is an alternative spelling of reflection ❑ *To cut across the reflex of a star* (*The Prelude* by William Wordsworth)

Reformatory NOUN a prison for young offenders/criminals ❑ *Even when I was taken to have a new suit of clothes, the tailor had orders to make them like a kind of Reformatory, and on no account to let me have the free use of my limbs.* (*Great Expectations* by Charles Dickens)

remorse NOUN pity or compassion ❑ *by that remorse* (*On His Mistress* by John Donne)

render VERB in this context render means give. ❑ *and Sarah could render no reason that would be sanctioned by the feeling of the community.* (*Silas Marner* by George Eliot)

repeater NOUN a repeater was a watch that chimed the last hour when a button was pressed–as a result it was useful in the dark ❑ *And his watch is a gold repeater, and worth a hundred pound if it's worth a*

penny. (*Great Expectations* by Charles Dickens)

repugnance NOUN repugnance means a strong dislike of something or someone ❑ *overcoming a strong repugnance* (*Treasure Island* by Robert Louis Stevenson)

reverence NOUN reverence means bow. When you bow to someone, you briefly bend your body towards them as a formal way of showing them respect ❑ *made my reverence* (*Gulliver's Travels* by Jonathan Swift)

reverie NOUN a reverie is a daydream ❑ *I can guess the subject of your reverie* (*Pride and Prejudice* by Jane Austen)

revival NOUN a religious meeting held in public ❑ *well I'd ben a-running' a little temperance revival thar' bout a week* (*The Adventures of Huckleberry Finn* by Mark Twain)

revolt VERB revolt means turn back or stop your present course of action and go back to what you were doing before ❑ *Revolt, or I'll in piecemeal tear thy flesh* (*Doctor Faustus 5.1* by Christopher Marlowe)

rheumatics/rheumatism NOUN rheumatics [rheumatism] is an illness that makes your joints or muscles stiff and painful ❑ *a new cure for the rheumatics* (*Treasure Island* by Robert Louis Stevenson)

riddance NOUN riddance is usually used in the form good riddance which you say when you are pleased that something has gone or been left behind ❑ *I'd better go into the house, and die and be a riddance* (*David Copperfield* by Charles Dickens)

rimy ADJ rimy is an adjective which means covered in ice or frost ❑ *It was a rimy morning, and very damp* (*Great Expectations* by Charles Dickens)

riper ADJ riper means more mature or older ❑ *At riper years to Wittenberg he went* (*Doctor Faustus chorus* by Christopher Marlowe)

rubber NOUN a set of games in whist or backgammon ❑ *her father was sure of his rubber* (*Emma* by Jane Austen)

ruffian NOUN a ruffian is a person who behaves violently ❑ *and when the ruffian had told him* (*Treasure Island* by Robert Louis Stevenson)

sadness NOUN sadness is an old term meaning seriousness ❑ *But I prithee tell me, in good sadness* (*Doctor Faustus 2.2* by Christopher Marlowe)

sailed before the mast PHRASE this phrase meant someone who did not look like a sailor ❑ *he had none of the appearance of a man that sailed before the mast* (*Treasure Island* by Robert Louis Stevenson)

scabbard NOUN a scabbard is the covering for a sword or dagger ❑ *Girded round its middle was an antique scabbard; but no sword was in it, and the ancient sheath was eaten up with rust* (*A Christmas Carol* by Charles Dickens)

schooners NOUN A schooner is a fast, medium-sized sailing ship ❑ *if schooners, islands, and maroons* (*Treasure Island* by Robert Louis Stevenson)

science NOUN learning or knowledge ❑ *Even Science, too, at hand* (*The Prelude* by William Wordsworth)

scrouge VERB to scrouge means to squeeze or to crowd ❑ *to scrouge in and get a sight* (*The Adventures of Huckleberry Finn* by Mark Twain)

scrutore NOUN a scrutore, or escritoire, was a writing table ❑ *set me gently on my feet upon the scrutore* (*Gulliver's Travels* by Jonathan Swift)

scutcheon/escutcheon NOUN an escutcheon is a shield with a coat of arms, or the symbols of a family name, engraved on it ❑ *On the scutcheon we'll have a bend* (*The Adventures of Huckleberry Finn* by Mark Twain)

sea-dog PHRASE sea-dog is a slang term for an experienced sailor or pirate ❑ *a "true sea-dog", and a "real old salt,"* (*Treasure Island* by Robert Louis Stevenson)

see the lions PHRASE to see the lions was to go and see the sights of London. Originally the phrase referred to the menagerie in the Tower of London and later in Regent's Park ❑ *We will go and see the lions for an hour or two—it's something to have a fresh fellow like you to show them to, Copperfield* (*David Copperfield* by Charles Dickens)

self-conceit NOUN self-conceit is an old term which means having too high an opinion of oneself, or deceiving yourself ❑ *Till swollen with cunning, of a self-conceit* (*Doctor Faustus chorus* by Christopher Marlowe)

seneschal NOUN a steward ❑ *where a grey-headed seneschal sings a funny chorus with a funnier body of vassals* (*Oliver Twist* by Charles Dickens)

sensible ADJ if you were sensible of something you are aware or conscious of something ❑ *If my children are silly I must hope to be always sensible of it* (*Pride and Prejudice* by Jane Austen)

sessions NOUN court cases were heard at specific times of the year called sessions ❑ *He lay in prison very ill, during the whole interval between his committal for trial, and the coming round of the Sessions.* (*Great Expectations* by Charles Dickens)

shabby ADJ shabby places look old and in bad condition ❑ *a little bit of a shabby village named Pikesville* (*The Adventures of Huckleberry Finn* by Mark Twain)

shay-cart NOUN a shay-cart was a small cart drawn by one horse ❑ *"I were at the Bargemen t'other night, Pip;" whenever he subsided into affection, he called me Pip, and whenever he relapsed into politeness he called me Sir; "when there come up in his* *shay-cart Pumblechook."* (*Great Expectations* by Charles Dickens)

shilling NOUN a shilling is an old unit of currency. There were twenty shillings in every British pound ❏ *"Ten shillings too much," said the gentleman in the white waistcoat.* (*Oliver Twist* by Charles Dickens)

shines NOUN tricks or games ❏ *well, it would make a cow laugh to see the shines that old idiot cut* (*The Adventures of Huckleberry Finn* by Mark Twain)

shirking VERB shirking means not doing what you are meant to be doing, or evading your duties ❏ *some of you shirking lubbers* (*Treasure Island* by Robert Louis Stevenson)

shiver my timbers PHRASE shiver my timbers is an expression which was used by sailors and pirates to express surprise ❏ *why, shiver my timbers, if I hadn't forgotten my score!* (*Treasure Island* by Robert Louis Stevenson)

shoe-roses NOUN shoe-roses were roses made from ribbons which were stuck on to shoes as decoration ❏ *the very shoe-roses for Netherfield were got by proxy* (*Pride and Prejudice* by Jane Austen)

singular ADJ singular means very great and remarkable or strange ❏ *"Singular dream," he says* (*The Adventures of Huckleberry Finn* by Mark Twain)

sire NOUN sire is an old word which means lord or master or elder ❏ *She also defied her sire* (*Little Women* by Louisa May Alcott)

sixpence NOUN a sixpence was half of a shilling ❏ *if she had only a shilling in the world, she would be very lilkely to give away sixpence of it* (*Emma* by Jane Austen)

slavey NOUN the word slavey was used when there was only one servant in a house or boarding-house—so she had to perform all the duties of a larger staff ❏ *Two distinct knocks, sir, will produce the slavey at any*

time (*The Old Curiosity Shop* by Charles Dickens)

slender ADJ weak ❏ *In slender accents of sweet verse* (*The Prelude* by William Wordsworth)

slop-shops NOUN slop-shops were shops where cheap ready-made clothes were sold. They mainly sold clothes to sailors ❏ *Accordingly, I took the jacket off, that I might learn to do without it; and carrying it under my arm, began a tour of inspection of the various slop-shops.* (*David Copperfield* by Charles Dickens)

sluggard NOUN a lazy person ❏ *"Stand up and repeat ''Tis the voice of the sluggard,'" said the Gryphon.* (*Alice's Adventures in Wonderland* by Lewis Carroll)

smallpox NOUN smallpox is a serious infectious disease ❏ *by telling the men we had smallpox aboard* (*The Adventures of Huckleberry Finn* by Mark Twain)

smalls NOUN smalls are short trousers ❏ *It is difficult for a large-headed, small-eyed youth, of lumbering make and heavy countenance, to look dignified under any circumstances; but it is more especially so, when superadded to these personal attractions are a red nose and yellow smalls* (*Oliver Twist* by Charles Dickens)

sneeze-box NOUN a box for snuff was called a sneeze-box because sniffing snuff makes the user sneeze ❏ *To think of Jack Dawkins—lummy Jack —the Dodger—the Artful Dodger— going abroad for a common twopenny-halfpenny sneeze-box!* (*Oliver Twist* by Charles Dickens)

snorted VERB slept ❏ *Or snorted we in the Seven Sleepers' den?* (*The Good-Morrow* by John Donne)

snuff NOUN snuff is tobacco in powder form which is taken by sniffing ❏ *as he thrust his thumb and forefinger into the proffered snuff-box of the undertaker: which was an ingenious little model of a patent* *coffin.* (*Oliver Twist* by Charles Dickens)

soliloquized VERB to soliloquize is when an actor in a play speaks to himself or herself rather than to another actor ❏ *"A new servitude! There is something in that," I soliloquized (mentally, be it understood; I did not talk aloud)* (*Jane Eyre* by Charlotte Brontë)

sough NOUN a sough is a drain or a ditch ❏ *as you may have noticed the sough that runs from the marshes* (*Wuthering Heights* by Emily Brontë)

spirits NOUN a spirit is the nonphysical part of a person which is believed to remain alive after their death ❏ *that I might raise up spirits when I please* (*Doctor Faustus 1.5* by Christopher Marlowe)

spleen ■ NOUN here spleen means a type of sadness or depression which was thought to only affect the wealthy ❏ *yet here I could plainly discover the true seeds of spleen* (*Gulliver's Travels* by Jonathan Swift) ■ NOUN irritability and low spirits ❏ *Adieu to disappointment and spleen* (*Pride and Prejudice* by Jane Austen)

spondulicks NOUN spondulicks is a slang word which means money ❏ *not for all his spondulicks and as much more on top of it* (*The Adventures of Huckleberry Finn* by Mark Twain)

stalled of VERB to be stalled of something is to be bored with it ❏ *I'm stalled of doing naught* (*Wuthering Heights* by Emily Brontë)

stanchion NOUN a stanchion is a pole or bar that stands upright and is used as a building support ❏ *and slid down a stanchion* (*The Adventures of Huckleberry Finn* by Mark Twain)

stang NOUN stang is another word for pole which was an old measurement ❏ *These fields were intermingled with woods of half a stang* (*Gulliver's Travels* by Jonathan Swift)

starlings NOUN a starling is a wall built around the pillars that support a bridge to protect the pillars ❏ *There were states of the tide when, having been down the river, I could not get back through the eddy-chafed arches and starlings of old London Bridge* (*Great Expectations* by Charles Dickens)

startings NOUN twitching or nighttime movements of the body ❏ *with midnight's startings* (*On His Mistress* by John Donne)

stomacher NOUN a panel at the front of a dress ❏ *but send her aunt the pattern of a stomacher* (*Emma* by Jane Austen)

stoop VERB swoop ❏ *Once a kite hovering over the garden made a stoop at me* (*Gulliver's Travels* by Jonathan Swift)

succedaneum NOUN a succedaneum is a substitute ❏ *But as a succedaneum* (*The Prelude* by William Wordsworth)

suet NOUN a hard animal fat used in cooking ❏ *and your jaws are too weak For anything tougher than suet* (*Alice's Adventures in Wonderland* by Lewis Carroll)

sultry ADJ sultry weather is hot and damp. Here sultry means unpleasant or risky ❏ *for it was getting pretty sultry for us* (*The Adventures of Huckleberry Finn* by Mark Twain)

summerset NOUN summerset is an old spelling of somersault. If someone does a somersault, they turn over completely in the air ❏ *I have seen him do the summerset* (*Gulliver's Travels* by Jonathan Swift)

supper NOUN supper was a light meal taken late in the evening. The main meal was dinner which was eaten at four or five in the afternoon ❏ *and the supper table was all set out* (*Emma* by Jane Austen)

surfeits VERB to surfeit in something is to have far too much of it, or to overindulge in it to an unhealthy degree ❏ *He surfeits upon cursed* necromancy (*Doctor Faustus chorus* by Christopher Marlowe)

surtout NOUN a surtout is a long close-fitting overcoat ❑ *He wore a long black surtout reaching nearly to his ankles* (*The Old Curiosity Shop* by Charles Dickens)

swath NOUN swath is the width of corn cut by a scythe ❑ *while thy hook Spares the next swath* (*Ode to Autumn* by John Keats)

sylvan ADJ sylvan means belonging to the woods ❑ *Sylvan historian* (*Ode on a Grecian Urn* by John Keats)

taction NOUN taction means touch. This means that the people had to be touched on the mouth or the ears to get their attention ❑ *without being roused by some external taction upon the organs of speech and hearing* (*Gulliver's Travels* by Jonathan Swift)

Tag and Rag and Bobtail PHRASE the riff-raff, or lower classes. Used in an insulting way ❑ *"No," said he; "not till it got about that there was no protection on the premises, and it come to be considered dangerous, with convicts and Tag and Rag and Bobtail going up and down."* (*Great Expectations* by Charles Dickens)

tallow NOUN tallow is hard animal fat that is used to make candles and soap ❑ *and a lot of tallow candles* (*The Adventures of Huckleberry Finn* by Mark Twain)

tan VERB to tan means to beat or whip ❑ *and if I catch you about that school I'll tan you good* (*The Adventures of Huckleberry Finn* by Mark Twain)

tanyard NOUN the tanyard is part of a tannery, which is a place where leather is made from animal skins ❑ *hid in the old tanyard* (*The Adventures of Huckleberry Finn* by Mark Twain)

tarry ADJ tarry means the colour of tar or black ❑ *his tarry pig-tail*

(*Treasure Island* by Robert Louis Stevenson)

thereof PHRASE from there ❑ *By all desires which thereof did ensue* (*On His Mistress* by John Donne)

thick with, be PHRASE if you are "thick with someone" you are very close, sharing secrets–it is often used to describe people who are planning something secret ❑ *Hasn't he been thick with Mr Heathcliff lately?* (*Wuthering Heights* by Emily Brontë)

thimble NOUN a thimble is a small cover used to protect the finger while sewing ❑ *The paper had been sealed in several places by a thimble* (*Treasure Island* by Robert Louis Stevenson)

thirtover ADJ thirtover is an old word which means obstinate or that someone is very determined to do want they want and can not be persuaded to do something in another way ❑ *I have been living on in a thirtover, lackadaisical way* (*Tess of the D'Urbervilles* by Thomas Hardy)

timbrel NOUN timbrel is a tambourine ❑ *What pipes and timbrels?* (*Ode on a Grecian Urn* by John Keats)

tin NOUN tin is slang for money/cash ❑ *Then the plain question is, an't it a pity that this state of things should continue, and how much better would it be for the old gentleman to hand over a reasonable amount of tin, and make it all right and comfortable* (*The Old Curiosity Shop* by Charles Dickens)

tincture NOUN a tincture is a medicine made with alcohol and a small amount of a drug ❑ *with ink composed of a cephalic tincture* (*Gulliver's Travels* by Jonathan Swift)

tithe NOUN a tithe is a tax paid to the church ❑ *and held farms which, speaking from a spiritual point of view, paid highly-desirable tithes* (*Silas Marner* by George Eliot)

towardly ADJ a towardly child is dutiful or obedient ❑ *and a towardly child* (*Gulliver's Travels* by Jonathan Swift)

toys NOUN trifles are things which are considered to have little importance, value, or significance ❑ *purchase my life from them bysome bracelets, glass rings, and other toys* (*Gulliver's Travels* by Jonathan Swift)

tract NOUN a tract is a religious pamphlet or leaflet ❑ *and Joe Harper got a hymn-book and a tract* (*The Adventures of Huckleberry Finn* by Mark Twain)

train-oil NOUN train-oil is oil from whale blubber ❑ *The train-oil and gunpowder were shoved out of sight in a minute* (*Wuthering Heights* by Emily Brontë)

tribulation NOUN tribulation means the suffering or difficulty you experience in a particular situation ❑ *Amy was learning this distinction through much tribulation* (*Little Women* by Louisa May Alcott)

trivet NOUN a trivet is a three-legged stand for resting a pot or kettle ❑ *a pocket-knife in his right; and a pewter pot on the trivet* (*Oliver Twist* by Charles Dickens)

trot line NOUN a trot line is a fishing line to which a row of smaller fishing lines are attached ❑ *when he got along I was hard at it taking up a trot line* (*The Adventures of Huckleberry Finn* by Mark Twain)

troth NOUN oath or pledge ❑ *I wonder, by my troth* (*The Good-Morrow* by John Donne)

truckle NOUN a truckle bedstead is a bed that is on wheels and can be slid under another bed to save space ❑ *It rose under my hand, and the door yielded. Looking in, I saw a lighted candle on a table, a bench, and a mattress on a truckle bedstead.* (*Great Expectations* by Charles Dickens)

trump NOUN a trump is a good, reliable person who can be trusted ❑ *This lad Hawkins is a trump, I perceive*

(*Treasure Island* by Robert Louis Stevenson)

tucker NOUN a tucker is a frilly lace collar which is worn around the neck ❑ *Whereat Scrooge's niece's sister—the plump one with the lace tucker: not the one with the roses—blushed.* (*A Christmas Carol* by Charles Dickens)

tureen NOUN a large bowl with a lid from which soup or vegetables are served ❑ *Waiting in a hot tureen!* (*Alice's Adventures in Wonderland* by Lewis Carroll)

turnkey NOUN a prison officer; jailer ❑ *As we came out of the prison through the lodge, I found that the great importance of my guardian was appreciated by the turnkeys, no less than by those whom they held in charge.* (*Great Expectations* by Charles Dickens)

turnpike NOUN the upkeep of many roads of the time was paid for by tolls (fees) collected at posts along the road. There was a gate to prevent people travelling further along the road until the toll had been paid. ❑ *Traddles, whom I have taken up by appointment at the turnpike, presents a dazzling combination of cream colour and light blue; and both he and Mr. Dick have a general effect about them of being all gloves.* (*David Copperfield* by Charles Dickens)

twas PHRASE it was ❑ *twas but a dream of thee* (*The Good-Morrow* by John Donne)

tyrannized VERB tyrannized means bullied or forced to do things against their will ❑ *for people would soon cease coming there to be tyrannized over and put down* (*Treasure Island* by Robert Louis Stevenson)

'un NOUN 'un is a slang term for one—usually used to refer to a person ❑ *She's been thinking the old 'un* (*David Copperfield* by Charles Dickens)

undistinguished ADJ undiscriminating or incapable of making a distinction between good and bad things ❑

their undistinguished appetite to devour everything (*Gulliver's Travels* by Jonathan Swift)

use NOUN habit ❏ *Though use make you apt to kill me* (*The Flea* by John Donne)

vacant ADJ vacant usually means empty, but here Wordsworth uses it to mean carefree ❏ *To vacant musing, unreproved neglect* (*The Prelude* by William Wordsworth)

valetudinarian NOUN one too concerned with his or her own health. ❏ *for having been a valetudinarian all his life* (*Emma* by Jane Austen)

vamp VERB vamp means to walk or tramp to somewhere ❏ *Well, vamp on to Marlott, will 'ee* (*Tess of the D'Urbervilles* by Thomas Hardy)

vapours NOUN the vapours is an old term which means unpleasant and strange thoughts, which make the person feel nervous and unhappy ❏ *and my head was full of vapours* (*Robinson Crusoe* by Daniel Defoe)

vegetables NOUN here vegetables means plants ❏ *the other vegetables are in the same proportion* (*Gulliver's Travels* by Jonathan Swift)

venturesome ADJ if you are venturesome you are willing to take risks ❏ *he must be either hopelessly stupid or a venturesome fool* (*Wuthering Heights* by Emily Brontë)

verily ADV verily means really or truly ❏ *though I believe verily* (*Robinson Crusoe* by Daniel Defoe)

vicinage NOUN vicinage is an area or the residents of an area ❏ *and to his thought the whole vicinage was haunted by her.* (*Silas Marner* by George Eliot)

victuals NOUN victuals means food ❏ *grumble a little over the victuals* (*The Adventures of Huckleberry Finn* by Mark Twain)

vintage NOUN vintage in this context means wine ❏ *Oh, for a draught of vintage!* (*Ode on a Nightingale* by John Keats)

virtual ADJ here virtual means powerful or strong ❏ *had virtual faith* (*The Prelude* by William Wordsworth)

vittles NOUN vittles is a slang word which means food ❏ *There never was such a woman for givin' away vittles and drink* (*Little Women* by Louisa May Alcott)

voided straight PHRASE voided straight is an old expression which means emptied immediately ❏ *see the rooms be voided straight* (*Doctor Faustus 4.1* by Christopher Marlowe)

wainscot NOUN wainscot is wood panel lining in a room so wainscoted means a room lined with wooden panels ❏ *in the dark wainscoted parlor* (*Silas Marner* by George Eliot)

walking the plank PHRASE walking the plank was a punishment in which a prisoner would be made to walk along a plank on the side of the ship and fall into the sea, where they would be abandoned ❏ *about hanging, and walking the plank* (*Treasure Island* by Robert Louis Stevenson)

want VERB want means to be lacking or short of ❏ *The next thing wanted was to get the picture framed* (*Emma* by Jane Austen)

wanting ADJ wanting means lacking or missing ❏ *wanting two fingers of the left hand* (*Treasure Island* by Robert Louis Stevenson)

wanting, I was not PHRASE I was not wanting means I did not fail ❏ *I was not wanting to lay a foundation of religious knowledge in his mind* (*Robinson Crusoe* by Daniel Defoe)

ward NOUN a ward is, usually, a child who has been put under the protection of the court or a guardian for his or her protection ❏ *I call the Wards in Jarndyce. They* are caged up with all the others. (*Bleak House* by Charles Dickens)

waylay VERB to waylay someone is to lie in wait for them or to intercept them ❑ *I must go up the road and waylay him* (*The Adventures of Huckleberry Finn* by Mark Twain)

weazen NOUN weazen is a slang word for throat. It actually means shrivelled ❑ *You with a uncle too! Why, I knowed you at Gargery's when you was so small a wolf that I could have took your weazen betwixt this finger and thumb and chucked you away dead* (*Great Expectations* by Charles Dickens)

wery ■ ADV very ❑ *Be wery careful o' vidders all your life* (*Pickwick Papers* by Charles Dickens) ■ *See* wibrated

wherry NOUN wherry is a small swift rowing boat for one person ❑ *It was flood tide when Daniel Quilp sat himself down in the wherry to cross to the opposite shore.* (*The Old Curiosity Shop* by Charles Dickens)

whether PREP whether means which of the two in this example ❑ *we came in full view of a great island or continent (for we knew not whether)* (*Gulliver's Travels* by Jonathan Swift)

whetstone NOUN a whetstone is a stone used to sharpen knives and other tools ❑ *I dropped pap's whetstone there too* (*The Adventures of Huckleberry Finn* by Mark Twain)

wibrated VERB in Dickens's use of the English language "w" often replaces "v" when he is reporting speech. So here "wibrated" means "vibrated". In *Pickwick Papers* a judge asks Sam Weller (who constantly confuses the two letters) "Do you spell it with a 'v' or a 'w'?" to which Weller replies "That depends upon the taste and fancy of the speller, my Lord" ❑ *There are strings . . . in the human heart that had better not be wibrated* (*Barnaby Rudge* by Charles Dickens)

wicket NOUN a wicket is a little door in a larger entrance ❑ *Having rested* here, for a minute or so, to collect a good burst of sobs and an imposing show of tears and terror, he knocked loudly at the wicket (*Oliver Twist* by Charles Dickens)

without CONJ without means unless ❑ *You don't know about me, without you have read a book by the name of The Adventures of Tom Sawyer* (*The Adventures of Huckleberry Finn* by Mark Twain)

wittles ■ NOUN wittles is a slang word which means food ❑ *I live on broken wittles–and I sleep on the coals* (*David Copperfield* by Charles Dickens) ■ *See* wibrated

woo VERB courts or forms a proper relationship with ❑ *before it woo* (*The Flea* by John Donne)

words, to have PHRASE if you have words with someone you have a disagreement or an argument ❑ *I do not want to have words with a young thing like you.* (*Black Beauty* by Anna Sewell)

workhouse NOUN workhouses were places where the homeless were given food and a place to live in return for doing very hard work ❑ *And the Union workhouses? demanded Scrooge. Are they still in operation?* (*A Christmas Carol* by Charles Dickens)

yawl NOUN a yawl is a small boat kept on a bigger boat for short trips. Yawl is also the name for a small fishing boat ❑ *She sent out her yawl, and we went aboard* (*The Adventures of Huckleberry Finn* by Mark Twain)

yeomanry NOUN the yeomanry was a collective term for the middle classes involved in agriculture ❑ *The yeomanry are precisely the order of people with whom I feel I can have nothing to do* (*Emma* by Jane Austen)

yonder ADV yonder means over there ❑ *all in the same second we seem to hear low voices in yonder!* (*The Adventures of Huckleberry Finn* by Mark Twain)